Smooth Sailing or Stormy Waters?

Family Transitions Through Adolescence and Their Implications for Practice and Policy

Smooth Sailing
or Stormy Waters?

Family Transitions Through Adolescence and Their Implications for Practice and Policy

Rena D. Harold
Michigan State University

Lisa G. Colarossi
Fordham University

Lucy R. Mercier
Saginaw Valley State University

LEA LAWRENCE ERLBAUM ASSOCIATES, PUBLISHERS
2007   Mahwah, New Jersey   London

Lawrence Erlbaum Associates, Inc. Publishers
10 Industrial Avenue
Mahwah, New Jersey 07430-2262
www.erlbaum.com

Cover design by Kathryn Houghtaling

Cover photo by Jo Ann McFall: "The 'Namasté' in the North Channel of Lake Huron"

Library of Congress Cataloging-in-Publication Data

Harold, Rena D.
  Smooth sailing or stormy waters? : family transitions through adolescence and their implications for practice and policy / Rena D. Harold, Lisa G. Colarossi, Lucy R. Mercier.

    p. cm.

ISBN 978-0-8058-4907-3 — 0-8058-4907-6 (cloth)
ISBN 978-0-8058-6305-5 — 0-8058-6305-2 (pbk.)
ISBN 1-4106-1552-9 — 1-4106-1552-7 (e book)
BF724.2.H37   2006
306.87 — dc22   2006020066
                                              CIP

Books published by Lawrence Erlbaum Associates are printed on acid-free paper, and their bindings are chosen for strength and durability.

Printed in the United States of America
10 9 8 7 6 5 4 3 2 1

January 4, 2008

*To all of the people in our lives
who reside within the inner and outer
circles of our own eco maps and give us
support, love, and good counsel.*

Contents

Preface

The primary purpose of this book is to enhance understanding of the family's transition through adolescence by relating the experiences of parents and teens. A secondary purpose is to demonstrate the use of a qualitative methodological approach, *eco mapping*, that helped participants organize their thoughts and comments about relationships within the family itself and between the family and its social environment as they sought to "weather" this developmental transition. This book offers unique information in two ways. First, other research has not examined both parents' and teens' views across multiple relationships and social contexts. Second, this book follows the same families that we described in our first book, *Becoming a Family: Parents' Stories and Their Implications for Policy, Practice, and Research* (Harold, 2000).

In that book, we presented qualitative data from 60 families who were participating in a larger, longitudinal study of parents, children, and teachers. Six years after these initial interviews about parents' decisions to marry and have children, we asked the same parents and their teens to meet with us again and discuss the family's transition from childhood to adolescence. Fifty-four of the original families agreed to be interviewed again, and six additional families participated, for a total of 60 families interviewed. These 60 families yielded individual interviews with 59 mothers, 41 fathers, and 117 adolescents ages 12 to 17. This book presents these new data, utilizing a different methodology than described in the first book. Taken together, the two books provide a longitudinal perspective on family systems development and different techniques for collecting this kind of information from multiple informants. This qualitative, longitudinal perspective is an important addition to understanding change processes over time.

This work is interdisciplinary in nature, drawing on theory and practice from the fields of social work, psychology, and sociology, as described in chapter 1. It uses a similar theoretical framework as is described in the first book, but focuses more specifically on adolescent development and family ecology. Family systems theory and developmental life span theory are used to consider individual and family internal, psychological processes. Sociological perspectives are utilized to understand how social roles, structures, and gender impact our participants. Lastly, and most importantly, ecological systems theory and person-in-environment models lend a social work perspective to understanding how adolescents and families interact with their environments.

Adolescence is typically portrayed as a time of "storm and stress," both for the individual adolescent and for his or her family. This phrase led to the book's subtitle and chapter headings. We began to think of both the research process and adolescent development in terms of navigating change through "smooth sailing or stormy waters." Much has been written about the influence of hormones and peer groups during this developmental period, about relationships with parents, and about the need to become one's own person. However, there are multiple influences on the kind of transition that adolescents and their families experience. The data analyzed for this book present a picture of the transition to adolescence as it is influenced bi-directionally inside the family through parental and sibling relationships, and outside the family through relationships with a variety of systems including peers, school, and work.

This book presents interview data gathered using an eco-map technique and a semi-structured interview protocol to obtain both a drawing and a verbal description of the participants' family and social system relationships. A full description of the interview process and the coding procedures for the data is provided in chapter 2. In general, the interview consisted of a set of questions and subquestions, or probes, to assist participants in describing information about pubertal changes, the influence of becoming an adolescent on their relationships with peers and adults, inside and outside the family, and on school and work environments. Line drawings on the eco map were used to represent different relationship qualities between individuals and with environmental systems.

While the first two chapters of the book lay a foundation for understanding the data, proceeding chapters present the participants' stories, which are organized by context: developmental changes, interpersonal relationships, education, and work. Each chapter follows a similar format. Literature reviews are provided to overview research in each topic area, followed by a brief description of coding for that chapter's particular themes. Then, parents' and/or teens' descriptions are provided and interpreted, with a special focus on gender issues. Each chapter concludes with implications for practice and policy. The final chapter summarizes the findings from the earlier chapters and discusses limitations of the research as well as future research needs. Suggestions are offered for ways to make the developmental transitions to adolescence, and from adolescence to adulthood, a productive time for both the youth and their families.

ACKNOWLEDGMENTS

Research funding for the data collected and presented here was provided by grants from the National Institute of Child Health and Human Development to Jacquelynne S. Eccles, Phyllis C. Blumenfeld, Rena D. Harold, and Allan L. Wigfield, and by a grant from the Director's Discretionary Fund at the Institute for Social Research at The University of Michigan to Rena D. Harold and Jacquelynne S. Eccles. We thank all of our colleagues on the Childhood and Beyond Study, especially Jacque Eccles, for their support and the opportunity to collect these qualitative data from a subgroup of parent and adolescent participants of the larger, longitudinal study on child development. The authors are listed in order of their longevity with the project. This was truly a collaborative work. We acknowledge the many parents and adolescents who willingly gave of their time and energy to share their experiences. Needless to say, they made this book possible, as did the help of several graduate students and staff who helped interview parents and transcribe their stories. Particular thanks go to Cle Milojevic and Dana Johnston for their work in the early stages of this project, to Cathy Macomber and Brian Ahmedani for their work in the latter stages, to Bill Webber and Lori Handelman, Executive and Senior Editors at Lawrence Erlbaum Associates, and to Nancy Proyect for her excellent work in producing this book. We would also like to thank our respective Directors and Deans whose support was essential as the project neared its completion.

Each parent and teen presented a unique picture of their perspective of transitions and family life development. While each is distinct, there is also a more generalizable experience that is represented, one that caused us to reflect on our own life experiences as the children we were, and as the partners and parents we became.

Our love and thanks go to Linda, Fabio, and Linda, Lonny, Ilyse, Hannah, Noah, Robert, and Andre.

1

Checking the Compass: Looking at the Family Inside and Out

Adolescence is typically portrayed as a time of "storm and stress," both for the individual adolescent and for his/her family. Much has been written about the influence of hormones and peer groups during this developmental period (e.g., Steinberg & Levine, 1990), about relationships with parents (e.g., Luster & Okagaki, 1993), and about the need to "separate and individuate" (Erikson, 1982). Few, however, consider the multiple influences on the kind of transition that adolescents and their families experience. The data analyzed for this book present a picture of the transition to adolescence as it is influenced bidirectionally inside the family through parental and sibling relationships, and outside the family through relationships with a variety of systems including extended family, peers, school, and work.

As we showed in our first book, *Becoming a Family*, the movement from young adulthood, through partnering, and the transition to parenthood may be among the most universal adult developmental transitions. The transition from childhood through adolescence to adulthood, however, is not only universal, but is seen as perhaps the most crucial that we each undergo. This transition impacts not only each individual, but the entire familial and ecological system with which individuals interact, thus existing at the interface of individual and family systems models of understanding behavior (Goldberg, 1988). To really understand this developmental life transition, each person should be viewed both from an individual psychological perspective and within his/her own family system, with all its powers to mold and influence attitudes, values, and behavior, and to be influenced in its turn by the changes its members experience.

Once again, we have gone to the "source" to explore this developmental stage, from the perspectives of the adolescents themselves, and their parents. The qualitative methodology, described in chapter 2, allowed us to inquire about the inner subjective perceptions of self from the perspective of each individual (Borden, 1992). Through the use of a structured narrative tool, the study participants were able to define their lives, relationships, and experiences, sharing interpretive systems for explaining themselves in relation to the world as they move through the life span in their ecological environments (Laird, 1989).

Progress in the use of a narrative method as a tool for exploring the subjective nature of individual and family life transitions has occurred within the context of the "new epistemology" and of the constructivist movement in family research. This signifies a movement away from the traditional positivistic approach and from standard notions of family structure and functioning, from the search for "truth" to a search for meaning, and toward new ways of comprehending how families construct their worlds (Laird, 1989). One of the richest sources of meaning lies in the narratives through which individuals and families explain themselves, their thinking, and their behavior. Within family narratives are indicators of individual and family identity, as well as descriptions of connections to others.

Fiese and Sameroff (1999) report that there has been an increase in the study of narratives, particularly as a way to glimpse an individual's thought processes and how they put together pieces of their life story. There has been less work done on using narratives with families as a whole. This, they suggest, would "move beyond the individual and deal with how the family makes sense of its world, expresses rules of interaction, and creates beliefs about relationships" (p. 3). Further, it appears that "meaning-making" for a family may be related to adapting to stressful situations as well as to normal life transitions, such as the changes accompanying adolescent development.

The primary purpose of this book is to look at one of those "meaning-making" times, to explore the transition through adolescence, as experienced by the teens themselves, and by their families, in relationship with the rest of their social worlds. This exploration will enhance understanding of family-life development as we seek to give voice to the experiences of each generation, looking within and across families, as they transit through this important life stage. Sixty families, each with at least two children, who were part of a much larger longitudinal research project, were asked if they would be interested in participating in our first study where we gathered and analyzed their stories about becoming families. For this book, we recontacted those families, as described in chapter 2. It is their views of life, the strengths and struggles of adolescence, that we use to highlight issues that families deal with in the course of this family-life developmental transition.

The specific issues that are discussed in the book emerged through the process of qualitatively analyzing the expressions and explanations of the study participants. The first two chapters of the book place the stories in context, describing the theoretical foundation of the study and the methodology used in collecting and analyzing the data. Chapters 3 through 6 present particular issues and developmental themes that were important to different members in the family and include a review of seminal literature and participants' comments and ideas about the topic.

Steinberg (1985) suggests that there are five key psychological issues in adolescence: identity, autonomy, intimacy, sexuality, and achievement, and these are certainly represented in these chapters. He also states that "development during adolescence is the result of an interplay among three fundamental forces—biological, cognitive, and social—and the context in which young people live" (p. 3). Each chapter sheds some light on these psychological issues and fundamental forces. We also explore relationship dynamics between family members, as well as individual and familial patterns of presenting the relationships within the family, looking at the consistency between how family members chose to graphically (that is, the types of lines they used) describe relationships and the words that they used in talking about those same relationships (Harold, Mercier, & Colarossi, 1997). In addition, each of these chapters includes some interpretations of the issues presented in a discussion of practice, policy, and research implications that are relevant to the topic. The final chapter summarizes the themes and issues that were important in the lives of our participants, and offers a developmental glimpse into the future.

FAMILY

The first issue that must be addressed in any discussion of family development is what we mean by "family." Despite the fact that in recent years, the definition of family has entered the arena of political debate, it has always been a concept that is somewhat difficult to pin down. White and Epston (1990) suggest that this is due to the many levels of analysis with which one can view the family. Thus, we can talk in terms of "a family"—a single group or organization; we can talk in terms of "families"—a population of such groups; or we can talk in terms of "the family"—a social institution. Elkind (1994) might say that the difficulty in defining family has to do with the fact that "the modern nuclear family, often idyllically portrayed as a refuge and a retreat from a demanding world, is fast disappearing. In its stead we now have a new structure—the postmodern permeable family—that mirrors the openness, complexity, and diversity of our contemporary lifestyles" (p. 1).

Today there are "traditional" (that is, heterosexual) two-parent nuclear families, multigenerational families, single-parent families, blended families, gay and lesbian families, extended families, families of choice, and so on. However, there is some consensus among family researchers that a necessary characteristic of a family is that it be *intergenerational* (White & Epston, 1990). According to this definition, the affinal relationship between two adults does not constitute a family. It is only when a child is brought into the adult dyad for long-term nurturing and socialization that a family is formed. Although we would argue for the broadest, most inclusive definition of family possible, and have done so in our earlier work (Harold, 2000), the families represented in this book all began as "traditional" intergenerational groups, and it is this particular relationship, that is, parent and adolescent children, on which we focus.

ADOLESCENCE

Steinberg (1985) tells us that the word *adolescence* comes from the Latin verb *adolescere*, meaning "to grow into adulthood" (p. 6). Although there may be cultural differences in how adolescence is defined, when it begins, and what markers are considered, adolescence is a time of coming of age, both literally (chronologically) and figuratively (the meaning we ascribe to this life passage) in all societies, a bridge or crossroads from being a child to being an adult (Nurmi, 2004). In considering the impact of the transition to adolescence on both the teen and the family as we are in this book, we include Steinberg and Levine's (1990) advice to parents: "Your relationship with your child will not change for the worse in adolescence, but it will change" (p. 3) and that "friends don't subtract from the adolescent's affection for his [her] family but add to his [her] circle of significant others" (p. 4).

Adolescence is a developmental period when individuals are faced with many tasks that intersect and influence one another, for example, increased desire for autonomy, salience of identity issues, peer orientation, self-focus and self-consciousness, and a continuing need for a safe environment in which to explore autonomy and identity. Many factors make distinct and potent demands on adolescents. These include rapid biological changes associated with puberty, cognitive changes associated with more sophisticated thinking abilities, new psychosocial and sexual demands such as beginning intimate peer relationships, identity development, and changes in social roles that may bring with them such environmental transitions as movement into the work world and moving away from the family of origin. In addition, there are educational changes as teens enter middle and/or high school and legal changes as they attain certain statuses.

Theories have postulated that the stress of these demands produces vulnerability to mental health problems, and research studies have linked these changes, as well as other, more chronic social factors such as poverty and discrimination, to problems of low self-esteem, depression, and academic difficulties (Simmons & Blyth, 1987). An additional concern is the widening of sex differences during adolescence in the areas of mental health and academic achievement. Pipher (1994) writes, "Something dramatic happens to girls in early adolescence. Just as planes and ships disappear mysteriously into the Bermuda Triangle, so do the selves of girls go down in droves. They crash and burn in a social and developmental Bermuda Triangle" (p. 19). She suggests that there are three factors that account for vulnerability in adolescent girls: First, that fact that it is a developmental level where everything is changing; second, American cultural stereotypes such as body image and gender roles; and third, the expectation that girls will distance them- selves from parents at a time when they need their support the most. Adolescence, Pipher says, is "a time for cutting bonds and breaking free" (p. 24).

> There exists one real cure for adolescence, and only one, and this cannot be of interest to the boy or girl who is in the throes. The cure for adolescence belongs to the passage of time and to the gradual maturation processes; these together do in the end result in the emergence of the adult person. (Winnicott, 1965, p. 79)

THEORETICAL MODELS

Family Life Span Development

As in our earlier work, this book also has its underpinnings in three theories that can be used to interpret the data (see Fig. 1.1). For this book, however, the first two models can be seen as a backdrop for the third and most important model, which focuses on ecological systems. The first model draws on social and developmental psychological literature, including a model that considers family development across the life span, milestones or transitions in the life of the family, for example, a family life cycle, and the family's internal processes (Carter & McGoldrick, 1988, 1988; Steinberg, 1985; Thomas, 2001; White & Klein, 2002).

This developmental lifespan/family life course development model includes a conceptualization of the nuclear family as a three-generational system that reacts to pressure from generational tensions as well as developmental transitions, depicting this interactive process with a vertical and horizontal axis in their model. It also con- siders that the family may have its own "adolescent" period, during which it may go through development stresses and strains that correspond to those of the adolescent member, and that threaten the family's cohesiveness and primacy for its members.

In assessing families, Carter and McGoldrick (1988) incorporate activities of the entire three-generational system as it moves through time. Relationships with parents, siblings, and other family members go through stages as one moves along the life cycle. This is a useful framework to consider as we look at the impact of the transition to adolescence on the individual and his/her family, as well as looking at the impact of family life issues/events (e.g., birth, death, moving, divorce, going off to college) on the adolescent's development and interactions with his/her fam- ily and social environment. The family life cycle, then, interacts with the individ- ual members' life cycles such that to understand the changes in relationships that occur during this transitional period, we must consider the adolescent's develop- ment as well as that of his/her parents and the family. This model that looks across individuals and across time, also fits with the notion expressed by Fiese and

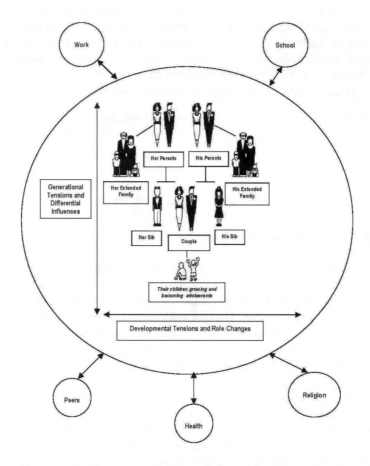

Figure 1.1.   Each child's transition to adolescence both impacts and is impacted by the multi-generational interactions and dynamics in this depiction of a family as a three-generational system moving through time at the center of a larger ecological systems model where examples of outside systems impact and are impacted by the central family system.

Sameroff that "the process of creating family narratives and the themes inherent in the stories may be shared across generations, regulating family beliefs and interaction patterns" (1999, p. 3) over time.

Carter and McGoldrick (1988) do not consider the influence of the family to be restricted to the members of a particular household or to a given nuclear family branch of the system. Although they acknowledge the stereotypical American pattern of separately domiciled nuclear families, there are subsystems within the larger family system, including the extended and intergenerational family, which react to past, present, and anticipated future relationships. In addition, they recognize the interplay between the family system, social roles, and the larger environment as discussed in the next sections.

Social Roles

The second model borrows from sociological theory as it looks at roles and social structures in the family and suggests that these are socially constructed (Feld & Radin, 1982). That is, notions of family and parenting, and "being" an adolescent, are important because of the meanings that they have for the individual within her/his social context. Further, these meanings are created through a social process that reflects expectations about what an adult should do (e.g., have a job, marry, have children) and what an adolescent should do (e.g., go to school, strive for separation and individuation), that is, the roles and behaviors in which adults and adolescents should engage, and when these should take place. Role theory and role analysis consider both the individual and the social system in which the individual exists to explain his/her experiences and behaviors (Wapner & Craig-Bray, 1992).

People's behaviors are influenced, in part, by the expectations, rewards, and sanctions that are associated with a given role or position. Further, these expectations come from a variety of sources, e.g., society, family, community, class structure, and so forth, and may change depending on the particular context. Parental behavior vis à vis their adolescents will also be dependent on how parents' own roles are transmitted and defined. If we consider Carter and McGoldrick's (1988) model, again, role expectations for parental as well as adolescent behavior may also be transmitted across generations, vertically (that is, from grandparents and parents) as well as horizontally (that is, from extended family, aunts, uncles, cousins). This points out that role expectations can help define members' roles at a given point or across the family life span. Further, these are impacted by a given culture's definition of family-developmental tasks. White and Klein (2002) give the example of launching an adolescent where the move toward adulthood does not mean that the parenting role comes to an end, but rather that the role is changed based on the "spatial and interactional organization of the members" (p. 97).

Being an adolescent also may have a different set of behavioral expectations depending, for example, on gender, sex role stereotyping, birth order, signs of physical development, and so on. In addition, the expectations will vary, as indicated previously, as a result of the adolescent's own conception of the role, her/his family's and peers' ideas, the environment in which she/he lives, whether the teen has a work and/or a student role, and so forth (Feld & Radin, 1982; Wapner & Craig-Bray, 1992). Steinberg tells us that "the social redefinition of individuals at adolescence has important implications for their behavior and psychosocial development. As adolescents come to be seen as adults, they begin to act and see themselves differently, and are treated differently by others" (1985, p. 93).

There are age markers, some universal, some tied to specific cultures, such as 13 (Bar or Bat Mitzvah), 16 (driver's license), 18 (adult status and voting age) that are tied to new roles, responsibilities, and expectations for the adolescent. These new activities and statuses may cause change in both the adolescent and his/her family, and lead to or are characterized by (a) real or symbolic separation from the family, (b) the highlighting of gender differences, and (c) the conveying of knowledge necessary for performing adult roles. It is an important role for adult family members to assist adolescents in gaining the knowledge and training necessary to take on new roles.

Examining families, then, from a role perspective, allows us to look at the role demands that parents and teens in our study articulated. Some participants described the role conflict that they felt when there were contradictory expectations about how they should behave, for example, wife, mother, or professional worker; student, child, new worker. In trying to hold two or more roles simultaneously, the participants in our study had to deal with their own definitions, those of their extended families, as well as societal definitions of what constituted appropriate role behavior for those positions, that is, which need or role takes priority in which situations, as well as what to do about conflicting expectations.

Elkind (1994) suggests that in post-modern times, a belief in human diversity is leading to role de-differentiation. He suggests that recognizing individual interests, abilities, and talents is breaking down gender barriers, but many of our families tell stories that suggest that while this is true for some, others are still occupying fairly stereotypical social roles within their nuclear families and in their outside environments. This perspective is particularly important because it suggests a way of analyzing problems that does not focus on a personal inadequacy, but rather considers roles and structures in the family and outside of it as being socially constructed, and therefore in need of examination and perhaps re-creation.

Ecological Systems

The third and most important theoretical model for this work, then, utilizes a largely social work perspective in that it examines the family as it interacts with its environment. This ecosystems approach (e.g., Bronfenbrenner, 1979; Harold et al., 1997; Hartman, 1978) is very helpful in understanding the interactions between family-developmental processes, roles that family members assume, and the institutions and other systems external to the family unit. It is this final framework that primarily directed this research and the collection and analyses of the data, allowing for the examination of such issues as relationship processes within and outside the family, the role of work and education in the lives of the family members, the transitions from childhood to adolescence and beyond, and the impact on the individuals as well as the family group. This fits particularly well with the study of adolescence, as the teens' development takes place in the context of multiple social and institutional systems (Nurmi, 2004). Parke and Kellam (1994) sum up the need for this ecological perspective: "it is no longer 'news' that families do not operate independently from other social organizations and institutions. Instead, it is generally recognized that families are embedded in a complex set of relationships with institutions and contexts outside the family" (p. 1).

Ecosystems theories stress that individuals and their environments are mutually influential and in dynamic interaction (Bronfenbrenner, 1979; Bush & Simmons, 1981). Thus, they have the advantage of providing a holistic framework for understanding and intervening with individuals while considering their environmental contexts. This approach best fits lifespan theories of development like Carter and McGoldrick's, which posit that development is not irreversible, unidirectional, or universal, but should be viewed as an interaction between the individual and the social context that involves both continuity and change from birth to death. "Since each developmental transition builds, to some extent, on earlier ones, there is continuity. However, each turning point contains the potential for varying degrees of change" (Bush & Simmons, 1981, p. 159). Further, to understand this developmental period, we must use an ecological model that focuses on the child's relationship to other parenting figures, for example, across generations (Sameroff & Fiese, 1999), as well as across other systems.

Clinician D. W. Winnicott also wrote of the vital importance of considering adolescent development in the context of the teen's ecological system:

> The part played by the environment is immensely significant at this stage. … Many of the difficulties of adolescents for which professional help is sought derive from environmental failure, and this fact only emphasizes the vital importance of the environment and of the family setting in the case of the vast majority of adolescents who do in fact achieve adult maturity, even if in the process they give their parents headaches. (1965, p. 80)

Urie Bronfenbrenner is one of the best known theoreticians in the area of ecological systems and human development. He detailed a theoretical framework that focused on people within their environment. Bronfenbrenner (1979) described the importance of the interconnections between different contexts such that experiences in one context (e.g., parents' peer experiences) moderate the influence that another context has on the developing child (e.g., parental support to the child). Bronfenbrenner describes the individual's environment as a "set of nested structures, each inside the next, like a set of Russian dolls" (1979, p. 22). This "nested" framework includes four types of systems that expand in terms of complexity and size.

The first is the *microsystem* that refers to individual interactions with their immediate environment. Next is the *mesosystem* that expands to relationships between contexts. Although, in our study, the family is the principal context in which adolescent development takes place, it is only one of several settings in which the teen is involved. The *exosystem*, then, involves systems that impact an individual's development indirectly, that is, environments in which the adolescent spends time, such as school, and where parents may spend time, for example, work. And finally, the *macrosystem* relates to the larger culture, and the broader values and practices of society, in which the individual, family, schools, and so forth exist. This framework can be applied to many aspects of psychosocial inquiry and practice, including the nature of social support, peer relationships, and adolescent and family development. Leaper (2000) also contends that this model can be used to understand gender development by considering that the type of socialization practices for boys and girls will reflect the existing macrosystem (e.g., values, opportunities, structures) of a given culture and historical period. This book uses what Bronfenbrenner (1986) called a "person-process-context" model in that we explore the impact of particular external environments on the family, taking into consideration the personal characteristics of the individual family members and the dynamic interactions that occur (p. 725).

Historically, the social work profession has encouraged the use of an ecological systems perspective in social work practice, and assessment/evaluation tools such as the "eco map" (short for ecological mapping technique and described more fully in chapter 2 as it was used in our study) have been developed to help clients and social workers assess strengths and weakness in relationships across multiple levels of their social system (Hartman, 1978). Many casework theoreticians have discussed the adaptations of systems perspectives, including early social work pioneers like Mary Richman (1917) who discussed the importance of making a social diagnosis based on individual, school, neighborhood, work, and family information. Later social workers elaborated on "person-in-situation" models (Hamilton, 1951; Hollis, 1972; Perlman, 1957) and the "life-model" of practice (Germain, 1979; Germain & Gitterman, 1980). These theories all encompass a similar ecological perspective described by Carel Germain where "[The goal of ecological systems interventions is to] improve the transactions between people and environments in order to enhance adaptive capacities and improve environments for all who function within them" (1979, p. 8).

Whittaker and Garbarino (1983, pp. 36–37) sum up five aspects of social work practice within a systems perspective and the importance of social support within such practice:

> [Social work practice with an ecological systems perspective contains] a view which: (1) recognizes the complementarity of person-in-environment, and seeks to strengthen each component; (2) accepts the fact that an exclusive focus on either the individual or his/her immediate environment will generally not produce effective helping; (3) acknowledges that interpersonal help may take many forms, as long as its goal is to teach skills for effectively coping with the environment; (4) views social support not simply as a desirable concomitant to professional help but as an inextricable component of an overall helping strategy; (5) recognizes the distinct and salutary features of both professional and lay helping efforts in an overall framework for services.

Family-in-Environment

"Families," writes Steinberg (1985), "are systems that must adapt to the changing needs and capabilities of family members. Adolescence presents a challenge to most families—not only because of changes in the adolescent but because of changes in the adolescent's parents as well" (p. 119). However, while the family is the principal arena in which individual development occurs, individuals and families are located within and interact with the levels of systems discussed previously (Bronfenbrenner, 1979, 1986). Further, according to ecological systems theory, change in relationships with one part of the interacting systems may impact on or result in a shift in all other relationships (Bronfenbrenner, 1979). This concept is central to diverse philosophies of change, including most family therapy work. In this book, many issues are examined that impact not only a specific family member, but also the family as a whole. For example, an adolescent's behavior and demeanor may impact the way she/he is treated within the family, which may in turn affect her/his ability to form relationships in the school setting. A parent's work life can certainly influence his/her behavior in the home, just as events in the home can impact his/her work life. Similarly, parents' access to social support can have a positive effect on their children, for example, financial aid, adult outlets for expression of feelings, appropriate expectations for adolescent development, role modeling, giving and receiving of help with family and friends, and so on. Thus, using an ecosystems approach to understanding families acknowledges the interactive influences and connections between individual members as well as between individuals, families, and their environments (McMahon, 1990).

Each variation within and between systems interacts to affect the individual's and the family's development. The focus of ecological systems theory, then, is on the interface where the person or family and the environment come together (McMahon, 1990). This person-in-environment perspective and the "fit" between the person or family and their surroundings is a characteristic of our stories. Families define who they are, anticipate and relate to their adolescent children, feel supported or not supported, and occupy multiple roles including worker and parent in the context of their extended family, peer group, community, and so forth.

Within this framework, and similar to the one described in Bronfenbrenner's (1979) work, the family is viewed as a *system*, a set or arrangement of people related or connected in such a way that they form a whole. Within that system there are *subsystems,* parts or components of a larger system, which may include parents, siblings, one parent and one child, et cetera. Equally important is the *suprasystem* to which the family belongs, the larger, more encompassing whole like a nation or culture. Each family has *boundaries* that keep the system enclosed (e.g., allowing people to identify themselves as part of that family), but these boundaries are also permeable, and some families may choose to let in nonfamily members. Families may, however, also have *barriers* that tend to prevent movement in and out of the system (Minuchin, 1988).

In using this model to understand the adolescent transition in the context of family development, the following assumptions are made:

- All members of the system are interconnected.
- Change in one person in the system affects all other persons.
- To survive, a system must have goals and strive to achieve them.
- Systems must have input—some form of energy from the external environment.
- Systems must have a way of processing input.

- Systems must produce output, which then becomes input for other systems and reinforces the cyclical or interactive nature of systems.
- There must be feedback from the environment.
- Systems are self-regulating and can adjust and readjust as needed.
- Systems have boundaries that may be permeable or fixed..

"Elements [people] in a system are necessarily interdependent, contributing to the formation of patterns and organized in their behavior by their participation in those patterns" (Minuchin, 1988, p. 9). This work recognizes and highlights that families and their members impact one another, and that outside systems, such as school and work, both influence individual and family group development and experiences and are influenced by them.

> Unidirectional models of development have been replaced by bidirectional ones, where on the one hand children are affected by the families that raise them and, on the other hand, children actively influence the way they are being raised by their families. From a general systems perspective, both children and families are rule governed systems that seek to maintain stability, at the same time engaging in developmental changes and transitions. (Fiese & Marjinsky, 1999, p. 52)

It is with these understandings that we used this systems framework and, specifically, the eco map as an interview tool, to explore the transition to adolescence for the teens themselves and for their families.

THE CHAPTERS

The authors in this book were all involved in some aspect of developing, collecting, and/or analyzing the family stories. We are all social workers and have additional training in developmental psychology and anthropology. We work in three different academic settings, but we also consult with a variety of practice-based institutions, and have taught adolescent and family development theory and research as well as worked clinically with adolescents and families. Each author has examined the data against the backdrop of the theories that were briefly described earlier, and has looked at parents' and teens' stories for the implications they may have for practice and policy. In presenting the stories themselves, names of parents, their children, and employers have been substituted with a description of the relationship (e.g., my husband, my wife, my son/daughter, etc.) or given a pseudonym to maintain and preserve the confidentiality of the participants.

Chapter 2, "Navigating the Research Process: Methods and Processes," documents a description of the development of the project on which this book is based, and the eco map as an interviewing tool, as well as the data collection and analysis processes unique to the qualitative research approach that was utilized. In particular, it describes a process for investigating the transition to adolescence in the context of the development of families as described by parents and teens in an open-ended narrative using the eco map as a guide.

Parents and teens were asked to talk about their family, including whom they define as members, how they interact with one another, and to which outside "systems" each or all of the family members relate. We utilized this technique to give "voice" to parents and teens allowing the meanings that they impart about how they interact with and are impacted by the systems in their environment to emerge from the data. There is also a discussion of the broader uses of the eco map for practice and research.

Chapter 3, "A Sea Change: Developmental Changes from Childhood to Adolescence," looks at the developmental changes that take place as individuals transist from childhood to adolescence. It looks at the life tasks that must be completed during a successful transition. These tasks include coping with bodily changes, learning new roles and behaviors that prepare them for adult activities, thinking in more complex and symbolic ways about the world, and forming relationships that take on adult qualities. These tasks can be described as falling into specific domains of behaviors, cognitions, emotions, and physical maturation.

The chapter describes the changes in these developmental domains, which were experienced by parents and children in our study over a five-year transition from childhood into adolescence. It focuses on individual-level adolescent changes and their timing, whereas later chapters focus on the social context of adolescent family transitions, including relationships, education, and work experiences. The basic developmental processes described in chapter 3 provide a foundation for understanding the individual-in-context, in which relationships, work, and education take place.

Chapter 4, "All Hands on Deck: Relationship Processes Within and Outside the Family," deals with issues of relationship and social support. Due to developmental changes during adolescence, such as role shifts, cognitive development and emotional perspective-taking, teens' relationships with family, peers, and other adults change dramatically. The quality of these relationships, though, continues to have important effects on mental health and academic outcomes. This chapter includes both parents' and teens' descriptions of intra- and extra-familial relationships that may provide social support for the adolescents. It explores how social support can be used as one way to understand relationship processes that develop and change across adolescence.

Teens spend the largest percentage of their away-from-home time in school, and research has shown the powerful influence that aspects of the school context can have on adolescent development. Chapter 5, "Learning the Ropes: Education," provides dual perspectives on the school context: teens' experiences from the inside and parent's views of the school from the outside. A description of parents' levels of involvement in their child's school and their feelings about the school context are given. Teens' views of teachers, classes, parental involvement, academic anxieties, and future academic plans are related.

The sixth chapter, "Taking on Provisions: Work," deals with the world of work that makes up a major focus of the adults' lives and is gaining new significance for the adolescents. Parental employment serves as a model for teens and plays an important role in parents' lives. Many mothers in our sample left the workforce after their children were born but had returned to work by the time their children became adolescents. As the debate continues about the pros and cons of maternal employment for child development, chapter 6 presents views of maternal and paternal employment and how it impacts the family. Additionally, for the first time in their lives, adolescents are entering the workforce. They must learn new roles and participate in new social relationships to adapt to this context. This chapter describes parents' feelings about their children entering into this new social context.

Chapter 7, "Sailing Toward the Horizon: Moving Into Adulthood ," highlights themes that go across all the chapters, summarizes the findings noting the ways in which they support the theoretical foundations of our work, and considers implications for risk and resilience during adolescence and for the transition to emerging adulthood and adulthood. Limitations of the research are discussed and suggestions are offered for ways to make the developmental transition to and from adolescence a productive time for both the youth and their families.

2

Navigating the Research Process: Methods and Processes

The family, when viewed in context and over time, is a complex and integrated whole whose patterns of interaction and negotiation are circular rather than linear (Minuchin, 1988). Again, this is in keeping with our "nautical" theme. Navigating the family system raised the question about how to navigate the research process, that is, what is an appropriate strategy for studying the family's developmental and interactional processes, especially in the context of its environment? How do we best explore the way families strive and survive one member's developmental transition through adolescence while the rest of the members' lives continue on their own trajectories?

We looked for a method that would allow us to take a snapshot of the individuals' experiences and the family relationships and dynamics, while still acknowledging the importance of the context in which all this takes place. We were also cognizant of the fact that in representing a static moment in time, we would only be presenting a slice of their lives. Similar to the methodology used in the first book, we wanted to examine the family as a naturally occurring unit, gathering data from multiple family members, and documenting the nature of their interactions over time (Minuchin, 1988). We were especially interested in capturing each member's individual perceptions of the family system, and thus wanted to find a tool that would make this possible, and guide the research process.

We adopted a Constructivist approach (Rodwell, 1998) that assumed that there was no objective "truth," but rather that the participants' realities cannot be understood in isolation from the contexts that give them meaning. This guiding principle was especially relevant for a study that wanted to look at the transition of family members within the context of their ecological environment. Further, we wanted to capture the "lived experience" of the family members, taking their perceptions and attempting to create meaning from them (Padgett, 1998). This emic approach—taking the respondents' perspective, together with an etic approach—a more objective outsider perspective of the researchers, allowed us to look at the meaning people gave to their experiences as well as to compare these data with the literature on adolescent and family development.

Giving "voice" to parents in the first book, and to parents and their adolescent children in this book, allows them to define themselves, their family members, and the way they interact with their world, all of which impacts the thinking, affect, and behavior of individuals and the group (Watzlawick, 1996). The challenge in investigating families and their relationships both within and outside the family structure is to assess both the behavior of the participants and the experience or meaning that their interactions have for them (Radke-Yarrow, Richters, & Wilson, 1988).

According to Fiese and Sameroff, "Family narratives are considered part of the dynamic process of imparting family values, family beliefs, and family expectations that will affect family functioning" (1999, p. 16). Our interest in the ways in which families develop stems from this notion, for example, that family dynamics and relationships affect the ideas and beliefs of children, the choices they make, and how they learn to define themselves within a family system (e.g., Eccles [Parsons], 1983). This was the driving force behind the research that we began quantitatively with a set of ideas about how family environments affect children's self-perceptions and their achievement motivation. As we collected data from the families, however, we became intrigued by the themes the families themselves identified as important, and this led to an addition in our methodology and a broadening of our emphases.

The study presented in this book, then, is an outgrowth of a larger, longitudinal study (Eccles & Blumenfeld, 1984; Eccles, Blumenfeld, Harold, & Wigfield, 1990) that was designed to assess the development of self-perception, academic achievement, and activity choices of school children. The original study involved approximately 900 children and began when they were in kindergarten, first, and third grades. The children attended 12 schools located in four Midwestern school districts in primarily White, lower-middle to middle-class communities surrounding a large metropolitan center. In addition to student participation, parents and teachers were also involved in completing questionnaires and interviews.

In the third year of the project, an additional sample was developed by adding the siblings of some of the original subjects to the group being studied (Harold & Eccles, 1989). These siblings were limited to brothers and sisters of the original children who were also in elementary school, but were not included in the original project because they were not in the targeted grades. The siblings were added in order to facilitate the study of family development, family characteristics, and similarities/differences between family members. This project resulted in the development of a story board that guided the interview process as well as the analysis of the data collected in the interviews and presented in our first book (Harold, 2000; Harold, Palmiter, Lynch, & Freedman-Doan, 1995). In the sixth year of the study, these same families were contacted about participating in a second wave of qualitative data collection. This book uses data collected from the second contact made by the researchers with these "sibling families" to explore the experiences and changes lived through by families as children develop into adolescents.

PARTICIPANTS

For the study presented in this book, families with more than one child who had been targeted as part of the larger project were contacted and asked to participate in a study regarding child and adolescent development and the roles that families play in these processes. Members of 60 families participated in this substudy, including 100 parents representing 41 parental couples along with 18 additional mothers whose current or ex-partners chose not to participate (that is, 41 fathers and 59 mothers were interviewed). In one family, only the teens participated. Among the 60 families, 50 couples were married to the same partner as they had been during previous contact with the research group, three were remarried, six were divorced and currently single, and one had remained single. The mean age of the mothers in the sample was 40 years old, and the mean age of the fathers was 46. A total of 117 adolescents participated. There were 62 boys and 55 girls, ages 13 through 18. The vast majority of the sample identified itself as Caucasian with one adolescent identifying as biracial, Asian-Caucasian.

The average education level of the mothers in the sample was "some college." The average level of fathers was "completion of a college degree." During the earlier study (Harold, 2000; Harold et al., 1995), many of the parents talked about their educational preparation for the workforce and the subsequent dilemma of having children and working (that is, whether to work and how much). Several women, in particular, talked about changing or beginning work when their children got older. It is not surprising then, that of the 55 mothers who were interviewed, 29 (52%) now worked full-time. Another 17 (30%) worked half or "part-time," and 9 (18%) reported that they did not work for pay. All of the fathers reported working full-time. In terms of religion, almost half of the sample identified itself as Catholic, another third as some denomination of Protestantism, and the rest indicated no preference. Income was reported by parents in $10,000 intervals. The possible range was from "under $10,000" to "over $100,000." The mean and median for the group was $60,000–70,000 per year. The mode was $50,000–60,000 (23% of the participants).

PROCEDURES

Letters were sent to identified families asking parents and adolescents to participate in the study and indicating that they would be contacted by phone to request
interviews. The families were then called to schedule in-person interviews in their
homes. Whenever possible, all targeted members of the family were encouraged to
participate in the interviews (e.g., both parents and two or three siblings). Interviews were scheduled to accommodate the families' schedules as much as possible, with many of the interviews occurring in the evening so that working parents
and teens who were involved in outside activities could participate.

Prior to meeting with the families, interviewers completed a training program
designed to maximize the qualitative nature of the data collected. In-depth,
semi-structured interviews were conducted with adolescent and parental consent,
each participant meeting privately with a trained interviewer in the family home.
Adolescent participants were paid $10.00 for their participation. All interviewers
held a Bachelor of Arts or Master of Social Work degree and were guided by an interview protocol. Interviewers signed agreements to protect the confidentiality of
the subjects. They were also trained on reporting laws regarding child abuse and
neglect, suicidality, and homocidality. Interviewers were asked to identify and report any information that concerned them in this regard to project coordinators to
determine whether a protective services report should be made.

Interviewers were encouraged to use clinical and communication skills to obtain accurate and in-depth information about the families being studied. However,
they were also trained to distinguish between the goals of interviewing for research purposes and interviewing for clinical intervention and to be cognizant of
the potential for subjects to reveal information that might require follow-up with a
helping professional. Although some of the interviewers had substantial clinical
training, and all interviewers used clinical skills in collecting information, the
data-gathering interviews were quite different from assessments typically conducted in practice settings. For example, no effort was made to elicit deep emotion
during the interviews, nor was any attempt made to create change during the relatively brief encounter between interviewer and subject. A resource sheet regarding
social services that might be relevant for family and adolescent issues was given to
each participant.

Interviewers were also trained regarding the specific goals of the study as reflected in the interview questions and the eco map as an interview tool (Harold et
al., 1997; Hartman, 1978). The interview itself was developed with a semi-structured set of questions and a series of subquestions, or probes, to assist the participants in focusing on the research questions. Interviewers were encouraged to
develop familiarity with the interview process through practice interviews during
role-playing exercises but were reminded that the participants' unsolicited comments would be recorded as a valuable part of the qualitative study as well. The interview process was also modified during this period after receiving feedback

from the interviewers about their experiences with the protocol during the training exercises.

Most interviewers worked in teams while conducting the face-to-face interviews. Each participating member of the target family met with a trained interviewer in the home. Participants were asked to sign consent forms that explained the rationale for the study, parameters of confidentiality, and the voluntary nature of the interview. Permission to tape-record the interviews was obtained. Parent and child interviews were slightly different, but both were guided by an interview protocol that included the completion of an eco map and focused on the transition from childhood to adolescence and subsequent changes in the structure and the quality of the relationships within the family.

Eco Mapping

As part of the interview, participants were shown a blank diagram of an eco map (Hartman, 1978) as seen in Fig. 2.1, containing a central oval or circle surrounded by several additional ovals/circles labeled with the names of institutions, relations, and systems that might be present in the participants' lives and might offer social support or be a source of stress. Participants were asked to help the interviewer complete the eco map by describing the nature of the relationships between family members and between the family and systems outside of the family. Starting with

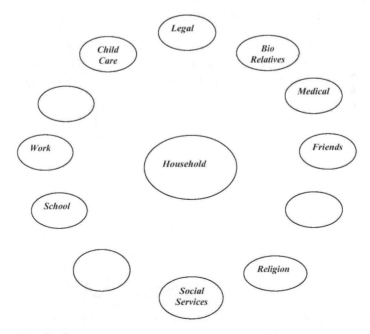

Figure 2.1.   Family eco map.

the central oval that represented the household, participants were asked to complete a "mini genogram" (Hartman, 1978) by naming members of the family and representing the nature of the relationships by choosing a type of line to symbolize the interaction between the family members. As shown in Fig. 2.2, five types of relationships were symbolized by lines as non-interactive, strong-positive, stressful-negative, tenuous-strained, and changed relationships.

The eco map was introduced over 20 years ago as an assessment tool for families in the child welfare system (Hartman, 1978). Originally devised as a simulation or model of an ecological system, the eco map highlights the connections between a family and its environment. When completed, an eco map is a graphic representation of a family's relationship to the world. Hartman (1978) asserted that the eco map's "primary value is in its visual impact and in its ability to organize and present concurrently not only a great deal of factual information but also the relationships between variables in a situation" (p. 472).

After diagramming the intra-family relationships, participants were asked to identify systems outside the family and to choose lines to represent relationships between the household and the social systems. Some ovals were labeled to suggest potential sources of extra-family relationships (e.g., extended family, work, school) while others were left blank and could be filled in with any person, system, or institution suggested by the participant. For each oval, participants were asked to identify a line that best described the relationship between the participant and the outside oval. Then participants were also asked to identify a line that best described the relationship between the whole family and the outside oval. Thus, completed eco maps had two lines between the central oval and each surrounding oval.

Questions and probes were also tailored to the specific system that was under discussion, or specific interpersonal processes. For example, many questions asked subjects to reflect on their social relationships and the importance of differ-

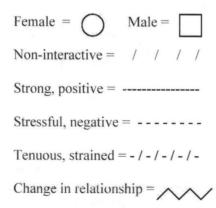

Figure 2.2.   Key used in coding of eco maps showing gender and five types of relationships that were symbolized by different lines.

ent people in their lives. Social support was not defined for the participants, but was left ambiguous in order for them to describe what they view as supportive. Interview questions for the youth that elicited information about social support included, "How have your relationships changed since becoming an adolescent?" (probe about peers, adults, and family members); "Who will help you meet your future educational and career goals?"; and "How do your family members support you?" (probe about mother, father, and siblings separately). This last question was repeated for nonfamily relationships (e.g., peers, teachers, extended family, and other adults).

While working on the eco maps, participants were encouraged to discuss the diagrammed relationships in greater detail. Interviewers asked open-ended questions to probe for additional information about the quality and history of the relationships. Many of the probes were also intended to elicit information about the availability of resources during the children's transition into adolescence. Other questions explored specific sources of stress and/or support for the family. Interviewers wrote pertinent, additional information on the eco maps as indicated by the participants and as space allowed.

After each interview was completed, interviewers were asked to reflect on the experience and to give feedback to the research team on the process. Regular meetings were scheduled to encourage the interviewers to discuss their experiences with each other and to modify the interview protocol, if necessary. Interview techniques that resulted in rich, descriptive data were encouraged, while questions or probes which yielded sparse information were discontinued. All identifying information contained in the transcripts was masked. Therefore, any names and places reported in this book are pseudonyms.

The general eco map process between interviewer and subject was explained in easy terms and followed this template (instructions/reminders for interviewers are in italics):

> I'd like to show you this drawing and have you complete it. It's called an Eco Map, and it's a way of drawing a picture of the connections or relationships that family members have with one another as well as with various institutions, persons, and systems in their environment. I'd like you to pick different lines connecting yourself and your family to each other and to the other circles on the page. *(Note: Give participant the card with the line drawings.)* The type of line you pick will differ depending on the nature of the relationship. *(Note: Explain each line.)*
>
> *Inner Circle.*
>
> What are your relationships like with your brothers and sisters? *(Note: Probe each separately.)*
>
> What are the relationships like between your siblings? *(Note: Probe each separately.)*
>
> In many families, kids have different relationships with their parents, for example sometimes they feel that they have a closer relationship with one of their parents for a variety of reasons. Can you describe what your relationship is like with each of your

parents? *(Note: Let participant answer in an open-ended way and then probe re: To which parent do you feel closer? Why? In what ways are you like your mother, e.g., personality, behavior, interests, values? In what ways are you like your father? How has your relationship with your parents changed in the last 5 years?)*

What is the relationship like between your siblings and each parent? *(Note: Probe each separately.)*

How would you describe your parents' relationship with each other? *(Note: Probe each separately.)*

In what ways is your family supportive to you?

In what ways is your family stressful for you?

Outer Circles.

Now I'd like you to describe what your relationships are like with the people outside of your family. I'd like you to pick which lines connect you to each of the circles outside of your family. *(Note: Now ask about each community circle outside of the family separately. For each circle probe re: How have these relationships affected your shift into adolescence? In what ways is this group supportive to you and/or your family? In what ways is this group stressful for you and/or your family? After probing about the above for each circle, probe other specific issues related the following circles: How does the participant interact with the school? To what extent do parents and adolescents get involved in or try to influence the school? How much time does the participant spend with extended family members? How often do they see them?)*

THE CODING PROCESS

Following the collection of data in the form of audio-taped interviews and completed eco maps, the research team met to develop methods for analyzing and interpreting the data. Entire interview transcripts were analyzed using a grounded theory approach to qualitative data. Accordingly, analysis attempted to saturate categories through constantly comparing incidents with incidents through the sampling of informants that led to the development of categories and themes (Strauss & Corbin, 1990). The aim was to be systematic and analytic, but not rigid. Categorical codes were used to initially guide the identification of certain types of content, but a secondary analysis allowed themes to emerge from the subjective reality of the individual participants.

An initial etic analysis of the data organized text into 12 broad categories derived from theories guiding the larger research study (see Table 2.1). Interview text was then read sentence by sentence for properties that fit into the categories. This first level of coding was conducted with the assistance of a computer software program entitled NUDIST (Qualitative Solutions, 1997). This program is designed to aid in the management of qualitative data, allowing content to be highlighted, identified, and copied into codes. This program allows the same data to be analyzed in a variety of ways and coded in as many categories as are related. It supports the flexibility necessary in qualitative research by providing an efficient way

TABLE 2.1
Initial Categorical Coding Scheme

Category	Properties
1. Work life	Mother's, father's and teen's work
2. Family life and social network	Nuclear and extended family relationships Social support structure, function, and satisfaction Friendships of mother, father, and teen Parent–child relationship and sibling relationships Romantic partners of parent and/or teen Relationships with currrent and/or former spouse(s)
3. Future expectations	Education, career, family life
4. Developmental changes and child characteristics	Personality and/or behavioral characteristics Puberty Emotional states/dynamics Gender characteristics Interests, values, beliefs Birth order
5. Educational/academic	Course work Teacher and/or school information Achievement in academics or sports
6. Events and transitions in family life	Deaths Moves and/or school changes Divorce, marriage, and/or remarriage Child move out of home Illness/injury Birth of additional child
7. Parent's family of origin	Parent's adolescence Parent's prior family history/upbringing
8. Counseling/social services	School counseling Individual, couple, and family counseling Mental health services Psychotropic medications Alchohol/drug counseling
9. Religion	Practices, beliefs
10. Family secrets	Information reported to interviewer that subject explicity stated was unknown by other family members.
11. Worries about child's future	Financial, educational, health, family
12. Miscellaneous	Anything that does not relate to other categories

to maintain systematic organization and record keeping, as researchers search for categories and common themes.

For example, and as is described in chapter 3, data from particular categories, such as that from the category called "Family Life and Social Network," was then selected for further analysis. In fact, over 50% of the text for each interview was coded into this category. This content was re-read for each individual interview with an emic approach to organizing data into indigenous support categories. This text was outlined by hand through sentence-by-sentence comparisons across subjects and emerging categories until themes were clarified. No further computer assistance was used. Once themes were identified, they were also explored for subthemes, such as gender, and frequencies were calculated to show the degree to which themes that were developed from the data emerged repeatedly. The intent is not to generalize to the larger population, but only to describe the experiences of the sample at hand.

A preliminary assessment of the eco maps also revealed the exceptional quantity and quality of data recorded on the diagrams completed with the interview participants. As a result of this abundance of data, the research team spent considerable time further organizing, encoding, and systematizing the information presented. A primary consideration in the process was that the richness and individual nature of the information not be lost in the research process or by reductionistic data analysis techniques. Further, the research team hoped to make the data more coherent by organizing the material in such a way that it was easily understood and useful in making inferences about the families being studied.

An initial coding scheme was developed for the central, that is, household, oval in which the type and frequency of relationship lines were recorded for each eco map. In addition, key issues were identified using an emic approach, and the presence or absence of these themes was recorded. A refinement of that process yielded the coding scheme/sheet illustrated in Table 2.2. One sheet was used per family unit to record each family member's reported themes and each person's assessment, that is, line choice, of intra-familial relationships. Using this coding method, it was easy to visually identify (a) developmental themes that were important to different members in the family, (b) relationship dynamics between the members such as alliances, conflicts, unspoken tensions, and cut-offs, as well as individual and familial patterns of presenting the relationships within the family, for example, some members chose a strong positive line to represent *every* relationship regardless of their verbally reported appraisal of the relationship.

Another type of coding involved looking at the consistency between the types of lines that family members chose to describe relationships and the words that they used in talking about those same relationships (Harold et al., 1997). Examining line choices and subjects' verbal descriptions yielded three categories of consistency. The first, the mother who chose a conflictual line to depict the father–son relationship and described it as follows, illustrates "high consistency":

TABLE 2.2
Perception of Family Relationships Coding Scheme

Relationships between	*Mother*	*Father*	*Oldest*	*2nd*	*3rd*
Mother and father					
Mother and oldest					
Mother and 2nd					
Mother and 3rd					
Father and oldest					
Father and 2nd					
Father and 3rd					
Oldest and 2nd					
Oldest and 3rd					
2nd and 3rd					

Note: Indicate the choice of line made by each participant for each of the relationships.

"Relationships between them have always been stressful. There's not too much in common. It never seems like anything is good enough for his father. [Son] tries his best to make his dad happy, but his expectations are too high. [Dad] can't accept him for who he is."

The second category, "low consistency," is shown in this quote from a mother who depicted the parental relationship with a strong positive line and then said, "We've been married 22 years. We tolerate each other. If he were home more often, it would be more stressful, we'd probably be divorced."

"Ambiguous/mixed consistency" describes the third category where subjects chose a line that represented their feelings some of the time, but clearly did not encompass the total relationship. For example, one teen indicated a strong positive line, and said about his sibling, "We do things together, but it is stressful with petty arguments."

Yet another type of coding that was done involved looking at the verbal and graphic descriptions of relationships between the subject, the family, and the outer systems. It is interesting to look at which systems individuals feel impact their lives, how they describe the relationships with these systems, and the similarity or difference among family members' views. Comparison of the eco maps within a family also exposes family secrets. For example, in one family, all but the youngest member talked about the family's involvement in counseling, and indicated that the youngest did not know about it. Indeed, the counseling oval was left blank on the youngest child's form, either because she truly did not know, or because she knew she was not supposed to know. This child's statement regarding counseling was, "not that I know of."

THEORETICAL AND PRACTICAL
CONSIDERATIONS AND IMPLICATIONS

The exploratory nature of qualitative studies minimizes the role of theory in the research process, but a "theoretical sensitivity" is required to provide a conceptual understanding or framework for the data (Glaser, 1978; Strauss & Corbin, 1990). Ecological systems theory, as described in chapter 1, provides the framework for this study, proposing that individuals and their environments are mutually influential and in dynamic interaction (Bronfenbrenner, 1979). From an ecological perspective, adolescence can be characterized as a period during which interdependencies in familial relationships continue, but often in different forms than in earlier life, whereas interdependencies with friends become more substantive. Navigating through the adolescent years can be both exciting and challenging for the youth themselves, and for their families. Qualitative methods have proven useful in the study of adolescents' peer and family networks and have helped to ground theory in people's actual experiences and to identify unexplored areas for future research. They have also been useful for gaining a more complex understanding of social processes that involve class, race, and gender and impact adolescent development.

Using qualitative data provides personalized views of the concepts, issues, and themes presented in this book for further validation, revision, and development of theory. Furthermore, the data provide in-depth information that will aid in practice with adolescents and their families. In fact, recent research has shown that 30% to 50% of family support workers rate their training and knowledge in the area of adolescent development and the promotion of social network assets as inadequate or poor (Scales, 1997), indicating a need for practitioners to be able to read adolescents' own verbal accounts of their family and other relationships within the context of their ecological environment.

The eco maps, specifically, were used for enhancing the way in which data were gathered from and about the families being interviewed. Eco maps lend themselves easily to the task of gathering information in both practice and research settings. Hartman (1978), in her introduction of the eco map as a practice tool, suggested that the eco map was developed primarily to assist in concisely presenting complex data. This study demonstrated that the eco map also lends itself to applications in the research field, and in fact, can provide a bridge for the practice–research gap.

Interviewers were impressed with the amount of information gathered within the time constraints of a typical interview. The eco map information took less than an hour to collect and provided both a guide for the interview and a convenient outline on which to note important information about the individual and her/his family. In addition, because of its standardized format, the information gathered was easily relayed from the interviewers to the research team who interpreted the data.

The process of analysis and of interpretation previously presented, highlights the importance of this tool for research and for practice. The eco map has value for the helping professional in his/her understanding of individual and family perceptions, dynamics, patterns, and themes, and enables the practitioner to present a summary picture to a supervisor or consultant who can also examine the data and either corroborate or challenge the worker's assessment. Additionally, the worker can use the map to visually feedback findings to the family/client. In fact, at times during an interview, a subject did look at the map in progress, and change his/her initial response as she/he reflected on the emerging picture. As a metaphor for the ambiance of a particular family environment, the eco map provides a graphic tool for the family.

As it did for us in our research, comparison of eco maps within a family in a practice situation can assist the family in recognizing the different perceptions and experiences of its members. Such awareness naturally leads to interventions that assist families with improved communication and more realistic expectations of its members. The use of eco maps as a tool for family members to relay information to each other is particularly applicable to nontraditional clients and those who are less verbally articulate by virtue of age, ability, ethnicity/culture, or personality. For example, our study interviewed teens who are often prone to verbal responses such as, "I dunno" and shrugging shoulders. The eco maps offered them another form of expression that provided some structure and guidance without reducing their thoughts to answers on a scale or to "yes" and "no" responses.

Eco maps reveal patterns of behavior and relationships that can inform intervention on many levels. For example, using one set of relationships as a symbolic representation of the family's characteristic method of giving/receiving support can help members of a family to work on identified problems. Imber-Black (1988) describes graphically representing an isolated family who overuses intra-family support. This visual representation could help family members gain insight into the family dynamic or pattern as well as help them identify outer systems of support that may be available to them. Such graphic representations of functional and dysfunctional modes of coping may be enough to induce a desire for change in families, or at least allow practitioners to use the evidence of patterns to focus and design interventions.

Much has been written in the social service literature about the multi-problem family. Practitioners confronted with clients who are experiencing difficulties in every sphere of their lives may become overwhelmed and ineffective. In a similar way, clients who exist in chaotic and hostile environments may approach intervention with pessimism. In such situations, using the eco map to focus on a single relationship or situation may present a more manageable picture. Such an approach is more likely to result in positive change that can then be generalized to other relationships or situations.

According to systems theory, change in one part of the eco map should result in a shift in all other relationships on the map (Bronfenbrenner, 1979). This concept is central to diverse philosophies of change, including most family therapy work (Gray, Duhl, & Rizzo, 1969). Using eco maps developed by the family members themselves, practitioners can strategize about the relationships most amenable to change when constructing service plans. Focus on the most effective arena for change should work to lower frustration, decrease length of treatment, and increase positive outcomes in practice.

In addition to its use as an assessment and intervention tool, the eco map can assist in developing relationships between interviewers and subjects (Hartman, 1978). In this study, collaborative relationships were quickly built when eco maps were used as devices for study participants to "introduce themselves" to the interviewers. Similar situations, in which a relatively unknown interviewer seeks detailed information from a service recipient, are common in the practice field, especially in agency settings in which a worker is assigned to intake and assessment for purposes of streamlining, triage, or other systemic needs. Also, solution-focused and strength-based practices rely on "exceptions" in clients' lives for initiating resolution to presenting problems. Looking for strengths illustrated on the eco map may result in changed perceptions about the client's or family's relationship skills, social supports, or patterns of communicating.

For research purposes, the eco map has several applications. As demonstrated in this book, it can be used to look at the dynamic relationships that exist within a family as one member transitions from child to adolescent, perhaps testing out existing developmental theory as well as generating hypotheses (Mauzey & Erdman, 1995). It also could be used to produce in-depth case studies of individuals within a family system to broaden knowledge about individual emotional and behavioral symptoms and how they affect and are affected by family systems.

In addition, eco maps provide the opportunity to compare and analyze relationship patterns or themes and issues over time and/or within certain populations, across many families. By using a coding scheme similar to the one presented in Table 2.3, frequencies can be obtained across many subjects, providing systematic information for descriptive research studies based on qualitative data. For example, in this study's sample, 10% of families reported high levels of conflict when the child became an adolescent. Using a simple *t* test and correlations, the data suggested that these families also were more likely to have teens with behavior problems in school and problems with depression. Research findings such as this can help practitioners develop treatment strategies based on an understanding of factors that contribute to individual and social problems. Eco map data could also be used to analyze which aspects of the social system, outside the family, when impoverished are associated with what kinds of child difficulties, allowing helping professionals to focus treatment, case management, and/or social policy efforts on these systems.

As an evaluation tool, a worker could use eco maps as a pre- and post-treatment measure by assessing relationships or comparing intra-family perceptions at the beginning of treatment and upon termination. Using a standardized eco map pro-

TABLE 2.3
Intra-Family Relationships Coding Scheme

	Mother	Father	Oldest	2nd	3rd
Parent–parent relationship better					
Parent–parent relationship worse					
Parent–parent relationship—no change					
Parent–child relationship better					
Parent–child relationship worse					
Parent–child relationship—no change					
Sibling relationship better					
Sibling relationship worse					
Sibling relationship—no change					
Child pushes limits/does not like rules					
Child is more independent					
Parent–child talk about problems					

cedure, the practitioner could monitor or evaluate her/his practice and perhaps share findings with the client through visual presentation and comparison of maps. The social worker and client can see how individuals and systems change over time with the use of different treatment modalities, such as family therapy, individual therapy, and intervention with outside systems. A worker can use the maps as part of a single system design with one family or individual, or compare data across families and individuals to assess the differential impact of treatment modalities on similar social problems.

Lastly, the eco map can be used as a qualitative research tool for developing theoretical knowledge across a large sample of clients. For example, once the information was encoded on the standardized code sheets for each family in this study, Harold, Colarossi, and Mercier (1996) used eco map data to examine what changes parents and teens themselves described as important experiences during the shift from childhood to adolescence. Conflict and stress between teenagers and parents has long been portrayed as a characteristic of the transition from childhood to adolescence. Although past research describing these parent–child interactions has focused on linear effects, emerging theories are postulating that parents and teens are part of a larger, more complex and reciprocal family system, as can be depicted using the eco map methodology. Contrary to the storm-and-stress model of adolescence and research on struggles between parents and children over independence, more parents and teens who commented on parent–child relationships reported improved relationships with the onset of adolescence. Changes in sibling relationships were also reported as being more positive than negative. Maturation seems to lead to more tolerance for differences in personality and interests, although some stated that the sibs no longer engaged in activities together and this was seen as negative.

In sum, the guided interview and eco map can produce data that are deep and real in the lives of those being interviewed. It is our hope that the qualitative research presented in this book provides unique information about the active role people have in shaping their world as well as explores the interrelationships among conditions, meanings, and actions (Strauss & Corbin, 1990).

3

A Sea Change:
Developmental Changes From
Childhood to Adolescence

I'm still not sure I have a clear picture of what adolescence is. Adolescence is, uh, a time of major, major changes. And, uh, learning to deal with transitions from being a kid to trying to think and act like you're an adult, and going through that wonderful separation phase from parents. Um, asserting their own unique adult minds. Young adult minds. It's interesting. I don't know. I need to do a lot of learning about it. I try to read about it. And I probably should keep reading until I get thorough it. I see a lot of anger sometimes, a lot of fear, and a lot of disliking of limits. I don't envy them, I wouldn't want to be a teenager again, it's very hard.
—Mother of three adolescents

As described in chapter 1, adolescence is a time when parents and children face multiple interlocking tasks that demarcate the transition from childhood to adult status. These tasks include coping with adolescents' bodily changes, learning new roles and behaviors that mimic adult activities, thinking in more complex and symbolic ways about the world, and forming relationships that take on adult qualities. These tasks can be described as falling into specific domains of behaviors, cognitions, emotions, and physical maturation. This chapter describes the changes in these developmental domains, which were experienced by parents and children in our study over a five-year transition from childhood into adolescence. This chapter focuses on individual-level adolescent changes and their timing; later chapters focus on the social context of adolescent family transitions, including relationships, education, and work experiences. The basic developmental processes described in this chapter provide a foundation for understanding the individual-in-context, in which relationships, work, and education take place.

We began our interviews with adolescents as follows:

> You began participating in our study when you were young, but now you're older and have moved from childhood into adolescence. People often experience many changes during this time. We want to hear your views about what it's been like for you and your family over the past 5 years.

Participants were allowed to respond in an unstructured way to elicit their first thoughts on the topic. Then follow-up questions were asked:

> How do you think you have changed over time? What about physical changes? During adolescence people go through one of the most major changes in their body that they'll experience in their whole life. What was that experience like for you? How did it make you feel about yourself? Did other people in your life react to you differently?

We asked parents:

> You were last interviewed for our study about 5 years ago. At that time, we asked you to tell the story of your family, how it developed from before the birth of your children up to that time, and about similarities and differences between your children. Your children are older now and have developed from childhood into adolescence. Families often experience many changes during this developmental time. We'd like you to describe what it has been like in your family over the past 5 years.

Participants were allowed to respond in an unstructured way to elicit their first thoughts on the topic. Then follow-up questions were asked:

> What sorts of things have changed since we last saw you? What is your family like now?
>
> How do you think your children have changed over time?

The answers to these questions are related throughout this chapter. Participants' information is organized according to the topics and themes shown in Table 3.1.

PUBERTY: BODILY CHANGES AND SOCIETAL REACTIONS

Physical changes are most frequently used to demarcate the end of childhood and the beginning of adolescence. The age at which pubertal changes take place varies, but they typically happen between 10 and 15 years of age (Tanner, 1962; see Table 3.2). Although these changes are often credited with causing the myriad difficulties that parents and children experience during adolescence, physiological changes are just the catalyst for the dynamic, multi-level interactions that take place in the social environment, creating the whole of the "adolescent experience." The combination of physical and social processes impact the behavioral and emo-

TABLE 3.1
Category: Developmental Changes From Childhood to Adolescence

Topic	Themes
Puberty	• Pubertal timing impacts boys and girls differently • Body image becomes important for girls and boys • Parents interpret hormonal effects differently for boys and girls • Puberty and sexuality difficult topics to discuss • Parents concerned about teen pregnancy
Cognition	• Uncertainty and self-consciousness result from new ways of thinking • Teens better able to understand others' views • Parents and teens enjoy more adult-like conversations
Autonomy	• Rough waters, not stormy seas for most families • More conflicts with younger adolescents over independence • Helpful and unhelpful parenting strategies • First born children experience different family adjustments than later born siblings • Parent–teen relationships taking on adult qualities
Emotions	• Teens experience mood variability • Teens at high risk for depression and suicide • Open communication, support, and counseling services helpful
Behavior problems	• Number-one worry for parents is car accidents, followed by substance abuse and victimization • Teen criminal behavior minimal • Victimization of girls a worry for parents • Teen runaways return home

TABLE 3.2
Typical Timing of Adolescent Pubertal Development

	Age in years	
Pubertal change	Females	Males
Height spurt	9–15	10–18
Genital development	11–14	10–17
Menarche	10–17	
Breast growth	8–18	

tional experiences that parents and adolescents face. After puberty, the world begins to change for an adolescent and, in turn, adolescents begin to have greater effects on the world around them. This dynamic interplay between the adolescent and his/her family (and with their broader community of friends, teachers, and other adults) shapes adolescents' experiences for better or worse.

Timing

Pubertal changes are set in motion by a complex interaction between the brain, pituitary gland, and the reproductive organs. Genetics, nutrition, hormonal changes, and overall health status all impact the physical growth process. In turn, the timing and sequencing of these changes is reacted to by peers and adults in ways that signal role changes to adolescents, who are now expected to engage in different behaviors than they did as children.

Pubertal timing has an important impact on social responses. For example, early maturation for girls and late maturation for boys may be risk factors due to different societal reactions to boys' and girls' physical development. Boys who develop mature physical characteristics early in the pubertal age range tend to gain more social status among their peers, have greater athletic advantages, and sometimes better academic functioning than late-maturing boys (Mussen & Jones, 1957). Late-maturing boys seem to be at risk for lower self-esteem and social popularity due to the value placed on physical strength, sports, and masculinity (Peskin, 1967; Petersen & Crockett, 1985). This mother describes her fear and the considerable steps she took to respond to her son's late development:

> He's late in starting puberty. The doctor said that he could start on [growth hormones] and it would help him catch up a little bit. My son was against it, he was angry about it. I took the brunt of it because I'm the one that gave him the shots every day. He said, "It's your fault, it's your idea." But I said, "No, your father and I talked it over with the doctor." And then, you know, he was so upset that I wondered if I was doing the right thing. I just wanted him to grow.

Alternately, this mother was concerned that medication for hyperactivity might affect her son's growth:

> He's at the point where he's developing rapidly, physically. And he was on Ritalin as a child. And I really did a lot of reading about what effect [Ritalin] would have on his physical growth. There's their whole hormonal system, it's in an uproar. So, I took him off of [the Ritalin]. He'd been on it a long, long time, but he's not having any problems off of it. He's studying and his behavior is OK.

These male teens emphasize the importance of developing on time or early:

> I was held back a year in school in junior high. And that really helped my confidence level because I was smaller and younger than all the [guys in my grade] and I was usually pushed around—before I had my growth spurt. Now I'm with kids my same size

and I started lifting weights. I started getting bigger and stronger and I was physically tough. That gave me more confidence. And that was right around the time I went to high school.

I'm a lot taller and stronger and stuff like that. I stood out five years ago because the bigger people used to pick on me sometimes. And no one does that anymore. I like it that more people are afraid of me.

When my voice changed, it like really cracked, and was really noticeable. And all of my friends made fun of me. So, now it's done changing and I'm happier than I was last year. I've also gotten stronger, faster, and taller. I'm better at sports and I don't get hurt as much.

Alternately, early maturation for girls is a risk factor for poor body image, eating disorders, difficulties in relationships with peers and adults, and earlier experiences of sexual harassment (Brooks-Gunn, 1988; Duncan, Ritter, Dornbusch, & Siegel-Gorelick, 1982; Graber, Brooks-Gunn, Paikoff, & Warren, 1994; Petersen & Crockett, 1985). The reasons for these gender differences are due to complex interactions of society and biology. More research is needed into attitudes and behaviors of peers and adults about the timing of puberty, but our study indicates a number of different social reactions to female puberty. A female teen describes the difficulty of early puberty this way:

Well, I'm like, held a year back. My parents held me back a year when I was younger. And so, I hit adolescence before everybody else did. It was like in fifth grade, and I remember being taller than everybody else, it was unbelievable. I remember like people thought I was kind of weird, like at school. I was thought of as different.

One mother described an incident of sexual harassment and her ambivalence about taking a position against it as causing trouble:

She's my little rebel. She had a teacher last year who would make inappropriate remarks to young ladies in class. And my daughter just catches on like this [snap of a finger]. She, I'm afraid her mouth is going to get her in trouble, she, you know, I believe she should stand up for herself, but there are times you have to weigh the situation. She was right to bring it to my attention and we did talk about it. And we talked to her school counselor, and I even talked to the teacher. But sometimes, you know, she's a rebel and ready to jump on a cause, and that's the only thing I worry about with her.

The younger girls are when they experience sexual harassment, often related to pubertal timing, the more difficult it is for them to understand how to interpret the attention and make decisions about how to respond to it. In fact, research has shown that pregnancy in young teen girls is most often a result of a sexual relationship with a young adult male, not a male their own age (Landry & Forrest, 1995), indicating that early puberty girls are particularly vulnerable to coercion by older males.

Body Image

Puberty, and the adolescent period in general, is a critical period for the development of body image and eating disorders (Graber et al., 1994). More females than males develop eating disorders, but the number of males with concerns about body image is rising (especially in athletes; Garner, Rosen, & Barry, 1998), and the overall rate of childhood obesity is rapidly increasing (Ozer, Park, Paul, Brindis, & Irwin, 2003). Body image is associated with pubertal time such that early-maturing boys have more positive body images, while early-maturing girls have more negative body images; the opposite is true for late maturers (Buchanan, Eccles, & Becker, 1992; Simmons, Burgeson, Carlton-Ford, & Blyth, 1987). This is due to differential societal reactions to boys and girls as discussed here and in chapter 1. Although no participants discussed eating disorders per se, body image was a concern for many parents and teens at some point during adolescence. This father describes the pressure from a wrestling coach for his son to lose weight and his wife's intervention:

> And it turned out that he was in a very low, you know almost the bottom end of, uh, you know, fat composition; and [my wife] sent [the school] the reports [from the doctor] and said he shouldn't be losing any more weight. So, I think she made some points there—the coaches think she's full of hot air or something, but she proved her point. So, they really couldn't say any more about his weight. She kind of bawled them out, you know.

These teens relate their concerns over body image:

> **Male:** I was heavier than I am now. I've grown a lot more and plus I've been trying to stay in shape, and not eat sweets or anything. It just feels a lot better, I'm not scared to go swimming, take my shirt off or anything. And I stopped watching so much TV, so I'm on my feet and doing stuff all the time.

> **Female:** I was supposed to become really tall. I'm supposed to be the tallest person in my family. I guess it was something that my mom and doctor said, because I have really big feet. But I only got to be 5'5" and, sadly enough, my growing's about over. So, I'm a little taller and I'm stronger, but I've become less physically fit, which is disappointing and I have to work on that. Because when I was little, I could eat all I wanted, and I was skinny. I didn't have to worry. But when I wasn't growing anymore, I started getting wide instead of tall. I guess it's our society that's shallow, in terms of looks. I guess I consider myself average.

Hormones

Congruent with our interview findings, other researchers have noted adults' and adolescents' discomfort talking about pubertal, bodily changes (Brooks-Gunn & Reiter, 1990). Almost no participants raised these changes in response to our open-ended questioning about changes over the preceding five years (a time period when all of our adolescent participants had begun puberty). When specifically questioned about bodily changes, most parents and teens responded evasively and did not want to elaborate. For example,

> **Father**: Oh, yes, they grew up. Mentally, emotionally, and … uh, physically. She's taller.

> **Father:** Hormonal changes? Yes, but I don't really talk to her about that.

> **Father:** Physical developments? Um, breast development. My daughters are looking more like young ladies than kids.

> **Boy:** My voice has gotten deeper. That's it.

> **Boy:** Physical changes? I've just gotten taller, that's it. It's no big deal. It wasn't hard. Nobody reacted to it.

> **Girl:** Yes, I went through "the changes." It's embarrassing to talk about, I guess. I don't know, it was the standard adolescent changes, nothing out of the ordinary.

> **Girl:** I went though physical changes. Guys notice me more, that's all I can say about that.

Research suggests that the effect of hormones on emotions is minimal for both boys and girls (Buchanan et al., 1992). Although not a widely expressed theme, some parents did communicate societal stereotypes about gender, hormones, and emotions. Hormonal changes were mentioned by some parents as explanations for girls' emotionality, while boys' emotionality was explained by maturity and intellectual development. For example,

> **Father:** My daughter is just, she's going through some heavy hormones in her life right now. So she's kind of temperamental right now; in fact, she's just started her periods, and so I think that's … well, that was what my wife said. She can just feel the hormones raging in the house right now. It means I really have to duck everybody .… My son is kind of moody and sassy, but I don't mind. I mean, I'm not that hard on him. But you know, like he'd give me a hard time over chores, [and I'd tell him] just do it, you know. I think he's just maturing. He realizes life is—you gotta do certain things; work to achieve certain things.

> **Mother:** With my daughter it's a battle of the wills right now. It's gotta be a hormone thing. In the last year the hormones just kicked in and she just slams doors and ignores you. With my son, I think hormones are working in his favor. He stomps around too, but he's more of an adult now.

> **Mother:** My son is having more conflict, fighting, and hormones. But a lot of it isn't just hormones, his mind is developing. My daughter is different, though. She is, you know, one minute, "I love you" the next she's slamming doors and she doesn't want to see me. I'm sure it's just hormonal peaks. It's her crazy hormonal anger.

Father: Reaching puberty is obviously a big step, especially for a girl. I think it's more significant for a female verses a male. [My daughter] going through her physical changes makes you feel older, and you know you're not going to have them for much longer. Um, they are growing up and it's scary. You have to, I think, look at her a little differently than I did before … . She's not a little girl anymore.

Mother: My son has matured, my daughter has a lot of hormones.

This father equated hormones with moodiness in one daughter, even though this was not consistent for both his daughters.

Father: Well, Jane's changing. She's getting older and moody. I tell my wife it's because of hormones. My other daughter never seemed to be that moody. I guess she just handled her hormones better.

It is noteworthy that no male or female teens discussed hormones as reasons for their behaviors or emotions, rather they discussed their emotions as related to stress from role changes and adjustments to new expectations, rules, and desires. Emotions and coping with stress are discussed later in this chapter.

Sexuality

With pubertal changes comes sexual development of the body, and, in turn, the development of sexual feelings, relationships, and dating. However, the gap between biological sexual maturation and the social acceptance of sexual behaviors creates a number of difficulties during adolescence. Sexuality is an interaction between many domains of development including puberty, social relationships, and identity. It is difficult to define normative sexual behavior for different ages, as these behaviors vary widely across history, cultures, and subcultures (Katchadourian, 1990). Therefore, researchers are trying to measure a moving target. Also, research has been overly focused on problematic results related to teen sexuality such as pregnancy and STDs, rather than more normative developmental changes that can be generalized across teens. What is clear is that this is a period of ongoing, varying sexual activity that entails increasing prevalence, explicitness, and intensity of fantasies, exploration of one's own body, and sexual interactions with others. Sexual timing is influenced by both onset of puberty and the sexual behavior of one's peers (Garguilo, Attie, Brooks-Gunn, & Warren, 1987), as well as their relationship with parents (e.g., teens with close, supportive relationships with parents, who share their values and feel connected to their families, are less likely to be sexually active; Inazu & Fox, 1980; Jessor & Jessor, 1975).

If puberty was an uncomfortable subject for our participants, sexuality was doubly so. Few parents and teens wanted to discuss sexuality, and the interview questions were not designed specifically to gain this information. A few ambivalent statements were made sporadically about sexuality:

> **Father:** She likes them tall and short, skinny and pudgy. She likes all boys. She likes to go to the mall and just sit and watch boys.

> **Father:** I don't know when, I don't know what age girls start showing an interest in boys. Um, I just thought that at fourteen, she would have made a little more mention of boys. But don't get me wrong, I mean, especially as a dad, I don't want to see them out and making out in cars.

> **Father:** I don't know if he's got a girlfriend or not. He might have, but he's not actually dating. He might have a girlfriend, but I don't think he's dating ... not to my knowledge.

> **Male teen:** Changes related to puberty? I guess I'm more interested in the opposite sex.

> **Father:** She likes to dress a little more risqué than my other daughter. She's showing her sexuality I think a little bit more than I think I like to see. But I think as long as she doesn't cross the line, she's responsible, I have to let her be who she is to a point.

Rates of teen pregnancy in the United States continue to be problematic, although they have declined in the past decade (Henshaw, 2003). However, only one teenager talked about sexuality, pregnancy, or birth control.

> **Boy:** I was with this girl that lived down the street from my buddy that I was living with when I got arrested and she stuck with me all through getting arrested. And she ended up pregnant like three days before I got arrested. You know, she came and told me. And, uh, stuff like that. So, I mean, I really had, I had some strong feelings, I had some real strong feelings for her. She was like the only one that, uh, I really cared about. As a girlfriend-wise. But, uh, when I got arrested, her parents had her get an abortion and then they moved her out. So, that pretty much is it.

A number of parents related their thoughts and concerns about teen pregnancy. For example:

> **Mother:** We talked to him about being smart, using a condom. We haven't actually bought any condoms for them, but if they have a question, we talk to them about it. His father talked to him about the plumbing and I talked to him about the feelings. It's a little embarrassing, but it doesn't last very long. I give them written information and newspaper articles and we talk about it at the dinner table.

> **Mother:** Boys' and girls' relationships are different, obviously. You're looking at different pictures, the shipping and receiving end. I worry about how she'll deal with boys' pressure. Boys, not always, but rarely have to deal with pressure from girls. It's just a matter of teaching my son to respect women, but teaching my daughter to respect herself, and that sex is not a way to prove your love to somebody.

Father: I worry about romantic relationships. You know, I'm like the kind of father, "Don't come near my daughter or ..." that kind of thing. I just really want them to achieve a college education and establish a career on their own. I don't want them to get pregnant before they do that. Because society makes it harder for females and I want them to be competent and successful before they take the plunge—I mean, my greatest fear is for my daughters to be barefoot, pregnant, and unskilled and their husband leaves them and not be able to make a living for themselves.

Father: Well, our faith is that we don't believe in preventing children from being born into our relationship. Each child is a gift from God. So, we have 15 wonderful kids. We accept them when they come. We feel very strongly about that. So, we don't encourage our kids to have relationships or to become close to the opposite sex. It's part of our religious teaching. They have to be in college before the can have a relationship.

Sexual Orientation

Sexual identity or orientation often consolidates during adolescence and early adulthood, although all aspects of identity formation (e.g., gender, career, sexuality, etc.) are a life-long process. Sexual orientation is commonly explored during adolescence; however, teens who identify themselves as gay, lesbian, or bisexual often pay a large price due to the social stigma associated with these orientations, including depression, low self-esteem, and higher rates of suicide (see review by Morrow, 2004). Very few parents and teens discussed the topic of sexual orientation or identity. Only one female teen discussed adjusting to her brother's gay identity. She notes the social stigma and risk of violence against homosexuals:

> Last year my brother told me he was gay. He's in college. So, I see him at Christmastime, and that's it. It got me more socially conscious, I guess. Like it does happen in small cities like this. I got more involved with stuff like AIDS at school. And I worry about him because he's not a big guy and he's turned into an activist ... which maybe is OK some places, but here he'd run into a lot of problems.

This father expressed his hopes that neither his son nor his daughter will want to have same-sex romantic relationships:

> I don't think there are any [romantic relationships] for either my son or daughter. I don't think so. If they were same-sex, I'd be real concerned. That's about all. Oh, I don't care [if they date], I accept—you know, I'd feel pretty bad if my son wanted to go out with his boyfriends or my daughter go out with her girlfriends.

This father and mother from the same family (in separate interviews) both expressed uncertainty about their son's sexual identity while implying that his choice of friends may be based on his own sexual orientation, and expressing their observations/concerns very differently:

Father: Yeah, I mean, God, I guess … [my son] doesn't date, but, I mean, he always has a girlfriend and he's always with girls. Yeah, he probably has a better relationship with girls … . The kind [of girls] that hate boys, really hate them.

Mother: [Our son] has not had any dates with girls. I did suggest that he should invite a girl to the prom, but he chose not to do that. He went and hung out with his friends. He doesn't know a lot about women. He doesn't have anything to do with girls—that's fine with me. You know, I just want them to be happy and healthy. I guess my perception is—I hope if they choose the gay lifestyle, that they keep themselves reasonably well. But I haven't seen any implications of the gay lifestyle. You know, you hope for the best, and we've talked about AIDS, and we've talked about school. You know, we had a real good health class. And the youth group talks about AIDS. He knows the cause of it. He knows what to do and what not to do. Whether he follows through on it, when the time comes, I can't do anything about it.

COGNITIVE DEVELOPMENT: THINKING, REASONING, CHALLENGING

In addition to bodily "growth spurts," it is theorized that the brain also has growth spurts during the adolescent period in terms of nerve cell growth and the connections between different brain regions; which is also referred to as increases in structural functioning of the brain (Baer, Connors, & Paradiso, 1996; Epstein, 1974; Thatcher, Walker, & Giudice, 1987). This spurt is thought to increase adolescents' capacities for memory and efficiency, as well as how the brain processes information. However, development of knowledge and more complex ways of thinking are also due to social processes such as education, intellectual conversation and stimulation with adults and peers, and other forms of learning (Byrnes, 1988; Piaget, 1972; Vygotski, 1978).

Research has shown that adolescent thinking differs substantially from childhood thinking across areas of logic, math, moral reasoning, interpersonal understanding, self-reflection, political thinking, and the ability to "think about thinking" (Keating, 1990). In early adolescence, teens start to think in abstract ways rather than concretely, they are better able to think about multiple perspectives of a topic, understand things in relative ways rather than in absolute terms, and to be self-reflective. Piaget (1972) referred to the development of these skills as formal operations, while others have used the terms critical thinking and information processing. This male teen describes changes in his thinking:

> I've become more mature, like I can realize and know how to deal with situations better. Like things that I did before that I now look back on and think, or when I see other people doing it, I think, "Oh, that's pretty stupid." And I just really don't do the dumb things that I used to do.

However, these skills can create stress, as new ways of thinking and understanding the world generate complex emotions and often require new coping skills (Chandler, 1987; Compas, 1987). These teens provide excellent examples of the interaction between thinking, feeling, and coping:

> **Female:** You tend to think about stuff a lot more than before. Just thinking about anything, like in-depth thinking. It just comes naturally. Like sometimes I wonder if I could not be smart, would I make myself not smart? I like being smart, but then you sometimes wish for a level of ignorance where you didn't have to care so much, like things didn't really matter. It can be stressful.

> **Male:** When I was in junior high I just wanted to blend in with everyone else, and be like everyone else. In high school I realized there's a lot of different people. I didn't look down on people for being different. So, I decided to be who I wanted to be, who I was, and if people didn't like it, then so be it. Now I can be more open with people and express who I am. I used to get angry with people and keep it all inside and it would really bother me. Sometimes I just couldn't handle it and would feel really bad. Now I just take it one step at a time; now I can tell people in a friendly way what I don't like—you know, constructive criticism, and I feel better.

Overall, though, both parents and teens in our study noted the gratification they felt from engaging in more adult-like conversations with each other:

> **Female teen:** I'm closer to them [parents] because I can, I feel like I can talk to them about like more important things. We can have discussions about what's going on, like issues, like homelessness and stuff, you know.

> **Male teen:** I'm closer to my parents because we can talk about more stuff. But it can be stressful. I'm often really confused about what's going on. And sometimes I can't explain it. And I get stressed out.

Fathers, especially, noted their satisfaction with more adult children and less responsibilities for young children:

> **Father:** She's grown up, you can talk to her like an adult. And there she's working her way to peer level [to me], rather than daughter level.

> **Father:** We took John out for his birthday and we sat there and we talked to him. I mean it was like sitting down and having dinner with a friend or something.

> **Father:** I can speak to him as more of an adult now. You know, that has actually been very positive. He understands when you tell him something, what you're saying, what I'm thinking and why. That's maturity.

Reasoning and Decision Making

Adolescence is a time when independence increases and teens make more autonomous decisions than many parents feel comfortable with. Are teenagers capable of making decisions that affect them in critical ways? Research suggests that young and middle adolescents (beginning around ages 11 and 12) can generate options, consider different perspectives on a situation, and anticipate consequences of their decisions; however, they are notably less skilled at these tasks than later adolescents and adults, with another spurt in this kind of thinking around ages 15 and 16. Again, the ability to make these kinds of judgments does not guarantee that either adolescents or adults will actually use these skills at a given time (Quadrel, Fishhoff, & Davis, 1993). One example of this is driver training courses for adolescents, which increase teens' knowledge and skills in practice driving tests. However, this training has not always been effective in reducing teen traffic accidents in real-life driving situations (Potvin, Champagne, & Laberge-Nadeau, 1988). Relatedly, our participants, by and large, discussed driving as a major concern:

Male teen: I think [my family] is scared [about my driving]. My mom especially thinks I'm a bad driver. My brothers think I'm a crazy driver. I don't think so. My friends drive much worse.

Female teen: I'm starting to have my own opinions, like she doesn't always agree with. And it still hasn't hit her, you know, that I'm almost an adult and I want to do what I want to do. That causes arguments, and we have our own ideas and things that I think are right, she doesn't necessarily think are right.

The good news is that teens can and do make good, reasoned decisions when they have supportive environments that provide guidance without being too restrictive. The following participants discuss this support for decision making:

Male teen: My mom has always given me a lot of freedom since I was little. That helped me because a lot of parents are really strict and their kids rebel. My mom doesn't let me do everything, but she gives me some choices and knows how to lead me in the right direction without telling me what to do. She's a good parent, I think.

Male teen: I never wanted to follow the rules because I wanted to be with my friends. Now I try to understand where she's coming from. And she gives me reasons why she has a rule and why she wants me to follow them. She doesn't just tell me, "because that's the way she wants it." There's always more to it and I try to understand why it's good for me. Things have gotten better, we can talk about it instead of arguing.

Father: I expect them to grow up and go through a lot of change. And the only thing I want them to be able to understand is they can always come here, you know, they ought to be able to come to one of us and say, "I got a problem," or "What do you think?" or "I don't understand, can you help me?" And that's the only thing that I expect through adolescence. I mean, God knows what they're going to try or what they're going to do or what situations they're going to be in, but they're going through all kind of changes, with a lot of pressures from peers and family and school and everything. I don't expect them to do anything other than just have the ability to think about what it is they're doing, maybe use [their brains] when they have real critical decisions that they're going through.

Perspective-Taking, Self-Consciousness, and Uncertainty

The work of Selman (1980) outlines the development of perspective-taking as part of social and moral reasoning. Selman notes that very young children see their own views and others' views as the same, but later (between ages 6 and 12) they are able to differentiate between their own view and that of someone else. Between the ages of 9 and 12, adolescents are able to understand even greater complexities between their own view, another's view, and a third-party view. Even later, they can conceptualize the social system and cultural views. Adolescents are more likely than children to describe internal or personality characteristics of a person over merely physical characteristics. They are also more likely to understand both personal and situational motives when assessing their own and other people's actions:

> **Female teen:** It's unusual to feel like you understand what's going on, like I'm getting older and I can think more on that level, instead of being young, like eleven, and not understanding the world—the concept of the world. I'm really open to any idea. I will take in all sides of the story first.

> **Male teen:** At nine, I only wanted my own way. Now I think I'm more understanding. Not all the time, but you know, I try to understand other people. My mom is going back to school and I try to understand that I have to help out around the house, that she can't do it all and study.

> **Mother:** They're much more aware and understanding of the world around them. There's a lot more out there. It's amazing how they'll talk about issues that are going on now … . Six years ago, things wouldn't bother them, like, someone saying something discriminatory about someone else, against someone else, and they [now] want to discuss it. Back then they wouldn't have.

Learning new ways of thinking is difficult to do, and adjustments are necessary. Adolescents often overcompensate or overapply new ideas; trying them out in ways that are not yet fine-tuned. For example, when adolescents learn concepts of relativism (e.g., that a problem can have many solutions, all of which may be correct), they tend to overapply the idea that there is never a right or absolute answer, even to problems where there are reliable conclusions based on consistent evidence. Consequently, they become uncertain about many things and can be overly skeptical (Byrnes & Overton, 1986; Chandler, 1987), needing to learn to balance skepticism and certainty. This mother provides an example:

> **Mother:** He's having a very hard time making decisions. Um, it's become almost a family joke and we've talked to him a lot about, you know, there are some very important decisions, like college, and there are some that aren't, like whether to go on spring break. He also has a hard time picking out clothes. From that and to making big decisions, he has a hard time. We tried to give him practice like make a grid with the pluses and minuses, you know. The ins and outs of things.

Another way this may happen is that the enhanced ability to take others' perspectives might lead to "adolescent egocentrism" and self-consciousness (Elkind, 1967; Shantz, 1983). When teens recognize that they are the potential focus of others' attention (e.g., the ability to think about another's perspective and that someone else can be thinking about you), they may over-generalize this and assume their everyday successes and failures are noticed by everyone else. Over time, these new skills balance themselves out and they learn to moderate; realizing that only a few people notice us some of the time. This young adolescent girls describes this kind of self-consciousness, while the older adolescent boy describes getting over these kinds of thoughts:

> **Female teen:** Like classes can be hard and you don't think you can get it right, or might think you're doing something stupid and then everybody's going to be laughing at one time and the next time they might forget it, but they might not. So, you never know.

> **Male teen:** I'm more sociable now and I don't have as much trouble speaking in front of people, like to people or in front of people or groups. I'm not really nervous or shy, like I used to be. I've also turned from being real pessimistic a few years ago to now being optimistic. Like before I would think when something bad happened, "Oh, it's the end of the world" and everything. Now, I just think, "So, live with it."

These fathers describe their adolescents' self-consciousness:

> It's difficult for him because he thinks he's different, and that people are picking on him, which is not the case, but he has what he's experiencing, and hopefully he outgrows that.

> John used to be very materialistic. I mean he was into the name-brand clothes or what other people were wearing. He had to have the right things. It was five or six years ago, it sounds funny, but that was sixth/seventh grade stuff. It's like this sudden shift from like Mr. Materialistic to I just want to be comfortable. He's extremely confident and that's grown more.

AUTONOMY AND INDEPENDENCE

With the development of critical thinking skills comes the push for independence and autonomy as adolescents begin to think and act more like adults (Smetana, Crean, & Camione-Barr, 2005). This takes many forms as teens assert themselves in a number of different ways from challenging authority to questioning values and taking on more responsibility. While the latter is praised by parents as mature, independent and responsible, not many parents were so pleased with other forms of individuation. For example:

> **Mother:** They're pulling away, and sometimes pulling in ways that parents don't want them to pull. And so it's almost, some days it's like a battleground, and then

some days it's real nice to be around them, seeing the people they're going to become. Sometimes you can see the people they're going to be peeking through. It's different. It's interesting. It's difficult. It's a struggle and then some days it's a pleasure, you know. I think some days I'm not going to survive it. Some days, I know I will because all parents do.

Mother: Sneaking. Sneaking behind your back. It's so unsettling, because you try to instill all these qualities in your kid, but then they follow [other kids]. They go out and cruise up and down [the boulevard] and find boys. So, it's unsettling as a parent. You want to keep them from making mistakes. You don't want them to fall. But, you have to let them grow into their own selves, and it's very, very hard. I do not like it. I do not care for it.

Father: Joe is starting to form his own ideas about things, and he and I sometimes differ on those. And rather than bring those up and have a confrontation, it's kind of like, I gotta, I say to myself, "Let him be his own person. Let him think his own things." You know, as long as he's not some radical that's gone off the deep end somewhere. But, you know, he's going to have a lot of different views and let's not force the issue and get things into a confrontation.

Female teen: Like when I got my nose pierced, my mom, she didn't want me to, and she told me not to, but I did it anyways.

Rough Waters, but Not Stormy Seas for Most Families

Although many of our families reported these kinds of experiences, very few families reported serious disruptions or deteriorations of relationships with teens. This is consistent with other research findings that illustrate that the vast majority of teens maintain close relationships with their family members and rely on them for advice and support, often more than they do on their peers (Offer, Ostrov, & Howard, 1981). Research shows that approximately one-fourth of families report serious disruptions during the adolescent period, and most of these also experienced problems prior to adolescence (Rutter, Graham, Chadwick, & Yule, 1976). A few of the families also experienced serious adolescent behavior problems and family disruptions such as running away, drug and alcohol abuse, school dropout, and criminal behavior. This is discussed further in the "Behavioral Problems" section of this chapter.

Controversies persist in defining the nature of autonomy in adolescence (for a review, see Silverberg & Gondoli, 1996). There is no consensus on what "healthy" autonomy for teens entails. Independence, distancing, and separation/individuation vary widely between families and across cultures. It is difficult to define the best place on the continuum from detachment, separateness, and complete self-reliance to enmeshment and willingness to sacrifice one's own goals for other's desires (Bowen, 1974; Furstenberg, 1990; McGoldrick, Pearce, & Giordano, 1982). Maturity, independence, and autonomy tend to be associated with social goals, tasks, or privileges in most cultures, rather than purely with age.

For example, in the United States we tend to conceptualize teens as children from around age 13 up, but another marker of maturity is set at 16, when teens are allowed to obtain a driver's license, then again at 18, upon high school graduation and the right to vote, and then 21, as teens move into even more formal adult status as they are allowed to buy alcohol, tend to live independently, get married, and have children. The elusive nature of such definitions is noted by these teens:

Interviewer: Do you feel more like an adult now than you did?

Male teen: Yeah, oh, definitely. I, well, it's funny, the thing I've always said, I've said to myself was like, "wow, I'm 10 years old now and when I'm 13, that's going to be when I feel old." And when I'm 13, I'm like, "when I'm 16 I'll be able to drive, wow, then I'll feel like I'm, you know, big and old." And then I get to 16 and I don't feel old, you know maybe when I'm 21. So, I don't know.

Female teen: And, um, college and stuff and realizing that I'm an adult, which is scaring me slightly but you know, I'm getting used to it. I feel more responsible. I have a driver's license now. I have more respect for adults, for what they have to do. I have more respect for myself. Discipline. I know my boundaries, I know the lines that I don't cross. I understand those a little bit better and I know I have to set them for myself rather than my mom saying what I have to do.

This chapter does not attempt to define or determine the causes and consequences of autonomy, of which there is much debate among researchers and theoreticians, but rather to present our participants' descriptions of independence and autonomy. The majority of families in our study reported more ebbs and flows than storm and stress per se. Other researchers have noted "temporary perturbations" and bumps and potholes in the family, which tend to take place around the onset of puberty and smooth out later in adolescence (Collins, 1989; Steinberg, 1990). This may be because early teens are testing boundaries and limits (that is, their own autonomy) without having developed a track record of reliability, responsibility, and good decision making on which parents can count, which creates a push–pull between parents and younger teens. This is certainly an area where the families described feeling the impact of their children's transition to adolescence, and the adolescents felt they were impacted by their families:

Mother: He's 14 and he doesn't like, he thinks he knows everything at this point. And he doesn't like to feel like he's being babied, I guess, I don't know. He doesn't like to take orders, he likes to spend a lot of time with his friends, and he thinks things that I say are dumb. He's testing his independence now.

Female teen: When you're little, they're making all the decisions for you. Then you start getting to the point where you want to make your own decisions. And they still think of you as their little baby, and stuff. There's, like, conflict over that.

Mother: There's more conflict because the girls are older and they're more apt to speak their minds, as opposed to doing what we want them to do. I think they're growing up and trying to break away and develop their own identities. At times it's not real pleasant. They're like, "I can think for myself, I can choose for myself, and I don't want to eat left-overs that you're having for dinner. I want to go out with my friends and I don't want to be with you."

Mother: She's like a typical teenager with the, you know, rebellious streak, and independent, you know, overly independent sometimes. "I'm in charge of me," and, you know, just—we've had a little bit of roughness there, nothing serious.

Female teen: My mom is Catholic. My dad doesn't really have a religion. I think I'm starting to change over more like my dad. My mom wants me to go to church and stuff, but she doesn't really go to church. She wants me to have the same beliefs she does and I don't and that's where some of the conflicts come in. That's pretty tense. She wants me to believe in certain things and I just can't. I just can't. And I agree with some things, but she doesn't want to agree with me.

Participants related that after they adjusted to these changes, there was less conflict over autonomy and independence with older teens:

Father (whose teens will leave home soon): Over a protracted period of time I really put a lot of trust in them. And, uh, they acted responsibly, and that's always been the biggest thing I've talked about—is wanting them to be responsible. And when they exhibited it, they get even more freedom, and they had to get old enough to understand that. So, ever since they did, it's been a joy to have these two guys around the house. I will miss having them around I think.

Father: In our opinion, well, that's one thing we always tried to stress with the kids is, you know, be independent, do what you want to do. And do what's right, and when everybody wants to go right, and you think you ought to go left, then go left and let the other people go whatever way they want.

Father: Watching them grow, there has been some signs of rebellion—their attitudes. And they voice their opinions a lot more. And, you get your arguments with them over what they think that they should be able to do and what you say they can do. Um, they've matured somewhat, knowing what it's like to have a job and be responsible for working—to earn money, not just be given it. Now they do a lot more, and they will argue their point more. Try to show you that what they think is right and you're wrong. And you have arguments back and forth about right and wrong. All of the kids are really independent.

Male teen: The biggest thing that's happened to me since I was 12 is that I got my driver's license. It gave me more freedom, also more responsibility. Now I got a good job where I can go to work every day. And I like go out with my friends without having like parent supervision and stuff.

Adjustment Strategies

Homeostasis is the tendency of family systems to regulate themselves in order to maintain cohesion in response to changes in the environment (Nichols &

Schwartz, 2001). Adolescence is an adjustment period for the whole family as roles and relationship characteristics are changing, leading to a disruption of homeostasis in the family. In fact, tolerance for disagreement and discord within close, trusting relationships, not avoidance or control of conflict, has been associated with positive teen outcomes. Disputes involving problem solving between parents and teens where empathy and acceptance is shown promote teen identity and ego strength; whereas arguments that are devaluing, judgmental or constraining, hostile, impulsive, and inconsistent are associated with poor outcomes for all family members (Hauser, Powers, & Noam, 1991).

These parents and teens describe interactions they found unhelpful:

Father: With Tommy sometimes … well, he's told me that the worst thing that can happen is when I yell at him. Just yelling at him makes him feel bad and he'll internalize it very quickly, and he goes away. Disappears. I think he feels intimidated by me, because I'm very opinionated.

Father: Our relationship is not as strong as it was because as he's gotten into this sixth through seventh grade period, he has been difficult to deal with. And he doesn't want to be told "no." And so I've got to tell him "no" a lot, because I'm not going to pamper him. And, as a result, he gets upset with me a lot. Because I'll say, "You have to do this. You have no choice." And he doesn't want to hear that ever. And so I've strained our relationship in that sense.

Female teen: He would tell me he's all for talking to me about stuff, but it was, if he didn't want to hear it, then, he wouldn't hear it. And it'd be something wrong and we'd just end up fighting more. So, it's like, I had no choice. I couldn't talk to him about it 'cause there was no effort of him like changing at all. So, there's no point.

Male teen: And he always tries to make me what he wants, instead of what I want. Become what he wants me to become. Like, he'll bring back stories of what he did when he was younger. And how I should be doing it now. Like for everything.

Alternately, these participants described more productive ways of adjusting to adolescent autonomy:

Father: It's taken a lot of patience at times to deal with them; and guiding and leading and so on. Well, it's more of a, again, it's more of a support, counseling-type role, pointing out the rights and wrongs rather than being, "This is the way you'll do it." Rather than more of the black-and-white-type position. We've tried to create an environment for learning.

Father: Our approach to childrearing? I don't know, if you're whiny, whatever your position is, you won't get it. Whiny means you get nothing. You don't get recognized as a person. However, if you give us a reason, we hold ourselves to stop and listen. And, if it is good, if we can afford it, you got it. And that goes for whatever. Kids are not dumb. If they can't get their way screaming, they learn to reason. And that's been since they were young, so it's continued [into adolescence]. Sometimes it drives you nuts, they become jailhouse lawyers. I mean, they can really whip up an argument and a rationale.

Female teen: They trust me a lot and they like let me do a lot more things than I used to be able to do. I think there's more communication because I'm like older, so they talk to me more about things, like they consult me. Like they ask me, not about their problems, but you know, like if something deals with me, they'll ask me for my opinions. Or, like, they ask me about topics that are more adult-like topics, like the news or stuff.

Mother: Once they hit the age where they think they have a voice, and they do have a voice, their own mind, you can't make them do things that you think [are] good for them. You can encourage and try to control and do whatever, but bottom line is that it has to come from them.

Birth Order Effects

Firstborn children have been found to experience more strain, suggesting that parents may have different expectations before their firstborns reach adolescence than they do for later children. Several of our participants noted this effect:

Father: With the first one we had to have tight rules and we had to enforce them all the time, because he's the type who, "give him an inch, he takes a mile." And so, this experience influenced how we dealt with all three other children right down the line.

Female teen: The hardest part with my parents was, that being the oldest child, you always have to break them into everything new. Like when I wanted to take driver's ed, it was like a struggle, I had to beg them to let me start driver's ed. You know, I needed to learn it. And they finally gave in, finally. I had to argue with them for a while. Then two years later my sister came along, when she turned fifteen, she was in driver's ed two weeks later. They thought it was a good idea. Like, I had to break down all their barriers.

Female teen: I feel like since I'm the oldest, I'm kind of the guinea pig. It seems like that me and my brother are really close in age and basically when I start to get to do stuff, he gets to do it at the same time. And, he's still two years younger. Two years ago, I didn't get to do all the stuff that he gets to. That's stressful.

Mother: I think that, um, we have a lot less control. Less influence. They've become very defiant. Just mainly the oldest, I think because she's the oldest. We went through the most rebellious time with the oldest. I know that had an impact on everybody, because it was constant fighting, self-doubt. I felt like a policeman.

Female teen: I get really stressed out with our family. Just, I think it's because I'm the oldest, and I was talking to mom one time and I said I feel like I'm the guinea pig of the family. She said I basically am, if you really think about it since I'm the oldest, they try all their parenting techniques out on me and everything.

EMOTIONS

Mother: I remember being a teenager, and I wouldn't do it again. You know, I mean, you talk about what point you would like to go back to in your life. I mean, I would not go back to being 13, 14, 15, or 16 years old. I mean, basically, most teenagers are not filled with a lot of self-esteem. You know, they look in the mirror and they don't like what they see, they're not happy with themselves, they're not sure if their friends really like them for who they are or for the fact that they're a cheerleader or football player or whatever. And it's a very insecure, very unhappy, emotional rollercoaster ride. I'm going through menopause right now, and going through puberty and adolescence is a lot worse, as far as I'm concerned. And as a parent, when you have to watch your kids go through this, and then, you're not only watching them, you can remember your own struggle with it.

Emotions have complex causes and are interrelated with thoughts, behaviors, physiology, and social context. As adolescents experience myriad changes in all these different areas, and are developing new coping skills that they did not use as children, varying and complex emotions arise and are difficult to regulate (Petersen & Spiga, 1982). Emotional variability and transient, mild depression is normal, while severe psychological turmoil is experienced by about 20% of teens (Offer et al., 1981; Powers, Hauser, & Kilner, 1989). These parents note their concern over teen emotionality:

Mother: They've been moody. Answering in monosyllables. Not wanting any comment or criticism or input on any part of their lives. So, probably I would say this was in the seventh and eighth grade, and it was like high school hit and it was, it was such a big change overnight in maturity level. I don't know why … . Before that, he'd blow up at anything. You know, at the drop of a hat. He'd just stomp through the house mad at you for anything. And he's calmed down a lot and he's easier to be around.

Mother: His feelings about himself have lowered. And that would probably be my biggest concern right now. Just that he's kind of lost his, um, respect, um, lowered his expectation. I don't think that's too normal, but I don't think it's too odd either for the age he is. With a little coaxing I think he'll be back up with it. He just doesn't think as highly of himself as he did probably a year ago or so. Maybe two years.

Mother: I worry that she'll stress herself out. She's hard on herself, on her own self-image of herself. She feels that she's fat.

Father: He was always kind of a moody child, but I think, he's now in seventh grade, he is even more moody than ever. Very obstinate, very stubborn … . He gets mad instantly, as an example. It's just like turning the switch to happy to mad.

Depression

Depression and low self-esteem are the most commonly occurring problems in adolescence (Lewinsohn, Hops, Roberts, Seeley, & Andrews, 1993). Despite its frequency, it should not be considered benign. Depression that begins in adolescence, rather than adulthood, is more likely to recur in the future and to increase the risk of other mental health problems (Kovacs, 1996; Petersen et al., 1993). While depression is a frequent problem for both male and female teens, females have double the rates of depression during adolescence and into adulthood (Angold, Costello, & Worthman, 1998; Lewinsohn et al., 1993). A combination of physical and social factors play a role in adolescent depression such that puberty, pubertal timing, discrimination, victimization, and poverty are all associated with depression (Buchanan et al., 1992; Nolen-Hoeksema, 1994; Roberts, Roberts, & Chen, 1997).

Signs of depression in teens include loss of motivation, poor concentration, insomnia or hypersomnia, poor motor skills, feelings of worthlessness, somatic complaints, suicidal ideas, and loss of pleasure in activities. Everyone experiences these problems from time to time, but it is a warning sign if several of these symptoms occur at the same time and last for more than two weeks (Allen-Meares, Colarossi, Oyserman, & DeRoos, 2003). Depression often co-occurs with substance abuse, anxiety, eating disorders, obsessive-compulsive disorders, conduct and oppositional disorders, and hyperactivity and attention deficit (Kovacs & Devlin, 1998), and this co-occurrence creates a much higher risk for suicide. The following participants relate more serious levels of depression. This is also an area where parents and teens sometimes mentioned their relationships with outside systems such as school counselors, therapists, and psychiatrists:

> **Mother:** He never talked about it as far as, "I'm feeling depressed," but he would come home from school, sleep until the next day, um, and I would wake him up to eat; he never wanted to eat and if he did come to the table, he'd eat very little or nothing and, um, did absolutely nothing. And my sister-in-law was the one that pointed out that's depression. And then I went and talked to his counselor in school—his grades had plummeted too, by the way. He went from being an honor student to his grades just plummeting.

> **Female teen:** I get depressed a lot. I come home and I cry sometimes. But that's just to myself. I don't let other people know. I've never been really depressed, I mean, I would go through periods, like, even at school I always showed that I was happy, and even if like me and my boyfriend broke up or something like that. I'd just act like I didn't care. You know. But I really would. It's just pride … . I don't know if you want to call them episodes, but the times when you're depressed, it's always like the same reason. Like, adults may say you're not in love, you don't know what love is, but that doesn't mean I don't have feelings. And so like I had really strong feelings for this guy, for a long time. And then we broke up and I'd get sad and I'd miss him. I just cry and sometimes songs make me cry. A lot of songs make me cry.

> **Male teen:** I was diagnosed with chronic depression and also ADD.

These mothers discuss frustrations and successes with psychiatric services related to depression:

> He's ADD and has learning disabilities. So, school has not been a good experience for him and, so, his self-esteem was very low and he failed most of his classes. We decided to send him to another school for learning disabilities. And at first, he did quite well, and then he was back into the drugs and the drinking and so he failed most of his classes again . … We took him to a therapist because one of his teachers thought he

was depressed. … [The therapist] didn't give me good information. I mean, he said, "Well, he could be depressed or he might not. Give him these pills and if they work, if they make him feel better, then he's probably depressed" sort of thing. I just didn't like that.

Mother: He's gotten a lot better with the ADD, and the medication and therapy [have] helped him. It was horrible before. How does one describe this totally negative person? Well, you look at the world through gray glasses instead of rose-colored. The glass is always half empty, it's never half full … . I'm not as afraid to leave him alone as I used to be. There were times [before he was in therapy] I wouldn't dare leave the kid alone for an hour. But now I feel half-way safe for a few hours, like telling him, "Call the hotline, if you're bottoming out … ." He's done damage to the house and to himself; he has self-mutilating behaviors.

This mother relates her son's reaction to his father's death and co-occurring ADD:

He's been to a psychiatrist and to counseling. He was diagnosed with ADD, and dealing with all that, today things have worked out. He's been diagnosed as being emotionally impaired, but his grades came up and he's off all the medications, and things have turned around. We involved him in church and extracurricular activities and camp, and that's helped him tremendously with his self-confidence … . Seeing the counselor also helped straighten him around, because he was depressed. He went through a stage of depression, and so we were able to work that out.

Suicide

Suicide is the second leading cause of death in people ages 15 to 25. Nine percent to 12% of teens will attempt suicide in a given year (Centers for Disease Control, 2003). A majority of teens who commit suicide also suffer from depression, conduct disorder, and/or substance abuse (Shafii, Carrigan, Whittinghill, & Derrick, 1985). However, the majority of teens who attempt or commit suicide are not mentally ill and there is no "suicidal type" of personality. Rather, there are risk factors that increase the likelihood of suicidality. Most suicidal teens who receive support through the crisis and/or depression do not remain suicidal into the future. Therefore, intervention, attention to warning signs, and dispelling myths can be critical for helping teens (McGuire, 1984). A suicide threat should always be taken seriously, as most suicidal teens mentioned their intent to others prior to the act. Other risk factors include feelings of helplessness and hopelessness, signs of depression (discussed previously), impulsive behavior, substance abuse, and a crisis event such as separation or loss, illness or injury, and/or a suicide attempt by a peer or family member (Blau, 1996). A number of families discussed suicidal adolescents:

Female teen: I think that after, like, my parents got divorced, [my brother] kept threatening to kill himself. I don't know. I didn't really know about it until my mom told me later. He and my mom went to counseling. It helped him and my mom.

Female teen: I had a chemical imbalance in my brain from the head injury (car accident at 13), and now I'm on medication because I was suicidal. I don't know, it's like when I did try to commit suicide a couple times. And then they took me to see all these psychiatrists and I don't think it was a chemical imbalance in my brain. But, um I didn't want to be dead. I just wanted to die, just for that day. Like one time it was from [due to] my boyfriend and one time [an argument] with my sister when I was 15, and I slit my wrists. Now my medication makes me really, like, passive about anything. I don't get mad anymore. I just don't care.

Male teen: My friend was suicidal. Basically he just left [was put in the hospital] and his parents didn't want to upset anybody, so they really didn't tell anybody. Because there were a lot of people who were wondering. I ended up calling him … I felt bad for him. I just took it as a decision that he made. And a decision that he couldn't handle because his parents were getting divorced. And I knew there was nothing I could do about it because he was somewhere I couldn't reach him. And like when he came back, I gave him as much support as I could. It's just that at the time I just didn't really concern myself with him because I knew there was nothing I could do.

Mother: He talked a lot about killing himself. He'd get angry. I think it was with himself. He'd get angry after his dad moved out. He would say, "It's not worth living. I'm not good enough." … He's done all the time, but, um, his judgment is pretty good. If he's going to do something, it's going to be 'cause he chose to. I just worry that, maybe, 'cause he is so moody and, you know, half the time has nothing nice to say, he's going to realize one of these days maybe that it shouldn't be this way or that maybe he shouldn't be this way. So, maybe my son doesn't like himself. Half the time you ask him why he's moody, he don't know. Because he's probably so used to feeling that way, he's probably not going to say, "I'm moody because I don't like myself." You know, but I think if he ever realizes why he's the type of person he is, he might kind of give up on himself even more, he might figure, "The hell with it all," and start doing things that maybe I think he would kinda stay away from. You know, one day he might go, "Oh the heck with it," and take some drug or something.

Father: He was diagnosed with ADD. He has gone through a lot of hard times in school. Extremely low self-esteem. It's been a tremendous hardship on the family. We've had problems with drugs, drinking, traffic violations, minor run-ins with the police. And this has been over a three- or four-year period. … We've taken him to psychiatrists, uh, we wanted to try different medications, such as Ritalin. He won't take his pills. Last semester he just quit going to school. We're doing everything we can to assist him and he's not accepting our assistance. And that's very hard. And I'm sure, it may or may not be valid, but he has extremely low esteem for himself … . There's a minor fear of suicide that, I hate to mention it, because it is minor. It's insignificant, but I know it's there. That bothers me.

Whether or not these risks are perceived, it is common for most teenagers to think about (but not necessarily intend) suicide at some point in their lives, and talking to them about it does not "put ideas in their heads." Open communication, information, and access to help and support are critical for prevention. These parents provide good examples.

Mother: She had a real bad reaction after her friend committed suicide. It didn't show up right away, but over a period of months, we noticed her getting more depressed. Pulling away from her friends, not wanting to be involved with any activities. That was scary. There was talk of suicide. That was scary. At first I wanted to ignore it, and then I thought, "No, you can't ignore those things, because who knows why her friend committed suicide. Was it because people ignored it?" So, we tried to deal with it head on and talk about it with her and with the family, and there was a lot of concern. I guess a big part of it was just trying to get her to talk about it, and trying to get her involved with friends and activities so that she wasn't alone and dwelling on it. So, that was a long process and over a period of months, and involving her, even forcing her to be involved in family functions.

Father: Oh, my son's friend accidentally committed suicide. That happened last fall, and it wasn't a real close friend. He shot himself by accident playing with the guns in the family, in the house or whatever. And he killed himself. It bothered my son a little, he never really talked about it to me, but he talked to his mother. He went to the funeral and all that.

Access to counseling can also be very helpful for both individual teens and whole families. Many of our participants discussed using counseling services. Here are some examples:

Mother: We took her to a psychologist, it had to do with perfectionism. She was, she's like a perfectionist, and it was, it was getting overboard. You know, she was getting really stressed. And we would reassure her about stuff, and it just, it didn't seem to work. She was having trouble sleeping at night, and so we went to our doctor and he recommended this guy, and she went to him once a week for several months. And whatever he said must have helped.

Mother: There were behavior problems. We sought counseling for her, had teacher conferences, various things. After about the third [counseling] visit, we just got into conversations about family interaction … . And we seemed to work it out. Actually, she had a real positive relationship with that because I think she felt special, that we cared enough to deal with some of the problems. And that it was just her, and that people were listening to some of her feelings.

Mother: He was in therapy for two years because he was depressed, and he couldn't really [explain] to us what was wrong.

Father: He seemed to have a significant lack of confidence in self. I always made it a point with the kids to tell them frequently, um, that I love them and I have a good close, you know, physical relationship, I've always hugged and kissed my kids and those kinds of things to let them know that they were loved and accepted and so forth. And one time he, I told him that, you know, "I love you," and he looked at me and said, "Why?" Like not, not a curiosity, but kind of like, you know, why would you love me? And we were going through some relationship issues and conflicts and he was having fights with it seemed like everybody, so we sought counseling. You know, we weren't sure we were coping effectively. So, we sought some outside help, it seemed to be positive.

BEHAVIOR PROBLEMS AND PARENTING CONCERNS

Although serious behavior problems such as criminal behavior, substance abuse, running away, and victimization are not the norm during adolescence, they do occur and have long-term consequences for teens into adulthood. Initiation of such behaviors are most likely to occur during adolescence and pose significant risks to adolescent development. Statistically, the most frequent risks during adolescence are depression, low self-esteem, suicide, violent victimization, accidents, and substance abuse. Other risks that are unique to adolescents are runaways and teen pregnancy (e.g., Westat, Inc., 1997). Many of our participants, especially parents, discussed their worries or experiences with the preceding problems. The number-one worry among parents was driving and the risk of car accidents, followed by drug and alcohol abuse, and then victimization, primarily of girls.

Driving safety and fear of accidents were mentioned by a majority of our families, and emphasis was placed on parents' talking to their teens about driving safely and teaching them how to drive. This father expressed his fear this way:

> You do the best you can do, but you hear those sirens on a Saturday or Sunday and, um, you just try to teach 'em to exercise their right to not place themselves in ... don't put yourself in a position where you're increasing the odds of something like, you know, unfortunate happening to you. That's all you can do.

A few minor accidents were experienced, but this teen describes the reality of parents' biggest fear:

> I had a cousin who died, she was 16 and I was 13. Now I'm 16. She died in a car accident. That was stressful and very emotional. I have noticed that since her death, my parents, like my mom, especially, and since I've been driving, they're a little more cautious about everything with us. Just making sure I do everything right when I'm driving.

Drugs and Alcohol

Although rates of adolescent illicit drug use have recently declined, overall rates of drug and alcohol use remain high. One of the largest, ongoing studies of adolescent drug and alcohol use has estimated that in 2003, 51% of twelfth graders, 41% of tenth graders, and 23% of eighth graders have used an illicit drug at some time in their lives (Johnston, O'Malley, Bachman, & Schulenberg, 2004). For alcohol, the rates are even higher with 77% of twelfth graders, 66% of tenth graders, and 46% of eighth graders using alcohol at some point in their lives, with 20% to 35% of teens using alcohol in the past 30 days. While some teens will use drugs and/or alcohol sometimes, others will abuse drugs, which is defined by failure to fulfill major obligations at school, work, or in relationships with friends and family; engaging in risky behaviors such as driving while intoxicated and engaging in unprotected sex; and legal problems related to intoxication (American Psychological Association,

2002). Still others will develop addictions or dependence on drugs or alcohol, defined by compulsive use, physiological tolerance, and/or withdrawal symptoms.

Those adolescents who abuse substances are at increased risk for delinquency, running away from home, academic failure, teen pregnancy, and poor mental health as well as physiological health problems, injury, and death (Newcomb & Bentler, 1989; Palmer & Liddle, 1996).

Female teen: My friend experienced alcohol for the first time, and she drank and drank like it was nothing. We brought her back to my house. I mean, she passed out like six times. And she walked right into my pool. And she just fell over just like that in the water, and I was like, "Oh, God." I was like freaking out. I jumped in and like held her up, but she had bubbles coming out of her mouth, her eyes were rolled back in her head, and I was freaking out. So, I had to go inside and get my dad and he called 911. They came and had to, like, resuscitate her and take her to the emergency room. And that was a pretty memorable thing.

Mother: I know he used marijuana. I could smell it. I caught him a couple of times out in the garage, and I'm sure there was more than that. He just, I just totally, it seemed like he became a stranger—a different personality.

Mother: She had an accident, and she was drunk, in the car. So, this is going to mean big changes in her life, as far as her curfew and, you know, her responsibilities. And she knows it. She didn't deny it or say she wasn't responsible.

Father: Sex, drugs, lies. That's probably the three main things I worry about. Uh, they are going to have sexual experiences they shouldn't have. Get into areas that are going to be damaging, even leading up to death. I worry about that. Drugs or alcohol, cigarettes you know, all those addictive things. That they could get into something that could force them to make life changing things that with the absence of them, their lives would be totally different. Our family has addictive type tendencies. I could very easily be an alcoholic, so I don't drink.

Father: They both had drugs on them (daughter and boyfriend). They had been doing acid with their friends.

Teen drug abuse is caused by a variety of factors, and no single factor stands alone as causal; rather, several cumulative factors probably create the biggest risk. For example, Hawkins, Catalano, and Miller (1992) review social factors such as availability of drugs, peer drug use, lack of community resources and activities for teens; family factors of parents' substance abuse, parenting styles and low parental monitoring, and conflictual family relationships; and individual factors such as low self-esteem, risk-taking, and difficulty regulating emotions. Of the many risk factors for teen substance abuse, the one most frequently discussed by our families was that of peer influences. For example:

Male teen: It's just that when we would usually hang out and do stuff, it's just that he likes to drink. And I just, I don't know, I'm kind of the oddity. All my friends are into it except for maybe a couple. But I'm not into it. I mean I've tried it before. I've tried a lot of things. So, when they drink I just kind of avoid them and we hang out when they don't want to get drunk. So, we don't hang out as much as we used to, but we're still close.

Mother: Some of his friends that he had in the beginning of the school year, I know now that they were smoking dope. There are some kids that are, that I've known since kindergarten, that are [into] the sniffing glue, paint cans in plastic bags sort of stuff. It's hard to be an adolescent and have friends that do that and not get pulled into it. But he [my son] just would not, his friends got into some of that stuff in junior high and he split.

Father: My biggest worry is them falling in with the wrong group of kids. Uh, you know, we've talked to them about alcohol and drugs, and stuff like that. And I feel that if it ever came down to it, they would come to us first, I mean they already have come to us and told us that this kid offered them drugs, and they refused. So, we had a good impression there.

Criminal Behavior

Despite a decline in teen crime over the past ten years, there is still a perception of a high level of youth violence. Media coverage of school shootings and other violent, but rare, incidents have succeeded in scaring and convincing the public that we need tougher juvenile laws (Center on Juvenile Justice, 2004). When teens do commit crimes, they are most frequently arrested for property crimes and thefts, followed by drug possession (Bureau of Justice Statistics, 2003). For males, arrest rates are higher than for females and include more assaults and vandalism. Our participants' reports reflect these statistics in that those who reported criminal behavior talked primarily about property crimes and thefts. For example, this mother relates her daughter's involvement with several outside systems (e.g., the legal system, community services):

My daughter was caught shoplifting once. And, um, she was with her friend. Well, I was shocked, but, um, she knew, you know she did wrong. She had to do community service, and she really enjoyed it. So, it turned out sort of okay. She went to a church nearby and did some secretarial services there. And they like her a lot. And even after she was done with her hours, she continued for a while because she felt that they needed her. So, that was a good experience for her.

A more serious example of criminal behavior is reflected in this teen male's inability to understand why his behavior was harmful:

I got in trouble by the police. And it was very memorable. Well, we didn't really get caught, I was over at my friend's house, we were throwing rocks at, like, cars and there were other people involved—one was a policeman's son. That guy got off and that really pissed me off.

Interviewer: *Why were you throwing rocks?*

I don't know. My parents had to go to these parenting classes. I don't think they like it. My dad didn't. And then I had community service, but that was—I actually had fun doing it. I worked at a haunted house and just jumped out and scared kids all day.

Interviewer: *What did you learn from all of that?*

Not to get into trouble.

This mother and son describe, in separate interviews, criminal behavior resulting in a prison sentence:

My older son started not wanting to participate in family events anymore. That was new. I think he also became involved in drugs and started skipping school. [His father abandoned him] when he was 14, and you need to be accepted and loved by both your parents. [He dropped out of school] and he got to the point where he felt he wasn't able to take a job. He wasn't being successful. He didn't like himself. We weren't getting along because he was coming home at all hours of the night disrupting the rest of the family. I told him [to] follow the rules, and he didn't want to do that. So, he felt like his dad had rejected him, school rejected him, work, and now I was rejecting him too. So, he figured, he just said that he was gonna move out of state and start over somewhere else. In order to do that he and another friend went into somebody's house to steal some things. They stole things from our house first. And they got caught. He went to jail for three months.

Me and this guy I was living with were just being stupid. It was a thrill. We did a B & E. We got in trouble for it. That's a good thing we got caught, though, 'cause it was starting to get carried away. Like, first we would just get into cars or whatnot. Steal speakers and radios. Sell them off. Whatever. You know. I never really had a job, so that was how we made money. It was cars except for that one time. One time it was a house. And we got in trouble for it. So, I'm glad we did too. 'Cause who knows where it would have went from there, if we would have got away with it. I was in jail for six months. Six and a half months. That had a pretty big effect. Made me realize, you know, I'm getting older. Gotta get your head out of the gutter. Well, I mean, I dropped out of school when I was 15. So, I never really was in school. When I got locked up, I started to realize, you know, it's not having fun anymore. You're getting older, you gotta start looking for your future.

Victimization

More noteworthy than teen criminal behavior is the fact that teens from 12 to 19 are victimized by violent crime more than any other age group (Bureau of Justice Statistics, 2003). This includes homicide, physical and sexual assault, and robbery. In a given year, 5% of teens will be victimized (a rate that has decreased from 13% a decade ago). However, the nature of victimization differs between male and female adolescents. Male teens are more likely to be physically assaulted and murdered by other males who are usually strangers or acquaintances, while females are more likely to be physically and sexually assaulted, and killed, by males they know well or with whom they are in a dating relationship (Tjaden & Thoennes, 2000). Almost no participants—parents or teens—related concerns about victimization of male teens (or male-to-male violence). In fact, very few teens discussed violence or victimization experiences, while parents frequently mentioned worries about the victimization of teen girls.

In the general population, similar percentages of male and female teens report being hit, slapped, or otherwise physically assaulted (about 9% in the last year), but about twice as many female as male teens report being sexual assaulted (12% vs. 6% in the last year; Center for Disease Control, 2003). The latter was the concern most often voiced by parents in our study.

> **Father:** I don't worry about the boys hardly at all, okay? I just mean, and not so much from a sex perspective (chuckle), but just going out and doing things. I mean when my son goes out with his friends, I'm not worried about what's going to happen to them, or who they're going to run into. Or if my son says, "I'm going up the street," you know, and he's got a friend who lives a couple of streets over, and he has to cut through some woods to get there, I don't worry about him doing that. Now if I had girls, I wouldn't want them to be doing that at night or by themselves.

> **Father:** [I worry about] people taking advantage of [my daughters], um boys. Um, being hurt. They've led pretty much, uh, kind of a sheltered life. They have been, they're not, they don't have a lot of street smarts. And because the girls have been restricted, I think they, they're not aware of a lot, and kind of naïve sometimes. And they're not aware of the, you know, problems with rape, problems with violence of any kind, and things like that.

> **Mother:** It's difficult having girls. I feel girls are more vulnerable at night and things like that. I don't stop them, but you know, it used to be, "Come in at midnight. I'm tired and I want to go to bed and I want you in." I don't like the girls being alone at night. I sometimes don't think they take me seriously … . And you worry about the typical high school stuff, um, pregnancy. You think, "I have two little girls here," you know, what if. It's just, it would be a very traumatic situation for my babies to be having babies.

Fewer parents, but some, noted concerns about victimization of boys:

> **Father:** One of my daughter's [male] friends from college was murdered. He got into a racial altercation up at Denny's and the guy chased him down and shot him or something.

> **Mother:** I think [my daughter] is almost too independent, which she thinks she can handle, she can handle any situation, and she can't, you know. And I just hope she is more aware of that as a girl because it doesn't take much—I guess I worry about her, like things like gang rape and things, because it existed when I was in school, we just didn't have a name for it. It happened … but on the other hand, I think, um, you know, guys had to learn that just because you spend time with somebody, it doesn't mean you're entitled to the, you know, whole thing … . And then, from a physical standpoint, my boys think that because they've watched a few Ninja cartoons and Chuck Norris movies that they know how to handle themselves if some bogeyman comes after them, and they cannot, you know.

This female teen does not describe a physical assault, but nonetheless, a risk posed to her at her job, which was not responded to by management in accordance with sexual harassment standards for the workplace:

> I get along [at my job] really well. But, except for the manager, because, um, my one manager, I came out one day and I went like behind the counter to get a pop, and he's like, he goes, "You look like a slut." I was like, oh I was like, I called him a dick. And so I got fired, and then my general manager re-hired me because the other manager is a pervert. You know, like he doesn't grab you or touch you or anything, just the things he says are really annoying. And it grosses me out and makes us want to puke. But, I talked to my general manager about it and he gave me my job back. He just says, "Just no more fighting with managers." Now, like, I'm kind of like, when I see that manager, it's like, I don't want to look at him, you know? Because I, you know, it's like I can't look him in the eyes anymore. I've got to get used to it.

Runaways

Running away is not an uncommon behavior during adolescence. About one in seven teens will run away from home before the age of 18 (Green & Ennett, 1999). Most teens return home or to the homes of friends or other family members, but some remain homeless (Hammer, Finkelhor, & Sedlak, 2002). The few participants (5 families) who discussed runaway behaviors described returning runaways (not teens who had been thrown out of their homes, abandoned, or who were homeless for any extended period of time). Although her explanation or understanding of the problem is oversimplified, this teen described her sister's running away:

> She's just mad because my parents won't let her see this guy. My sister got in a fight with my dad, and she started to hit him and swear at him and stuff, and then like, she ran away for like three days. And my mom went and got her, and she was still kind of upset, but she came back, put all her stuff back. And everything's been pretty calm since then. I mean, she's kind of grown out of her rebellious stage.

People often think of runaway teens as rebellious, but the reasons for running away can be varied and complicated. Teens run away for many reasons, but the commonality is that they do not perceive other ways to deal with problems at home; sometimes it is true that the problems are too great for a teen to continue living at home, but often it is faulty problem solving that can be corrected and resolved. This mother relates the use of counseling after her daughter ran away and returned:

> [My daughter's] been seeing a psychiatrist for about two years, something like that, she's had a lot of problems. She had run away from home. She was involved with people that were in trouble with the law, with drugs, and she was having a hard time with her father and getting along with others in the family.

Sixty-eight percent of runaways are between the ages 15 and 17 (the remainder are ages 7 to 14), and there is a 50:50 ratio of male to female runaways (Hammer et al., 2002). Runaway youth come from every kind of neighborhood, socioeconomic class, and racial background. Physical and sexual abuse are the most common characteristics of runaways, followed by substance abuse and school dropout (or serious school difficulties; Hammer et al., 2002; Schinke, Botvin, & Orlandi, 1991). This female teen describes the latter two problems for her stepsister's runaway behavior:

> She has a lot of her own ideas. She wants to go out and party. She could really care less about school. Skipping and letting it slide. She'll go out and come back the next morning or steal things. She's a rebel, I guess. I don't know the best way to put it.

This male teen used drugs, dropped out of school, and was involved in criminal behavior. He describes his running away this way:

> I've left several times since I was 15. The last one was when some friends got an apartment. I moved in with them at their apartment. Before that I was with friends and their families. I was like forget it, I'm leaving. You know, I'd pack a bag or whatever and I'd take off, and the longest period I stayed away was like two months. Then me and mom would start talking and I'd come back here. You know, we'd talk things out. And then I just, just kept recurring these arguments and I'd get fed up with it or I didn't want to follow her rules, so I'd take off.

Generalized Worries

In addition to the problems just discussed, parents often mentioned more generalized worries about preventing behavior problems.

> **Mother:** A lot of the kids that go to the high school are in trouble with the law. And it just blows my mind. To them [my kids], it's, ah, it's no big deal. They think that every kid kind of goes through this, and it's like, "No, they don't." You know, I don't know if kids are changing or if the laws are. I don't know if too many parents are throwing up their hands and saying, "Well, it's not my problem." I tell them [my kids] it's not acceptable. They're always saying, "Oh, he's not a really bad kid." It's like, well, if he's not a bad kid, why is he running around with a tether on his leg? Why is he in juvenile every weekend? You know. They find things that these kids do acceptable.

> **Mother:** You hope that you've brought them up right but you're never really sure once they're out of your sight. And, like my son, he thinks he's invincible or, you know, that nothing can happen to him. I worry about that, that he'll leap first, think later. I worry more about my son than my daughter at this point only because he thinks that he can do everything, everything will be easy, that he can do it and nothing will happen to him. He won't think of the consequences of his actions.

> **Mother:** I still worry about him because I think he finds it fascinating, you know, the "bad boy" image. So, I worry about him going with the wrong crowd because they're daring and they give him courage. I worry about my son more [than my daughter] falling into the wrong social group. Being involved in alcohol and drugs, probably sex later on.

Mother: I just hear so many horror stories of how kids get into stupid things. You know, drugs or smoking or drinking or sex or, you know, the whole gamut. So, I think, I feel my job is to keep them involved with a healthy variety of activities. And, what's frustrating, they don't want to do that stuff. He just wants to "chill" on a whole Saturday. Granted, he's tired from his week, football, but I want him to get out and do and taste and, you know what I'm saying, so that they know there's a life out there. You don't have to fall back on some junk. It's not going to prevent it necessarily, but I hope it will.

There are numerous ways parents can prevent or intervene in problem behaviors, and social programs and policies can substantially bolster parents' abilities to provide healthy environments for adolescents. The final section of this chapter reviews some of the key elements for healthy development.

SUMMARY AND IMPLICATIONS FOR PRACTICE AND POLICY

Although there are numerous, interlocking changes that teens and their families face during the adolescent period, overall, the family stories do not reflect broad "storm and stress" experiences. This is consistent with most developmental research that has found adolescence to be a time of rapid changes where cognitive, behavioral, emotional, and social factors overlap with each other; and these changes can cause "storm and stress," but it is not inevitable and may be short-term, longer term, or not occur at all. At this time, the importance of the person–environment fit discussed in chapter 1, becomes crucial. Teens need stability and a balance between autonomy and decision-making and guidance and safety.

Parents in our study described early adolescence as a more difficult time than later adolescence, which may be due to finding the right fit between how much a young teen can make their own decisions and how many rules should be applied to them. These teens are also trying on, and adjusting to, more new roles than later adolescents. Adults in their lives are also newly adjusting to the changes in young teens. Consequently, early adolescence may be a particularly good time to focus on family interventions and policies that affect families and school contexts. A variety of research has shown that fit across multiple contexts (e.g., school, peers, family, etc.) can impact development. Following subjects longitudinally from childhood to early adolescence to late adolescence can help us map this person—environment fit. Additionally, comparative cross-sectional studies of early adolescents and late adolescents can also address this question.

Autonomy and Parenting Strategies

There are autonomy-related factors during early adolescence that appear to have considerable impact on later development. For example, Goldstein, Davis-Kean, and Eccles (2005) found that teens who reported having too many restrictions at home, high levels of parental intrusiveness into their activities, and not enough decision-making input in seventh grade tended to seek out increased autonomy in negative peer relationships throughout mid- and late adolescence. On the other end of the spectrum, teens who reported high levels of freedom over their day-to-day activities in seventh grade (e.g., how late they can stay out at night, whether they can date), were likely to engage in higher amounts of unsupervised socializing in eighth grade, which predicted risky behaviors in eleventh grade. These findings point to the difficulty that parents experience when they seek balance in exercising control over their children's social behavior. When they allow too much freedom, they may risk putting their young adolescents in a negative peer situation, but they can also put their young adolescents at risk by being too controlling (Goldstein et al., 2005).

Such research can inform counseling practices as helping professionals suggest maintaining open communication, slowly introducing more and more freedom, and helping teens learn decision-making skills through discussions and negotiations with parents while their peer relationships and activities are still being monitored. This may be a helpful strategy for families with early teens. Maintaining positive parent–teen relationships (e.g., warm feelings, trust, and support) is also related to positive developmental outcomes. For example, as referred to earlier, a number of studies have found that negative family climate in early adolescence predicts later problematic peer relationships and risky behaviors (e.g., Goldstein et al., 2005).

In sum, levels of family decision making, autonomy, and warmth predicted peer orientations and the development of problem behavior; and this does not seem to differ by gender of the teen or between Caucasian and African American families (Goldstein et al., 2005; Smetana et al., 2005). Parents must struggle to find a balance between providing guidance, monitoring, and behavioral control, while not being intrusive, negative, or controlling. This balance shifts continuously throughout the adolescent period as individual teens are capable of more and more independence.

Activities/Programs

Structured and guided social and academic activities are a way to promote healthy developmental transitions between family and peers. Such activities provide teens with a context in which to interact with peers and make decisions within the boundaries of organized and supervised activities such as extracurricular school programs and community groups, classes and sports. For example, Eccles, Barber, Stone, and Hunt (2003) found that teens in extracurricular activities achieve better educational outcomes than nonparticipants even after controlling for social class, gender, and intellectual aptitude. Participation in service and religious activities predicted lower rates of drinking and drug use. Activities appear to assist identity formation, increase positive group membership and adult support (especially nonfamilial adults), which in turn enhances educational outcomes and prosocial behaviors. Alternately, research shows the potentially long-term harmful effects of unsupervised socializing between teens. Especially for early teens, unsupervised peer interactions influence later behavior problems, even after controlling for prior problems; and this appears to be true across gender and for Caucasian, African American, and Hispanic youth (Flannery, Williams, & Vazsonyi, 1999; Goldstein et al., 2005). Again, these findings may inform practitioners' work with families.

Schools

Finally, there is evidence that a good fit between teens and their school environment is also important for social, emotional, and intellectual development. Middle school contexts have been found to be particularly problematic for early adolescents. Many middle school policies and practices, as well as teacher behaviors, can have negative impacts on teens' mental health, motivation, and achievement. For example, like parents, teachers must find a balance between classroom management and opportunities for student input and decision making. Teachers who exert too much control, provide fewer decision-making opportunities, make comparisons, or create ability groupings or competition between students were associated with negative teen behaviors, peer relationships, and emotional health (Eccles et al., 1993; Roeser & Eccles, 2000). This may be a place where school social workers and psychologists try to mediate negative effects by working with both staff and students to try to create a better person–environment fit.

Early adolescence seems to be a particularly important time for impacting longer term outcomes, but the fit between an individual teen's needs and her/his environment continues to be important throughout adolescence and early adulthood. Whether at home or at school, policies need to be in place to provide teens with opportunities to engage in joint decision making, to feel cared for and supported (warmth), and to have access to structured peer activities and a safe environment. When problems do arise, access to self-referred, confidential health and mental heath care for teens can be critical for ameliorating or preventing serious problems and long-term impacts.

4

All Hands on Deck: Relationship Processes Within and Outside Families

Due to developmental changes during adolescence such as role shifts and cognitive development, teens' relationships with family, peers, and other adults change dramatically. The quality of these relationships, though, continues to have important effects on mental health and academic outcomes. This chapter provides both parents' and teens' descriptions of intra- and extra-familial relationships, including spousal, peer, extended family, and other adult relationships, that is, those relationships that occur within the central circle of the eco map and those that occur in the outer circles, as discussed in chapters 1 and 2. It also focuses on gender differences in these descriptions, as gender has been found to affect relationship processes over the lifespan (Antonucci, 1994; Furman & Buhrmester, 1992; Jones & Dembo, 1989).

UNDERSTANDING RELATIONSHIPS

Chapter 3 discussed a number of individual developmental changes that impact relationships such as perspective-taking, pubertal timing, and autonomy. However, once a relationship has developed, it becomes more than the sum of each individual's contribution or characteristics. Relationships are bi-directional; parents and adolescents influence each other reciprocally, and the relationship becomes a dynamic interaction. As such, relationships are understood not by studying the characteristics of the respective individuals, but by studying such things as dyadic engagement, reciprocity, complementarity, and the structure and function of social support (Shaffer, 1999) as can be graphically depicted and understood by using an eco map. This chapter presents two major theories for understanding developmental changes in these relationship dynamics: ecological systems and the convoy model of social support. Social support in adolescents' relationships is the primary focus of this chapter as one way to understand our participants' descriptions of their relationships.

Eco Systems Theory

Ecological system theory is discussed briefly in chapter 1 as a major force behind the study and data collection tool used in this book. As stated previously, Bronfenbrenner (1979) described the importance of the interconnections between different contexts such that experiences in one context impact the influence that another context has on the child and family. For example, parents' support from their own friends can impact their ability to support their children and also influence their teens' supportive relationships with friends (Colarossi & Eccles, 2000, 2003; Colarossi & Lynch, 2001). From an ecological perspective, all these domains, micro-, meso-, exo-, and macrosystems, are reciprocally related.

As such, ecological systems theories have been applied to adolescent development and changes in social relationships with family and peers. Socially, micro- and mesosystems become increasingly diverse with age; and with the broadening of social networks during adolescence, greater possibilities for interactive effects occur. Adolescents adopt new roles that change their behaviors toward others across systems. These relationships are likely to affect, and be affected by, other relationships across the social network. For example, behavior in the parent-child dyad and between siblings is often related to behavior toward friends (Cooper & Ayers-Lopez, 1985; Lockwood, Kitzmann, & Cohen, 2001). Also, in the cognitive-emotional domain, changes occur in the amount, content, and perceived meaning of the interactions occurring within relationships as well as the expressions of positive and negative emotions from early to late adolescence (see reviews by Collins & Russell, 1991; Parker & Gottman, 1989). For example, with age, positive feelings increase toward parents, and beliefs about oneself and others become more congruent with those of parents and peers (Alessandri & Wozniak, 1987; Furman & Bierman, 1984; Youniss & Smollar, 1985).

From an ecological perspective, adolescence can be characterized as a period during which interdependencies in familial relationships continue, but often in different forms than in earlier life, whereas interdependencies with friends become more apparent. One way this is evidenced is through the increasing proportion of time that is devoted to interactions with peers, although family relationships remain important in their nature and content (Csikszentmihalyi & Nakamura, 1989). Hence, there is both continuity and change from childhood to adolescence in relationships with friends and family members.

This balance between parents and peers is negotiated differently across families and cultural groups, but most theorists agree that change and continuity can be seen in the changing interplay of individuality and connectedness in family negotiation from early to later adolescence. Individuality involves processes that reflect the distinctiveness of the self and of autonomy. Connectedness involves processes that link the self with others. The interplay of individuality and connectedness carries over to attitudes, expectations, and skills in self and relational functioning in peer contexts (Cooper, 1994; Lockwood et al., 2001). Therefore, "Individuation is not something that happens from parents but rather with them" (Ryan & Lynch, 1989, p. 341). "Adolescent maturity is achieved through progressive and mutual redefinition of the parent-adolescent relationship and does not require that the adolescent leave or break away from the relationship. The balance between individuality and connectedness in the family and the encouragement of individuality and autonomy is crucial" (Noller, 1994, p. 55). These processes have been shown to differ by gender such that girls maintain a higher level of connectedness and are oriented toward communality while boys engage in higher levels of individuality and exchange orientations (Jones & Costin, 1995; Murstein & Azar, 1986).

Kahn and Antonucci's (1980) Convoy Model of social support specifies how different factors may shift over time. The Convoy Model is congruent with an ecological systems perspective, a family life span development perspective, and a social roles perspective, in that it emphasizes the importance of interpersonal interactions across various social systems (such as from family, peers, and school) that vary with life-course developmental needs, roles, and circumstances, as well as the dynamic nature of social systems.

The Convoy Model of Social Support

The Convoy Model posits that social support develops over time from person–environment interaction involving attachment processes, social role requirements, and characteristics of the social network composition and its support provisions. These interactions have aspects of both stability and change over the life course, where social context is an important moderating factor in addition to an individual's personality style, role demands, and emotional and behavioral responses. This life-course perspective is important for several reasons. An individual's needs for social support vary with age-related changes such as dependency on others (e.g., from childhood to adulthood), social roles related to occupational and social status (e.g., student, parent, employee/employer, friend, spouse, etc.), and changes in residence (e.g., living with family, living on college campus, living in different neighborhoods, etc.). As life circumstances change, individuals' social networks change as do their own needs for differing types and amounts of support. But patterns of social support also have some consistency over time based on past experiences that influence current and future support perceptions and relationships with others.

SOCIAL SUPPORT AND RELATIONSHIP QUALITY

Social support has been studied across disciplines and used in practice for decades as a way to understand helpful relationships in people's lives. Many aspects of social support directly affect health and buffer the negative effects of stress (Coates, 1985; Dubow, Tisak, Causey, Hryshko, & Reid, 1991; Sandler, Miller, Short, & Wolchik, 1989). Also, lack of social support is a risk factor for poor physical and mental health outcomes (Barrera & Garrison-Jones, 1992; Holahan & Moos, 1987). For these reasons, social support remains a critical area of study across the life span.

Conceptualization and Measurement of Social Support

An ongoing struggle in the area of social support research has been to specify and measure the concept in a way that can be understood in a unified manner across different methods and disciplines. Researchers view social support in a variety of ways: as a buffer in models of stress and coping, as an actual coping technique, as a risk factor if it is inadequate, and as an individual difference variable. These differing models use various conceptions and measures of support ranging from cognitive appraisals to behaviors and emotional states. This has proved problematic for gaining an understanding of the role of social support in individuals' lives. In the last two decades, though, major theoretical advances have been made in the area of social support. More fully developed theories of social support, stemming from multiple disciplines and conceptual domains, have guided research on the construct of social support itself and have produced a variety of reliable and valid measures (e.g., Procidano & Heller, 1983; Sarason, Levine, Basham, & Sarason, 1983; Sarason, Sarason, Hacker, & Basham, 1985; Slavin-Williams & Berndt, 1990).

Social support is fundamentally conceptualized and measured as falling into two types: structural support and functional support (Cohen & Wills, 1985; Kessler, Price, & Wortman, 1985). *Structural support* is considered to be the number of social connections (or relationships) within one's family and community (Cohen, 1992; Streeter & Franklin, 1992). It assesses the existence of a relationship, but does not speak to the depth or quality of those relationships. It is, therefore, purely a measure of network size or the potential for support availability from people with whom one has a relationship. There is some evidence that large networks can increase an individual's stress by raising the potential for negative exchanges or the number of members who ask for more support from the individual than they themselves provide (Antonucci, Akiyama, & Lansford, 1998; Belle,

1982; Kessler & McCloud, 1984; Kessler, McCloud, & Wethington, 1983; Rook, 1992). Most often, however, measures of structural support have been associated with positive outcomes (Cohen & Wills, 1985).

Functional support measures attempt to evaluate particular provisions of supportive relationships (Antonucci & Akiyama, 1987; Levitt, Weber, & Guacci, 1993; Weiss, 1974). Researchers have developed many different scales for measuring functional aspects of social support and there is some variation in the types that are measured from study to study. Several basic types are discussed repeatedly in the literature: (a) esteem support, also referred to as emotional or expressive support or ventilation; (b) informational support, also considered to be guidance or advice; (c) instrumental support, which is material or tangible in nature; and (d) social companionship, or time spent doing activities with someone. These are highly intercorrelated, and researchers often combine them to form a generalized functional support score (Barrera, Sandler, & Ramsay, 1981; Procidano & Heller, 1983).

Structural and functional support can be measured in two ways. The first focuses on actual *support received*, as evidenced by network characteristics and/or behavioral interactions. Received support is difficult to measure, and researchers often rely on others' reports of providing support and/or observer reports of dyadic interactions. Reliable measurement requires studies that provide direct observations or experimental manipulations of interactions to produce specific kinds of enacted support rather than subject reports. The second approach is to measure *perceived support*, which is often thought of as one's subjective perception or assessment of the satisfaction or availability of support provided by or available from network members (Cohen, 1992). This type of information can be obtained by straightforward subject reports via surveys or interviews about a variety of support functions or about network structure.

Perceived support has been found to be only weakly related to actual supportive behaviors performed by others (Barrera, 1986; Dunkel-Schetter & Bennett, 1990; Heller, 1979; Heller & Swindle, 1983; Heller, Swindle, & Dusenbury, 1986; Lakey & Heller, 1988; Sarason et al., 1991; Wethington & Kessler, 1986). Research shows that individuals' perceptions of support are more strongly related to well-being than are reports of actual support exchanges or received support (Cohen & Syme, 1985; Cohen & Wills, 1985; Henderson, 1981; Ingersoll-Dayton & Antonucci, 1988; Sandler & Barrera, 1984; Vaux, 1985; 1988; Wethington & Kessler, 1986). Therefore, what seems to matter is that people believe others care about them and will be there for them when needed. This chapter reports our participants' perceptions of support in their relationships.

Age Differences in Supportive Relationships

Descriptive research shows that social support is in dynamic transition from childhood to adolescence, which involves age and gender variations. Age differences occur in both the size and context of social networks (see Fig. 4.1). Feiring and Lewis (1991) used a longitudinal design to examine changes in the structure of children's networks from ages 6 to 13. They found that networks increased in size between ages 6 and 9 and became more age-segregated at age 13, as the proportion of peers compared to adults increased with age. Similarly, Levitt, Guacci-Franco, and Levitt (1993) found that social network composition changed with age such that children at age 10 receive more support from family members, while adolescents reported a larger number of and more support from friends. The results of this study were comparable across gender and ethnic groups. Congruent with both of these studies, Degirmencioglu, Urber, Tolson, and Richard (1998) found that support networks begin to take shape around age 11 such that childhood friendships change in characteristics and quality to reflect definitions of social support. These networks become moderately stable throughout the middle to high school years.

Ages 6–10

Size of network increases
More support from family members than peers
Same sex relationships preferred
More companionship than emotional support from peers

Ages 11–12

Friendship characteristics become more adult-like and provide more social support
Average number of friends increases
More emotional support provided in friendships in addition to companionship

---

Ages 13–14

Age-segregation and proportion of peers to adult increases
Relationships with grandparents and teachers decreases from childhood
More overall support from friends
Cross-sex friendships and interests begin
Sibling interactions decrease from childhood and become less intense

---

Ages 15–16

Dating and physical intimacy begin
Quality of friends begins to become more important than quantity

---

Ages 17–25

Maturing ideas of romantic partnerships and more complicated sexual relationships
Sibling interactions become more egalitatian and new quality develops into early adulthood

---

Figure 4.1.   Changes in relationship networks and qualities from childhood through adolescence.

Additionally, Berndt and Perry (1986) interviewed a cross-sectional sample of subjects ages 8 to 14 about features of their friendships and found that children verbally report more emotional support with age, with a significant increase in the mean number of reports between second and fourth grades (at about 10 years of age). Furman and Buhrmester (1992) further specified these relationships. They found, cross-sectionally, that parents provided more support than did peers to fourth graders, but peer support increased between grades four and seven. Also, perceptions of conflict with parents increased with age; relationships with grandparents and teachers were less frequent with age; romantic relationships were seen as more supportive with age; and relationships with siblings became less intense and more egalitarian with age (although this may reflect lower rates of sibling interaction with age). Other studies have reported similar results (Bigelow, 1977; Cauce, Reid, Landesman, & Gonzales, 1990; Jones & Dembo, 1989).

In sum, many studies of age differences in social support have found similar trends: network size and age segregation generally increase with age, and children perceive more support from family members while friends become the primary support givers by late adolescence. These changes reflect developmental patterns in autonomy from caretakers and the formation of more egalitarian and mutual peer relationships. However, further research is needed to explore the more complex nature of the balance between support from parents and peers, as these two groups of people may provide different support functions that influence different developmental needs. For example, parents may serve to provide more support for academic achievement and career goals while friends fulfill more emotional and intimacy needs during adolescence.

Gender Differences in Supportive Relationships

Research findings of gender differences in social support relationships are more equivocal than those of age differences. Most research on gender differences in social support has used adult participants, indicating a need for studies of child and adolescent gender differences in peer support; but the available descriptive data suggest that distinct gender differences in friendship patterns, especially those related to social support functions, exist across childhood and into adulthood (Winstead, 1986). Adult women report that they provide and receive more support than men and have more extensive, satisfying, and varied networks, while men tend to maintain close and intimate ties with only one person, such as their spouse (Antonucci, 1983; Bell, 1981; Hobfoll, 1986; Sarason et al., 1983). Research on adolescents has replicated some of these findings. Berndt (1982) concluded that adolescent girls' friendships are more intimate and more exclusive than those of boys. Specifically, girls mention intimate sharing of thoughts and feelings more often than do boys; girls seem less willing to include a nonfriend in an ongoing conversation than do boys; and if girls have a stable, reciprocated friendship, they are less willing to make new friends than are boys.

Sex differences in social support are due to a variety of factors, including (a) gender role beliefs and behaviors related to help seeking and use, (b) either support providers' gender-biased perceptions about males' and females' needs for support or their desire to provide support to them, and (c) actual differences in males' and females' needs for support. Researchers have only begun to study these causal factors, but preliminary evidence exists for the effects of gender-role beliefs and behaviors on supportive relationships during adolescence. For example, beliefs about communality versus exchange in relationships vary by gender and influence perceptions of support. There is some evidence to suggest that these differences in perceptions are due to socialization of girls toward interpersonal skills (such as empathy, reflective communications, and providing comforting messages) and cognitive orientations to relationships involving communality and expressivity, which have been found to relate positively to social support. Alternately, males lack particular skills related to supportive relationships and are more likely to have cognitive orientations toward relationships that involve exchange and instrumentality, which have been found to relate negatively to social support (Jones & Costin, 1995; Kunkel & Burleson, 1999; Murstein & Azar, 1986).

Gender-role related behaviors also have been found to influence support during adolescence and in adulthood. Females have higher rates of self-disclosure about feelings and problems and place greater emphasis on mutual support than males, while males are more likely than females to share activities and interests in their friendships (Berndt, 1982; Caldwell & Peplau, 1982; Wright, 1982). Cross-gender relationships seem to have some effect on these patterns. For example, females report deep intimate conversations with both male and female friends, but males report these types of conversations more with female friends than with other males (Caldwell & Peplau, 1982; Kunkel & Burleson, 1999). Also, both males and females report that they would go to a female friend rather than a male with a personal problem for emotional and social support. Thus, males do seem able to engage in emotional support with females, but are less likely to do so with other males.

Most researchers have found that adolescent females receive more support, especially emotional support, from peers than do males. However, results are more variable regarding family support. Some studies of family support have not found any gender differences in support from immediate family members (Vaux, 1985), while other studies report that adolescent males receive more support from parents and other nonfamily adults than do females (Colarossi, 2001; Cumsille & Epstein, 1994; Frey & Rothlisberger, 1996; Scheirer & Botvin, 1997). Additionally, the relationship between family and peer support has often been found to be additive rather than compensatory in nature (van Beest & Baerveldt, 1999; Wentzel, 1998). Peer support is usually unrelated to family functioning (Cumsille & Epstein, 1994; Kobak & Sceery, 1988), suggesting that even if teens are not getting adequate support at home, this deficiency is unrelated to their obtaining peer support outside the home. However, as noted in chapter 3, conflictual parent–child relationships can influence teens' choices related to negative peer groups and problem behavior.

Studies of age and gender interactions show similar findings. Studies that have examined the actual content of children's conversations have found that girls in the second grade were engaging in long, intimate conversations about events in their lives and providing each other active listening, support, and encouragement. Boys at this age talked about what activities they would do together. These patterns continued until the tenth grade when boys' time discussing personal problems increased, but in response to such disclosures they tended to downplay or dismiss the speakers' problem (Tannen, 1990). Studies by Bigelow (1977) and Jones and Dembo (1989) also found that scores on friendship intimacy increased from ages 9 to 15 years, with girls consistently scoring higher on levels of intimacy than boys across the time span.

What does seem fairly clear is that girls receive more support from nonfamily sources, especially peers, than boys, and that girls may possess some characteristics, such as engaging in conversations about more personal thoughts and feelings, that enable them to develop new supports more readily outside the family context. This may be because the typical female gender role involves more aspects of nurturing, communality, and affiliation than does the typical male gender role. In turn, these characteristics are more likely to lead to supportive relationships with peers than are characteristics associated with the male gender role. It may also be that girls need more support, due to more stress, and consequently seek it from many different sources.

THE STORIES

The eco map technique described in chapter 2 provided an organized and consistent way for participants to discuss many aspects of their relationships with immediate and extended family members, friends, co-workers, and others in their lives. Text that described any information about these relationships was initially coded into a category called "Family Life and Social Network." A second level of coding identified topics related to the function and structure of supportive relationships, including general developmental changes over the last 5 years; the current number of friends; and who provides emotional, companionship, and instrumental support to teens. Finally, the text was analyzed a third time for themes that emerged under each topic (see Tables 4.1 and 4.2 for adolescents' and parents' topics and themes). Themes related to teens' and parents' views of the adolescents' relationships, not parents' relationships with each other or their own peers, are the focus of this chapter.

TABLE 4.1
Adolescent Descriptions by Category, Topics, and Themes

Category: Family life and social network

Topic	Adolescent themes
Developmental changes	• Closer, more intimate and supportive friendships with peers • Fewer, closer friends better than quantity of friends • More mature relationship with parents • Dating relationships rarely discussed by teens • About half of teens report no changes in their relationships with siblings from childhood to adolescence • About one third of teens report that sibling relationships imiproved from childhood to adolescence • Teens rarely discuss content or quality of their sibling relationships
Support structure	• Most teens report four close friends • Differentiation between close friends and acquaintances
Support functions and providers	*Emotional support* • Equal emotional support from peers and parents • More emotional support from mothers than fathers • Female teens discuss emotional support more than male teens • Emotional support from nonparental adults mentioned by female teens more often than by males • Teachers and extended family members are available to talk to about personal problems *Companionship* • More compantionship support from peers than parents • More male teens discussed sports companionship with fathers than did females • More male teens discussed sports companionships with peers than did females • Male teens do not report companionship as associated with other kinds of support (i.e., sports and emotional support not discussed as co-occurring); however, female teens do mix activities and emotional support with peers and parents • More companionship related to activities, such as sports, with fathers than mothers *Instrumental support* • More academic support from parents than peers, such as help with school work and future academic goals • Tangible help and advice received more often from adults (parents and other adults) than from peers

(continued)

TABLE 4.1 *(continued)*

	• More male teens than females discuss receiving academic support from adults
	• More support from parents than peers for sports and hobbies
Negative effects of relationships	• Teens discuss stress in peer relationships due to bickering and gossip, but do not note that their peers influence negative behaviors

TABLE 4.2
Parent Descriptions by Category, Topics, and Themes

Category: Family life and social network

Topic	Adolescent themes
Developmental changes	• Closer, more intimate and supportive friendships with peers
	• Fewer, closer friends better than quantity of friends
	• More mature relationship between parents and teens, but teens want to be with friends more than parents
	• Dating relationships a source of concern
	• Dating and sexuality closely tied
	• Religion influences dating practices
	• Few parents equate teen dating with marriage
	• About half of parents report no changes in relationships between siblings between childhood and adolescence
	• About one third of parents report that sibling relationships improved from childhood to adolescence
	• Sibling relationships are strained and conflictual, but they care about each other
Support structure	• Teens have one to six close friends
	• Types of friends include close friends, acquaintances, and both same- and opposite-sex friendships
Support functions and providers	*Emotional support*
	• Parents do not have a lot of knowledge about the content or quality of their teens' emotional support from friends
	• Mothers discuss providing emotional support to teens more often than fathers
	• Teachers and extended family members are available to talk to or about personal problems
	Companionship
	• More fathers than mothers discuss doing activities with teens

(continued)

TABLE 4.2 *(continued)*

	• Parents note the importance of peer companionship for their teens, and how isolation from friends can create problems with depression
	Instrumental support • Tangible help and advice given to teens regarding academic planning and sports
Negative effects of relationships	• Parents concerned about negative peer influences on their teen's behaviors • Wide range of levels of parental monitoring of friendships • Drug use with friends the most common concern for parents

Developmental Changes in Support

Peers. One question asked during the interview was, "Has becoming an adolescent affected your relationships with other people?" Adolescents described becoming emotionally closer to their friends and parents. Their descriptions reflect developmental advances in the ability to engage in more complex, in-depth conversations with others about personal thoughts and feelings, to take another person's perspective and describe their own, and to give and receive emotional support (Denton & Zarbatany, 1996). This mother provides a good example:

> I think the older the kids get, the more supportive their friends are. I will say that. I think at Scott's age [12], they aren't really supportive. But I think at Dave's age [17], yes, they are. They are developing friendships that are more adult-like. They do help each other out and have that kind of give-and-take that adults have. At Scott's age, they don't do that.

Although more female teens than males discussed changes in their relationships with parents, the content of their descriptions was similar about peers and parents. This female student provides a description of changes in her relationships with peers:

> Back when I was in …, it was more like, the more friends you have, the better. Now it's the better friends you have doesn't necessarily mean the more friends you have. [I have] about four [close friends].

A male student described the change in peer relationships this way:

> Well, I've noticed that I have gotten better friends [since adolescence]. Stronger relationships with them, not just like, "Oh, we're buddies and we're going to do something" and that's all. Like, more, kind of friends you can talk to if you're having a problem or you just call and [they] talk to you and [you] tell them what's going on and everything. Just having someone to talk to, really. Like a more true friend. Not just like a buddy.

Another male said:

I would say I'm more open with my friends. Like, when I was younger, we didn't, we just kind of goofed around and stuff. And now, I mean, we sort of, we do the same thing, but it's like we're not afraid to talk about stuff. It's more serious. It's not just fooling around. We talk about more personal stuff.

Most parents agreed that their teens had more mature and closer friendships. This mother states:

[My son] always liked doing things in a group, being part of a group. I think, if anything, he became [in the last 5 years] more content with being with a smaller group than he had before. Or being part of a smaller, close circle of friends. I guess that's just part of growing up, that you start of realize that you can't be best friends with too many people.

Parent–Child. Descriptions of changes in relationships with parents were described in a similar way. One female teen remarks about her father, "When we have disagreements, we try to make each other understand. We're closer than we were [since childhood]." Another female states about her mother, "I've always felt comfortable, but I guess more now that I'm older. I talk to her more about things just because there's more to talk about." And about parents in general, a female comments:

I think I'm more honest with them now. Now my parents can actually just sit down and talk with me about the family. So, that was like a major change [since childhood]. And, um, actually I have more, like, conversations with my parents instead of just, like, we discuss things more.

Similarly, this male said about his parents:

I think I tell them more now than I used to. Just because I realize now more than I did, it won't be so bad, you know, if I tell them something. Like when I was younger, I used to think, hey, if I tell them something, you know, it wasn't such a good idea. But now that I realize, you know, so I tell them more, I think, than I did. Well, I don't know, like stuff with, you know, things that go on in school or girlfriends, stuff like that. Because I think, I don't know, I've grown more. So, it's like more understanding, very important, more so. But they realize, too, what's going on with me.

Parents' descriptions were more equivocal. Although many expressed more mature relationships with their teens (described earlier in chap. 3), parents also shared concern and some sadness about their children wanting to be with friends more than with parents. For example, this father states:

It's been difficult to communicate with him. I'm trying to find ways. Dads are uncool at this stage, or at least this dad is. But maybe we preach, maybe I preach. I don't know. Most of my time with him is just driving him here and there.

This mother expresses a similar concern:

He doesn't want to feel like he's being babied, I guess. I don't know. He doesn't like to take orders too much, and he wants to spend time with his friends. And most of the things I say are "dumb," and he laughs at me. He's more distant. He's moving away from me and his friends are more important at this point than family, and school.

Siblings. Sibling relationships are an integral part of family dynamics throughout the life span, but the nature and quality of these relationships have mostly been studied in childhood and adulthood, leaving a gap in knowledge during the adolescent period (Cicirelli, 1995; Stewart, Verbrugge, & Beilfuss, 1998). Additionally, many studies of developmental changes in sibling relationships have been cross-sectional rather than longitudinal. Available studies indicate that sibling relationships tend to mirror peer relationships in that they become egalitarian and more symmetrical from childhood to adolescence (Buhrmester & Furman, 1990). Further, early (middle-childhood) sibling relationships predict the quality of later adolescent peer relationships (Yeh & Lempers, 2004). However, during adolescence, siblings spend less time together in play and companionship and become more differentiated from each other, but also have less conflict than they did as children (Cole & Kerns, 2001; Feinberg, McHale, Crouter, & Cummsille, 2003); whereas relationships with peers become more of a focus of time and energy. In sum, as teens develop their own identities and more adult-like relationships with peers, they show increased autonomy and emotional separation from parents as well as siblings. Some researchers have best described adolescents' sibling relationships as ambivalent (Deater-Deckard, Dunn, & Lussier, 2002; Stocker, Lanthier, & Furman, 1997).

Interestingly, similar to dating relationships, teen participants had very little to say about their sibling relationships. They expressed more disinterest in the topic than about other relationships in their lives. There may be a similar reason for this as for dating relationships; that is, early and middle adolescents have some difficulty cognitively and emotionally understanding the nature of and changes in sibling relationships. The ability to reflect on the complexity of sibling relationships, and the renewal of the quality and development of more adult-like relationships with siblings tends to happen in early adulthood, not in adolescence (Scharf, Shulman, & Avigad-Spitz, 2005).

Our teen participants did provide some information. In line drawings on the eco map, approximately 30% of teens said their relationships with siblings improved from childhood to adolescence, 15% said they worsened, and the remainder had no opinion or said they were the same over time. Parents' opinions of sibling relationship improvement, worsening, or staying the same were almost identical to their children's reports. However, parents' were much more interested in describing and discussing the nature of their children's relationships with each other.

Parents most often described sibling relationships as tense and conflictual, but that sibs generally care for each other. For example,

Mother: One moment, they may be fighting like cats and dogs, and then the other, they will interact, like, one will come to the defense of the other—against, perhaps, what I am trying to do. To my irritation, they do that. But I understand and don't try to stop it. I let her speak her piece about that. Because I think sisters bonding like that is very good. So, I think they're supportive that way, in a sibling way. Where the two might be getting along, and then the other one might be the outsider. It constantly changes, where [the two brothers] might be teasing [their sister] a little bit. Then it will switch, and it will be the other two against one. But as far as support, I think as far as support of running the home, knowing that we are family, a unit, together, and to keep things running, uh, support whether it's borrowing money from one another, you know, um, things like that ... we have to be a family together and pull together. In tough times we do. They don't hold grudges long with one another. You may have had a spat, an argument. Someone lost their temper. Um, but it doesn't last long. Usually it's over within a relatively short period of time. Um, so yeah, those things change.

Mother: It varies. It's not always tenuous or stressful, even though they have their moments as siblings. Um, I think they're drawn a little closer, due to the fact that their personalities have changed a little bit. [My daughter] has grown. She's settled down a little bit more. She's, uh, as a teenager, say within, maybe six months to a year ago, going through that stage of being a little more mouthy. A little more defiant, perhaps. Um, that would upset my son. He thought she was being disrespectful. They would argue and things like that. But I think on a whole, their relationship is changing. They have good times where they laugh together and talk together, and other times it would be tenuous and strained. But on the whole, I'd have to say, it's a changing relationship—for the better. Yes. I would say it's changing for the better.

Dating. Dating and the formation of romantic relationships has long been considered an important part of adolescent development (e.g., Erikson, 1968). Much of the research on early romantic relationships has focused on sexuality and the problem of teen pregnancy and sexually transmitted diseases. Much less is known about the developmental timing of romantic love in terms of emotional and interpersonal peer dynamics. What we do know is that these relationships have complicated outcomes. Dating and positive romantic relationships (that is, those that provide support and developmentally appropriate emotional bonding and closeness) have good outcomes for teens such as secure identity development, less depression, fewer risk-taking behaviors, and decreased social anxiety. However, dating violence and negative emotional interactions between teens can have just the opposite effects and additional negative consequences such as delinquency (La Greca & Harrison, 2005; Montgomery, 2005; Nelson & Barry, 2005; Stanton-Salazar & Spina, 2005; Young & D'Arcy, 2005).

Studies of developmental timing of romantic relationships indicate fewer gender, race, and cultural differences than do studies focusing narrowly on sexual experiences. The majority of girls and boys describe falling in love, commitment-related beliefs, less romantic idealization, and emotional and physical intimacy as occurring between the ages of 15 and 18, with the most maturity and conceptualization of dyadic partnerships occurring between the ages of 18 and 25 (Montgomery, 2005; Nelson & Barry, 2005; Regan, Durvasula, Howell, Ureno,

& Rea, 2004). More immature first dates and first kisses are reported between the ages of 14–15. Alternately, nonromantic, platonic, cross-sex relationships have not been widely studied either, but it appears that non-romantic relationships between adolescent males and females are important for acquiring the positive benefits of emotional support, especially for boys (Stanton-Salazar & Spina, 2005). Also, students who report cross-sex friendships tend to have more ample and diversified peer networks in general.

Despite the importance of dating to the developmental process, it is a topic that almost no adolescents in our study wanted to discuss in any detail, even when probed by the interviewer. About half of male and female teens said that they had dated at some point, but most of them said that they did not have any serious romantic relationships. This may, in part, be due to research showing that mature conceptualizations of romantic relationships do not begin until late adolescence and early adulthood, and only 20% of our participants were 17 or 18 years old. Teens may have felt this area of their lives was more private than other areas we asked them about and/or may have had less of a cognitive understanding of these relationships and could not formulate clear or in-depth descriptions about these experiences. Also, the one-on-one interview format may have elicited less information about this topic than a same-sex focus group might have. This was not a problem, however, for parents. Parents' reports of nonserious dating relationships matched that of adolescent reports, but parents discussed their ambivalence, hopes, and concerns for their adolescents' current and future intimate partnerships.

Dating relationships, overall, were a concern for most parents, but parents' expectations of the age at which dating is appropriate varied widely from 12 to 18. Many parents expressed ambivalence about their teens' dating relationships, knowing that dating is developmentally normative, but were uncomfortable with this aspect of social development. For example:

Father: Oh, they've gone to the prom and whatnot. I would not say that they're seriously dating anyone. It hasn't really had an effect on me. You know, it's not that important. She's still young, she just turned 18. She's got a full life ahead of her. I'm relieved. It has cut my stress down that she doesn't have a steady boyfriend or anything of that nature. She has lots of friends, and they have good times. I wouldn't say she has any romantic interests—at least that she'd like to share with me at this point.

Father: They spend a lot of time, the two of them. I'm not sure I know what they do. I don't know if they're spending time necking or shooting pool …. And, and, no, I didn't want my parent's prying into it too much, so, I guess I don't either. I have no objection to [my son] at 15 having a steady girlfriend. I did and I thought it was healthy and I enjoyed it and, um, um, it, it certainly didn't lead to any, ah, any negative things. In fact, I thought going through all that, that whole process of building close relationships and then going through the emotion of, of having them break down, uh, it was a—it ends up being a positive thing. A learning thing. So, uh, I don't discourage that in either of I my kids.

This ambivalence might be due to many parents equating sexual behavior with dating.

> **Mother:** Well, I think for example this is her first actual dating relationship, and I suppose I worry like every parent does. I try to prepare her, you know, to not get herself into situations where her and [her boyfriend] maybe tempted to get involved sexually. I think they're much too young. And I've been trying to talk to her. That's a worry for me. So, I feel like I'm a real watch dog, you know?

> **Mother:** Um, so I think, um, with my children, I wouldn't let them date at 12. I dated at 12. I double-dated at 12. I wouldn't let them date at 13. [My daughter is] 14. If she said she had a boyfriend and wanted to go to a show, I would allow her to go to the show, but to come right home afterwards. She's 14. She's at that stage where she should obviously be able to interact that way. My other daughter is 15 and she has a boyfriend. We've discussed sex, we've discussed birth control. She's not having sex. She's told me that if she was, she'd want to come to me in order to have … um, she's very open, so, I know where she's at with this relationship. I know how she feels about virginity and so forth. At this point, as much as I can know and as much as I feel as a gut instinct as a parent, I believe she's still a virgin. I'm hoping that she remains a virgin through this relationship. Um, because I think other relationships will come along also, and she has to realize this isn't the end, to not give herself to someone because she thinks she's in love with him. So that … I guess as a mother, it's always a concern.

Religion was mentioned by some parents as related to their concerns about dating. For example:

> **Father:** It would cause a tenuous-strained relationship [if our son were dating], because we really don't want to encourage a relationship. Um, we try, and again, it's part of our teaching, part of our religious teaching is not to encourage children at this young age to become close, to have close romantic relationships. We've discouraged that. It's part of our value system, if you will. And, so we allow, I mean, we can't prevent these things from happening, but it's not a really, it's not something we encourage. Because he's 16, we'd much rather see him get through school and at least get in college before something serious happens.

> **Mother:** I just worry, maybe, like when he gets older, you know, in the near future, meeting girls and stuff. Like too soon, too young. So I discourage him, because I always because we're … you know, Christians you know, you don't go to bed until you're married, things like that. That doesn't mean that's realistic, but I'm going … like I don't want to condone it. You know what I mean?

Finally, very few parents equated dating with marriage, but some did:

> **Father:** Yeah, he's got a two-year relationship with someone he met through the church. Her parents, for a while, went to a different church, but they met at our church. And, they ended the relationship in January. [My son] felt, although we didn't know it at the time, he was making this decision to go into the Navy, that it would be better for her not to have a steady boyfriend in the Navy. So he ended the relationship. They have

subsequently restarted the relationship. And she was one that went down to Chicago, and we have photographs of her cow-eyed, looking up at him. And the different things they've said, it sounds like this could be a permanent relationship. They're seriously thinking about marriage.

Mother: They think that they're indestructible. And (pause) he's madly in love, (laugh) which he was not six years ago. Well, (pause) she's just like part of the family. I mean, I could see them getting married. I mean, not … they're just (pause), it's strange. I never thought I would really feel that way. But I was 16 when I started dating my husband and he's 16 and … and I can … it's all there. I said, "Don't they remind you of us?" (laugh). You know, they spend a lot of time on the telephone together, you know, and wanting to see, but they don't really go out that much, because that costs money. So they're more apt to have some kids over at our house or her house or some other place and they do group activities. He's always been a pretty good kid, and happy.

Support Structure: Number and Differentiation of Friends

Two themes emerged that fit the theoretical notion of support structure. First, teens often related the number of close friends that they had. There was a wide range of responses from 1 to 50 friends, but most responded by naming 4 close friends. Parents' responses were more widely varied. Parents seemed unsure about the number of close friends their children had, and responses ranged from 1 to 6. Second, participants also differentiated between close, supportive friends and those who are more like acquaintances. This kind of differentiation is believed to develop during early adolescence as cognitive views of friendships change from childhood characterizations based on overt characteristics such as members of their classroom and neighborhoods to adolescent views involving intimacy, trust, and commitment (Furman, 1982; Hartup, 1993). One male teen described the differentiation of friends this way:

> There's basically three friends that I've been close with forever, because I entered kindergarten, who I grew up with basically. We were just close. Now there's about five of us who hang out and do everything together. And then, that's my majorly close friends, I have a lot of other acquaintances.

Another male says, "[I have about] twelve [friends], and about six of them are really close friends. But I'll do stuff with about 25 different friends throughout a week." And this male describes:

> One kid, my closest friend, and so I tend to turn to him for all the stuff I do. Because I can trust him more than the others.

Females provide similar descriptions. One female states, "I have a lot of friends at school [that] I see. If I, like, see them somewhere, we'll do something, but I only have like a few close friends that I'll hang out with." Another says:

I have about, I guess that I have four close friends that I see in and out of school. And then I have a group of friends from my youth group that I see out of school. And then there's just a, I have a lot of friends that I see in school that are just school friends.

Several parents noted that their teens had friendships with peers of the opposite sex, which seemed unusual to them and they sometimes had trouble differentiating between dating relationships and friendships. Many commented that their teens "hung out in boy-girl packs, which I never did." This mother expresses a concern that several parents had:

[My son] has a handful [of friends]. [My daughter] has zillions. She has, you know, one really good friend, then a lot of other girls and guys. I don't mind girl and guy friendships, but I won't allow a boy-girl sleep over. Her friend had a mixed-sex sleep over, and I wouldn't let her go.

No thematic differences were observed between male and female participants' responses in this category.

Emotional Support in Relationships

Interview data were explored for intersections between support functions (that is, emotional vs. instrumental vs. companionship support) and which persons provided these kinds of supports to teens. A complex array of themes emerged about the nature of relationships that adolescents have with adults and peers. For example, parents and peers were discussed as the main sources of support by almost all students, but they are used for different functions. Male and female teens mentioned peers more than adults for companionship, while adults are mentioned more often than peers for academically related support (e.g., help with school work and future goals) and for other kinds of instrumental support (e.g., help with sports and hobbies). In terms of providing emotional support, parents and peers are mentioned about equally, but mothers are mentioned much more often than fathers. However, both female and male students mention fathers more often than mothers as providing companionship for sports-related activities.

Parent–Child. More female teens mentioned emotional support from different providers than did males, but mothers and peers stood out as main sources of support for both sexes. Mothers were discussed as providing emotional support by being understanding and giving students the feeling of being cared for and loved. This is a representative statement made by one male student, "Well, like, um, I don't know, I think it's because, I don't know, she's usually always there for me, and stuff like, you know, the usual. She'll listen to me and stuff and help me when I need it and stuff like that." Females similarly described emotional support from their mothers, "I talk to her about everything and she knows about like everything that goes on with me, and she's supportive of me if I have a problem." This male provided a more descriptive statement:

> Well, um, like if I'm having some sort of problem, she'll help me, because I remember I was having a problem in December because I kind of felt all depressed. And so, like in December I was talking about how I thought people didn't get along with me and stuff, and how I felt I was an outsider, and she was all supporting me and giving me suggestions of what I could do. And, so, she like, I can talk to her when I'm sad and stuff.

One sex difference that emerged in this theme is that females often discussed their mothers as "friends" to them and males did not use this terminology. For example, one female states:

> Like, I'm really close with my parents. Like, I tell my mom everything. And we talk like she's my best friend. Um, we talk about everything. We get along. She understands, like, if I say, like I'm like, "Mom, I'm trying to talk to you as a friend here, not like as my mom, or as an, or like as an adult would be fine, but just not my mom." She's like, "Okay." And she listens to me and she helps and she give me good advice. Because I get really stressed out from school and stuff. And she's always there to help me no matter what.

Another female states:

> We have a positive relationship because I feel that I can tell her anything and she'll listen to me. And she won't go around telling anybody. She's like a friend, you know? She won't tell anybody my secrets and stuff, and I feel that I can trust her with them.

Mothers also discussed providing emotional support to their teens, but to a lesser extent than teens. This mother relates, "She confides in me. Not everything, but you know. She does talk to me and we do things as mother–daughter."

Teens much less frequently discussed fathers as providing emotional support than mothers. Fathers, themselves, also rarely described aspects of emotional support. A few students provided descriptions of receiving emotional support from fathers, such as this female: "He's always there for me to talk to. I always tell him about, I'm really not scared to tell him about my boyfriends or friends in school, because he knows a lot of my friends in school, so he can really help me out there." A male student states, "He's always willing to help me. Always nice to me. He's always there when I need him." However, this male's description sounds somewhat ambivalent:

> Well, most the time we get along good. We can, you know, we can work together, like if we're doing something. And, you know, we can just talk, talk to each other about anything. But it's negative when he gets angry and compares me to my sister and all that mess.

Peers. Peers were discussed as similar to mothers as a major source of emotional support by male and female adolescents. One female states:

We're always there for each other whenever we need us, and they're really, I'm really close with them and I can tell them whatever. They won't, they're not like, they won't judge me or anything, they're just people that I can really talk to.

Another female comments:

I think I can talk to them a lot, but there's like with my five friends, I don't know, we just always hang around together. I can talk to all of them about, um, it's pretty supportive for me because there's always like one of them I feel comfortable talking to about our problems.

Similarly, these males state about their friends:

I think they're supportive. I mean, pretty much, you can like, we, you know, do everything together and talk about anything, no matter what it is. Let it out and talk about it.

You know, emotionally they can be [supportive]. You know, if I, if I'm ever down, they'll try to do something to bring me up or something, if I'm just, if I'm just not feeling very good.

Parents did not describe their teens' emotional support from friends with much depth. Many of them mentioned that their teens talked on the phone too much, but did not seem to know much about the nature of the support that friends were providing to their teens. However, one mother mentioned:

How are their friends supportive of them? Well, I know my daughter is having boyfriend problems. I know she'll just call her friends and sit with them. For [my son], I guess the only thing for support, um, his friends want to get together with him. The fact that they reach out for him, that's supportive.

Non-Parental Adults. Other adults were often mentioned as providing emotional support, especially by female teens. Teachers and extended family members were seen as being available to talk to and as caring about them as individuals. One female states about her extended family:

And all of my aunts and uncles, they've really been supportive. My aunt really helps me out. I talk to her about my boy problems, sometimes, and she'll help me with that. I always have people to talk to and I can count on in my family, that family [referring to her mother's extended family], to help me when I need it.

And this male says, "I'm real close to my mom's side of the family. Um, just everybody's nice to each other and supportive. And, um, we all get along." A mother describes support from a grandmother:

It's been supportive that Jenny called my mom to talk to her, because I wasn't home. I must have been at work and she didn't want to disturb me there, so she called my mom and discussed her boyfriend problems with her. She said, "I knew Nana would be able to help me." So, they're supportive. Plus, they didn't try to take over.

An example of support from teachers that is not just for academic assistance is given by this female student:

> And the teachers really help me out. There's a couple, my French teacher, she helps me out an awful lot. I talk to her about stuff, she's always, if I have a bad day she always, you know, even today, today was one of my off days. You know, she's real, "Is everything okay? Is there anything I can do? If there is, just tell me." And that's the way it's been all year and last year.

And this male states:

> I mean, I think it's kind of like, I don't know. They're more, they're like in a supportive role, too. They teach and then they, you know, if they have, like the majority of them are more willing to talk to you, too, about other stuff than in the classroom. I know now that some teachers are there that will listen to you and stuff.

Parents often discussed nonparental adult support to teens as important. This father notes:

> [My son] has just been blessed by friends and their parents. Their parents have been just unbelievable. There are any one of 15 families where he could go right now and stay with them and they'd look out for him. And their friends are welcome here [in my home]. We have a very strong, positive relationship with the families of [my son's] friends.

This mother says she likes adult support for her son who is having behavioral problems:

> At this point in this life, um, the best source for help is just someone from outside the family who has a genuine interest in Dan. And he can see that. And I'm not talking about a professional, I'm thinking more in terms of friends from church. People that he associates with through a youth group at church. They do have genuine interest in Dan, and I think that they're pretty good about letting him know that. I think, you know, an adult male from outside the family putting their arm around him and saying, "How are things going?" does a lot more good than anything else we can provide for him right now.

A number of parents also discussed providing support to their teens' friends, from major interventions to just talking to them and having them over for dinner. This father relates:

> Recently, one of [my daughter's] friends, who was in the church, her father was abusive and we had her stay in our home for two days while protective services worked with that. We intervened to help her with protective services. There is a cost to that,

it was stressful. And I was raised to live and let live, not to get involved. Keep a distance. But I'm happy to relearn that, that it's necessary to show compassion to other people.

Companionship

Having someone with whom to engage in activities was discussed as an important part of adolescent life. Activities involved engaging in sports, games, or hobbies together; watching sports together; going to movies; watching TV; "hanging out"; shopping; and eating. Males predominantly discussed sports-related activities with fathers and peers. Females discussed a wider variety of activities with mothers, fathers, and peers.

More males than females discussed sports-related companionship with fathers. For example, one male states, "We both play sports, or he used to play sports. So, my mom was never really athletic, but me and him, we do things." Other males say:

He was supportive of my archery and started taking me hunting, when I felt I wanted to. And doing stuff with me.

[I've always been close to him] because he's the one who takes me to all my sporting events and we go fishing.

Like he helps out a lot with, um, my soccer team. He's one of the assistant coaches. Just the fact that we have that common bond that I think we are real close. We like play pool, um, play sports. And go places. And talk.

Even though males discussed feeling close to their fathers through doing activities together, these same students said that they were closer to their mothers because of the emotional support that they provided. This will be discussed again later.

More females than males discussed engaging in non-sports-related activities with adults. For example, one female stated about her father:

We do a lot of stuff together. We go shopping, not for clothes, just for stuff. We like the same kind of stuff. Like books and TV and comic books and stuff, and I like to go on his motorcycle [with him].

And this student stated about her mother, "We go shopping, and to the movies and stuff." One student further described the way activities bring her closer to her family:

[In the last five years] my family was going on family vacations. And we always have to spend time together. And even though we, um, we fight a lot and argue, because we're together all the time, I really think it brings us closer together.

Male and female students similarly discussed peers as important companions for activities, but, again, males more often discussed activities that involved sports than did females. In fact, every description of males' activities with peers involved sports in some way. This male's description is common:

> Um, [we do] team sports, you know. We're in a lot of the same classes, we play video games, go to the movies, get something to eat.

Another male states:

> With my close friends? [With] some of them I play hockey. All of them, we just like we go to sports events, because we're going to one like this weekend. We go to concerts. Just basically bum around in the summer. Hang out and go swim. And, like, go to concerts.

Some males described engaging in activities as a way of feeling closer to their male peers:

> I've gotten closer to some of my friends. And, like, because I'm rather shy, so until, uh, about this year, this year all of a sudden I started doing a lot of stuff, played football or basketball or stuff. Normally I play sports because we all like to play sports.

However, some males did not define these activities as necessarily supportive in ways other than companionship. This statement reflects that idea:

> We go out more, because I can drive. And now, we go out and play soccer or something. We go out, and I'll play soccer with my friends, or play cards or watch TV. And, basically, I made friends on my soccer team. I talk to them a lot and go over to their houses.
>
> **Interviewer:** *Do these friends support you, if you have a problem?*
>
> Not really. No. We play cards and soccer.

For females, there was a greater link between companionship and emotional support. For example, this student states:

> We like go to movies, go bowling. Shopping, just normal teenager stuff. I don't know, they help me with like any problem I have. They're always there for me.

Similarly, another student says,

> Well, um, a lot of them are in cross country, so we're really close and can talk about anything. And, I don't know. We just do stuff all the time with other people.

Another typical example includes,

> Um, just talk, sit around, I don't know. Um, well we have dinner, go to the movies, play miniature golf.

Parents frequently discussed all the activities that their teens do with their peers. A typical example is this mother's statement:

> Well, there's usually a group of like five of them. Um, their version of chilling is riding their bikes, playing video games. They used to roller blade and play hockey a lot, but they've backed off that. Um, cards, whatever. You know, they listen to music, they're trying to get a band together (laughs), and then, of course, I'm sure calling girls falls in there now too.

This mother describes how important peer companionship is when you don't have it. Their family recently moved to a new town, and her son has a physical disability that limits him from playing sports:

> It seems that everyone likes him a lot, but as far as having any close friends, like he had in our former town, he doesn't. So, he's very alone, he doesn't have anybody to do anything with and I think that, um, doesn't help the situation. We suspect that depression is setting in, and he used to be an honor student and now he doesn't care. So, we're not sure what's happening. But how can [depression] not set in? He doesn't have any friends that he can come home and go outside and play baseball with and do things with. He's physically limited. He has nobody. That's a concern.

Similarly, another father says:

> There was a transition in friends [when he quit the sports team]. He had to make a new group of friends, and that bothered him because his old friends were leaving him out. Luckily he found a group of kids who were real nice, but at first it really bothered him that he wasn't hanging around the other kids anymore. It's amazing how they [his child's friends] can affect the parents also, because he was unhappy, he wasn't being accepted.

Instrumental Support for Academics

Students discussed tangible help and advice from a variety of adults more often than from peers. Instrumental support for academics included descriptions of involvement with the school such as parent-teacher meetings about progress, advice to students about how to do better academically, praising performance, and assistance with homework. Students mentioned a variety of adult sources for academic support including mothers, fathers, teachers, and extended family. More males than females mentioned academic support from all adult sources combined. This male student describes the way his parents provide support for academics:

> They, uh, they take us to school activities. They ask us a lot about what kind of stuff we do. And you know, they want to know what we're doing in school. They help me if I have homework, like they help me study for finals, and they ask me if I have homework, you know, and make sure I'm doing it.

This male describes help from teachers:

> Um, the teachers have been [supportive]. They're really supportive of, uh, of us and try, and uh, they, uh, they really want us to succeed, succeed. They, uh, they just make sure that, uh, that they, uh, they pay, uh, a lot of attention to me. They aren't, uh, they get to know you really well, and they talk to you a lot and make sure they, like, each individual student is doing well. And if they're not, they make sure they talk to them, make sure they start doing well.

And this male describes help from a variety of family sources:

> They've been supportive in school, and uh, they, they've helped me out with school. My dad and my aunt's husband, my uncle, he helps me in school.

Girls provided similar descriptions. For example, this female says about her parents:

> They're really supportive with my school. They're at my swim meets all the time. Um, just, they're pretty much supportive in all my academic things, because I'm a good student, and that would be it. They encourage me, I mean, they compliment me when I get good report cards, but it's pretty much, and then they're at my swim meets. They're really supportive in my academics, and that's it. And all the other decisions, it's just, it's like I'm pretty much on my own. Um, with my relationships with my friends, my boyfriend, sometimes, it can be stressful. I don't get a lot of support there.

Another way adults were supportive was by providing information and help for future academic and career goals. When asked who would provide support for their future academic and professional goals, one male stated,

> My parents have been really supportive. And money won't be a problem [for college].

Another male said

> My parents will help me. And my teachers. My teacher might recommend me.

And a female states:

> I think my mom will [help me with college plans]. Yes, I think both my parents will, actually. My dad is really strong. Well, number one, they probably will pay for college—part of it. And also, my dad is very supportive, and he's been planning. Like, when it's for school, I know he's preparing us for stuff like this. He's like, well, this is what you're going to run into. And I know he probably gets a lot of information. And I know my mom would support me mentally. But my dad would support me also, but my mom would, if I'm stressing out, she would support me and help me through it. And my dad will just support me by helping me with the knowledge, I guess. Helping me learn.

And this female says that her aunt is helpful to her goal of becoming a nurse:

My aunt, one of my aunts, my mom's sister, is in the medical field. And I talk to her sometimes about being a nurse and she kind of gives me some pointers and stuff when I ask her questions about how to go about things.

While more males than females discussed academic support from adults, more females than males discussed friends as a source of support for academic and career success. The few students that mentioned support from friends talked about friends being encouraging and helping them solve problems regarding teachers. However, several students' seemed ambivalent about the support they receive from friends in this area. For example, one female discussed who will help her with her future goals:

I mean, I talk to my friends about it, and they've, I guess they've encouraged me somewhat, but I mean, not really.

Another female thinks adults are better able to help her academically than are peers:

Oh, probably, I'm not sure. Probably teachers and family. I don't know about friends as much. I mean, I don't think, not my friends as much. I don't think how they can help me.

The one male's description of support from friends for his future goal sounds dubious:

Um, I'd, my, one of my really good friends is going to help me through it. He, he'll help me, um, most of my friends that I've had will help me in some way. Because they all agree that it's a big ball, at least most of them do.

Instrumental Support for Sports and Hobbies

Instrumental support for sports and hobbies included descriptions of buying equipment, driving students to events, helping/teaching/coaching students, praising performance, and paying for lessons. Parents were the only adult sources of support mentioned for this kind of support, and more males than females discussed help in this area. Peers were almost never mentioned as providing instrumental support for sports or hobbies. Regarding instrumental help for sports, this female says:

I think with no matter, like, what I want to do [they support me]. New things I want to try. It's like because I'm involved in a lot of sports and stuff like that, they always support it. They try their hardest to let me do it. They like encourage me. And I'm on the girls' hockey team, but it took a lot of their time because it was real, it was like an hour away. And so I practiced every weekend and one day a week. And, so they drove me out there all the time and basically everybody spent their weekend taking me to hockey.

Similarly, this male states,

They just support me [in soccer]. They give me rides, they pay for it. They try to help me if I have any problems with it, or with the team.

Another male says,

My dad's not [involved in soccer]. My mom plays a big part in the soccer program 'cuz we have to run concession stands to provide for like our new uniforms and stuff, so she's the head of that.

Male students did not discuss support from parents for non-sports related activities, but several females talked about support for hobbies like music, cooking, and sewing. For example:

Once in a while, if they hear me playing [the piano], they'll say it sounds nice, I guess. Well, she'll buy me music sometimes, and, um, she wants to find a teacher for me.

Support From Mothers Versus Fathers

During the interviews, students were asked to compare their relationships with different members of their family. When the transcripts were coded for social support content, a theme emerged that involved the importance of emotional support in comparing their relationships with mothers and fathers. Many students mentioned that their father's work kept him from spending time with them and from being available when they wanted to talk to him, because he was too busy or too stressed. Two females state:

Um, probably I'm closer to my mom. Just because she's around more. It doesn't mean, like, I don't get along with her as well as I do with my dad. But, she's around more and she knows more about me. Sometimes he's not home, he's a work, when I want to talk to him.

Because it's like my dad wasn't home a lot. He worked from early in the morning. Like, when I was really young, I really didn't see him until weekends. Well, now he's trying to do more stuff with us. But I don't know if it's really affecting me that much, if I'm getting closer to him, because I think it would have been better if he was closer with us and did more things with us when we were younger. Then we would be closer. But I don't know.

And these males relate:

It's just that my mom is always home. My dad hardly ever is. It's usually been cut-and-dry since I've been little. It's just that my dad is not going to be home and I have to just spend time with him when I can. Because, basically, my mom raised us.

Well, he spends like all the time he has [with us] because he works a lot. Like, he has two jobs. And, every time he like has to stop working for a day just to take us somewhere. And we really appreciate it. And he spends time with us whenever he can, because he doesn't have very much time. And I enjoy the time he spends with us.

Students tended to view fathers as more available for financial support than other kinds of support. For example, these females state:

[I'm closer to] my mom. Because I never see my dad. We [mother and daughter] just do everything together. Unless we, like, go out with our friends. Sometimes my dad can be generous, like give us money when we need it.

[My mother] talks about everything [with me]. We don't necessarily do a lot of stuff together. She goes to my soccer games. Basically the only things [my father and I] talk about is work and soccer and college. Like, I don't talk about my personal life with him. It's more financial then, so, I go to him for money.

Another reason that was given for feeling closer to mothers was that fathers were authority figures who might judge them. For example, this female says:

I don't know, we're pretty close [my mother and I]. Um, we talk about like everything. Or, like, I tell her about everything, and there's some things that I, you know, don't want her to know, but like I'm not, I mean there's like with my friends. Like, she knows basically everything about all my friends.

Interviewer: *What about your dad?*

I don't know, um, we're basically pretty close. It's the same thing, you know, I tell him about my friends and things like that. Um, I don't know him as much. He's more overprotective, and then if he found something out, he'd be like, "Oh, you're not going to see that person anymore." I'm more reserved with my dad. Um, I don't know, we talk about choir together.

Interviewer: *So, who would you say you're closer to?*

My mom.

And this male states:

My relationship with my dad is stressful. I mean, it never seems like anything is good enough for him. I don't know. I think he has a hard time accepting who I am. I'm always worried about what he's going to think and stuff.

A third reason for feeling closer to mothers, which boys mentioned more often than girls, was that they felt uncomfortable talking to their fathers. These males state:

I would say I'm closer to my mom than my dad. Um, I would say I can, I can talk to her about things, um, that I can't talk to my dad about. I guess I just feel more comfortable talking to my mom. Um, my dad, he just, not that I can't talk to him, I just, I never really did talk to him about a lot of things, so I guess I just, I just don't.

Yeah, my mom, definitely. I can tell her a lot more. Like I can go to her for like more serious things. Like, you know, like if I'm having problems or something, you know.

Interviewer: *Do you feel like you can talk to your dad like you can with your mom?*

Um, actually, no. Because he's more of a, a man. He's kind of, thinks of a, kind of a little insensitive. So, I tend not to want to talk to him about certain things.

Two females and one male said that they were closer to their fathers than to their mothers. However, these descriptions did not emphasize the same emotional closeness that was present in the descriptions about mothers. For example, one female states:

Probably I'm the closest with my dad. We watch basketball and football games ... [my mother] hangs out with my sister more than me. She hangs out with my brother more than me. It seems like she's paying more attention to them than me, but pretty much it's good.

This male says:

The time that I do spend with her, it's, she's just like, she's mom. She makes me dinner, or she pays for my dinner or buys me clothes or stuff like that. So, most of the time I don't get in like real serious, deep-rooted talks in conversation with my mom.

Interviewer: Who would you have these conversations with?

Probably my dad.

A few males described being equally close to both parents or somewhat ambivalent about their different relationships with each parent. This male provides a good example:

I've been real close to my mom and dad. My dad works a lot. So, I guess I see him for hockey and stuff. We have ties through hockey. And he taught me how to play golf. So, he's like basically where my sports have come through. And he's like a role model. I want to be a lot like him .... Yeah, I have a lot of fun with my dad. It's just, we're not as close as my mom. Because my mom has always been there for me since I was little. But my dad just kind of is there. He's just like a role model for me. Not so much as my mom. My mom, just like, she's just my mom. And she's the person I can turn to and the person that has always been there and the person who I think has actually raised me more than my dad.

Themes related to differences between mother and father support also emerged in both mothers' and fathers' interviews. Although some fathers did describe close, supportive relationships with their teens, it was more typical for them to rely on their wives to monitor their children's friends and provide emotional support. This mother compares herself to her husband:

He'll say hello (to the children's friends), and make some small talk. But if you ask him, like if we go to a football game or something and one of [my son's] friends comes to say hello, he can't tell you who they are or which friend they are to which one of our kids. But he'll be nice and talk to them.

When asked by the interviewer, "What kinds of things does your daughter do with her friends?" a father responds, "I'll have to show my ignorance there. Um, I don't know." Another father admits that his son turned to his mother for emotional support after his son's friend shot himself:

He never really talked to me about it, but he talked to his mother. His mother went with him to the funeral and all that. And you could tell that it bothered him a little bit, but he didn't seem to have that much reaction to it. You know, that it bothered him a lot or that he thought about it. Like I said, he talked to [my wife], he didn't talk to me.

The mother from this same family said:

I think it had a terrible impact on him, his friend's death. When you're 14, you don't expect someone to die like that. We went to the funeral home and the mass and the cemetery together.

Negative Peer Influences and Parental Monitoring

As described previously, parents continue to be important sources of support for adolescents despite the increases in time spent with peers. Adolescents in our study did not describe negative influences of their peer relationships, however, their parents described this as a frequent concern for how to supervise their teens. Adolescents did report that their peers could be stressful to them, primarily due to petty bickering, but friends' influence on their own behavior was not discussed.

As noted in chapter 3, peers can have both negative and positive effects on teens, and family relationships at home affect the quality of peer relationships. Too much or too little monitoring of adolescents can create problems. Parents discussed different levels of concern and monitoring of their teen's friendships. For example:

Mother: You know, she made some new ones along the way, but, um, I think she is learning more about her friends. Just … they're all growing up so we're just, I think we're just trying to keep our eyes open as to what changes in friends and which way they're going and how is it going to influence our kids. And so far I've had no problems. It hasn't been negative yet.

Mother: Um, to really get to know them [daughter's friends] as well … they're in the neighborhood … she goes to school with them … um, but I don't see them as much and get to know them as well as I would like to. They're different from say my oldest daughter's friends. They're more into the music that I don't like. They're, some are different with the hair. With the shaved hair and a little longer. The baggy clothes that I'm describing, which I'm not fond of, it's just their style. It's the style of the friends that she hangs out with. Um, they seem nice enough. They always seem polite, but I just don't know them as well; so, I'm uncomfortable with that. So, I would say, probably I don't know them, and what that causes me to feel is stressful.

Father: We communicate with their parents frequently. And they try to hide from us—the kids do. But I made a decision a long time ago that I'm going to find out where my kid's at, who he's associated with, where they live, their phone numbers, and I call these parents to find out information, to see what gossip they've got. Where is my kid? Where is your kid? And they call us too. And I'm talking about some problems that most parents don't want to admit to, (pause) drinking. Drinking's a big problem. These kids are drinking a lot. You know, they're 17, 18 years old. They drink a lot—more than I do. Well, where are they getting this stuff? What's going on here? What are you doing about it, Mr. Parent?

These fathers discussed setting expectations for his own teen and their friends:

I've terrorized my kids with things like, you know, sitting down with the guys and making sure they understand, um, that I expect that my daughters will be treated with respect and that doors will be opened and they will be home on time and I've, you know, gone out on the front porch to make sure that the guy opens the door for them and make sure the guy doesn't just pull into the driveway and honk the horn. I expect the same conduct on [my son's] behalf. And I've threatened to call the parents of the girls that he dates and to ensure that they he's doing the gentlemanly thing.

Father: Um, for the most part, they seem like good kids, all of them. There's obviously some bad apples in every basket. Um, the boys have an affinity for making a lot of friends in a lot of places. They seem to be very popular kids. Um, and, you know, not all the kids that they associate with would be people I choose to have them be friends with, but, you know, I'm not a parent that chooses their kids' friends. So, you know, I stress to them what to look for in friends and hopefully they take my advice.

The most frequently mentioned concern by parents was the connection between drug use and friendships.

Mother: Well you know, some of his friends that he had over here in the beginning of the school year, I know now that they're smoking dope. Um, there are some kids that are, that I could tell you that are walking down the street that I've known since they were in kindergarten with [my son], that are the sniffing glue, um, paint cans in plastic bags, I mean, the whole scenario is being done .... And I could probably tell you, pinpoint out, which kids are doing it. Um, those are the kids that I don't want him to be involved [with]. Those are the kids he knows since kindergarten. Um, (pause) it's hard to be in adolescence and have friends that do that and not get pulled into it, somewhat. I know he knows that it's wrong, but I don't know if he will always make the right choices.

Mother: Um, some of her friends I didn't really care for because of you know the drugs and the drinking that they were into. And I'm sure she experimented. I know she has, um, and then last year was even worse—with grades and drugs. Not now, nope.

Last year, definitely. Um, I know it was marijuana. And I'm … I'm not positive about other things. I know that some of the kids that she was around, she talked about them doing, um, LSD. Scary stuff. Um, if she did, it was maybe a beer or something. She never really did a lot of drinking and stuff. Um, so that … that definitely had a lot to do with her grades and … and the stress and when she was out at night, she … you didn't know what she was doing and, you know, wanting to help her in any way you can, but you can't because you're not there with her all the time.

A few parents, but not many, expressed concerns about negative influences of romantic relationships. This father describes signs of a dating relationship that are possible risk factors for dating violence such as increasing social isolation from friends and family, a drop in grades, and delinquent behaviors related to spending time with her boyfriend (Levy, 1998):

She has a boyfriend, which she is head over heels with. They've been going out now for a year and a half to two years, something I guess. My wife and I have talked about that situation and, ah, her boyfriend is a … I call him a professional liar. He's a nice kid to be around and I think he's got potential, but ah, he'll just lie straight to your face and not think two things of it. Um, we have always discussed college and looked at that, then about two weeks ago, we got, "Well I'm going to go to trade school." And we're going, "Wait a minute, what, what's going on here?" I don't believe her boyfriend has any aspirations whatsoever of going to college, um, the end of last year we had a real painful end of the last year in school. She ended up, basically flunking out, four Es, it was five Es, or four Es and one incomplete. Whereas she should be an A–B student without a problem. Um, she ended up skipping classes and this was with him. And more into not being here per say, to be with ah, her boyfriend. She had a real good group of friends that she would hang out with until she started going out with her boyfriend. That's done. She sees no one but her boyfriend. I consider that negative. Ah, and we've had, there have been discussions on that. She now hangs out with her boyfriend and her boyfriend's friends.

SUMMARY AND IMPLICATIONS FOR PRACTICE AND POLICY

Adolescents' descriptions of their support structure, or the make-up of the social network, revealed a large range of responses regarding how many peers made up the support network. Adolescents perceived from one to fifteen peer supporters. However, most adolescents reported about four supportive friends, and their parents reported teens had one to six good friends. Gender differences were not evidenced in these data, and results are consistent with other research on the nature of adolescent peer relationships (Frey & Rothlisberger, 1996). Reports of about four supportive friends is believed to reflect normative and beneficial patterns of supportive relationships such that a few close friends can often provide a greater depth in terms of relationship quality than many superficial friends. This is reflected in reports of how teens' relationships have changed since childhood. This age group is redefining the nature of their relationships with adults and peers from childhood expectations of many friends for companionship to a few friends for closeness and understanding.

As was discussed in chapter 1, this redefinition reflects developmental advances in cognitive and interpersonal behavioral skills that undergird supportive relationships (e.g., taking another's perspective, defining one's own needs for support, and using empathy and problem-solving skills to help others). Adolescents described different kinds of support functions that reflect theoretical conceptualizations of emotional, instrumental, and companionship support functions, providing qualitative support for current quantitative measurements. Adolescents' discussions of support also reflect a fit between individuals' developmental needs and provider capabilities. For example, peers were used for companionship, while adults were turned to for instrumental help with academic and extracurricular activities and future goals. This is true for females' and males' descriptions. However, descriptions of emotional support were more complex.

Teens described reaching out for emotional support equally from adults and peers, but reported receiving it from female adults (mostly mothers) more than from fathers and other male adults. Females and males similarly described emotional support from parents and peers, but females mentioned receiving emotional support from a larger variety of nonparental adults. Also, females' descriptions of companionship were frequently mixed with discussions of emotional support, while males' descriptions were not. This may indicate a more predominant use of emotional support across different activities and types of help by females, which has been found in other studies (Frey & Rothlisberger, 1996; Kunkel & Burleson, 1999).

The Need for Friendship and Support

The primary use of peers for companionship and adults for instrumental support is developmentally adaptive. Peer companionship is more likely to contain similar interests and abilities than companionship between adolescents and adults. However, peers are not yet capable of providing much instrumental support, as they lack the financial resources and experience to provide concrete assistance. In terms of emotional support, having both peer and adult providers may be particularly advantageous. Although peers can provide emotional support, these skills may as yet be underdeveloped and adult emotional support could be more effective or supplement current emotional needs. What most research has found is that support from different sources has an additive effect, rather than compensatory, on a variety of outcomes (van Beest & Baerveldt, 1999; Wentzel, 1998). Also, adult and peer support builds self-esteem and social skills for later adult relationships as adolescents move away from home and form intimate, primary relationships with peers (Franco & Levitt, 1998).

The data presented here raise the importance of considering the relevance of the seeming lack of support from fathers and other adult men in this sample, which has been found in other research (Frey & Rothlisberger, 1996; Kunkel & Burleson,

1999). In particular, findings reflect a lack of quality and mutuality in father-teen relationships, a lack of time spent together, and a restricted willingness to share emotions. This clearly has implications for any practitioners doing family work.

Evidence in other studies suggests that gender differences exist in the ability to provide support, rather than in receiving it (Kunkel & Burleson, 1999). For example, both women and men rate supportive behaviors in similar ways regarding what is supportive and the importance of receiving support. However, both genders prefer to receive support from a woman and agree that women are better at specific supportive behaviors such as empathy, person-centered listening, and expressing closeness and intimacy (Kunkel & Burleson, 1999). This difference has been attributed to differences in socialization of gendered behavioral skills related to empathy, communality, and affiliation (Jacklin & Reynolds, 1993; Maccoby, 1990). Thus, to the extent that adult men serve as role models for teenaged males, they are not reflecting supportive skills and may be sending messages that these skills are too feminine for men to engage in. Alternately, men may see support as a "woman's job" and feel that they do not need to develop the skills to provide support if they have women from whom to receive it. Ultimately, this leaves adolescent boys with skill deficits in the area of interpersonal relationships and girls and women to become overburdened with the cost of caretaking (Antonucci et al., 1998; Wood, 1994).

Finally, these data provide some clarification for theoretical questions regarding the importance of perceived versus received/enacted support. Adolescents' verbal descriptions of support primarily reflect cognitive-emotional perceptions of support rather than accounts of specific behaviors by others. The fact that most teenagers talked about support as a belief that others care about them and could help them when needed provides evidence for theories of support as a cognitive belief system about the self and others (Lakey & Cassady, 1990; Pierce, Sarason, & Sarason, 1992; Sarason, Pierce, & Sarason, 1990; Sarason, Sarason, & Pierce, 1990), which has more substantial benefits than does the actual support received (Cohen & Syme, 1985; Henderson, 1981; Ingersoll-Daton & Antonucci, 1988; Sandler & Barrera, 1984; Wethington & Kessler, 1986). For example, the two teenagers quoted next, poignantly define their views of social support. The first is a male who perceives strong support at home; the second is a female who perceives very low support from her parents. Both reflect a similar, cognitive-emotional (rather than behavioral) definition:

> Hmm, I don't know. I mean, they're usually, like, if I need something, they'll be there for me. Like anything, really. Like, you know, if I need money, if I need to talk to someone. If I need to, you know, if I just need something, they're there for me.

> I don't feel supported at all—in anything I wanna do. I really don't feel supported at all because, well, like, I'll do something and I'll be like, "Oh, I'm proud of myself." I have to, like, support myself pretty much. Like when I graduated from high school, I didn't get anything from my parents. But I know that it's wrong for me to expect some-

thing. And I really think their, their pride in me is sometimes fake, like when I do something good, like, they'll say, "Oh, that's good, that's great, that's good." And I really don't feel like there's anything behind the words.

The latter quote provokes an intuitive emotional response in the reader, summoning the need for interventions that increase support to such adolescents. In fact, research has shown that lack of support from parents can have particularly damaging effects, which accumulate over time (Garnefski & Diekstra, 1996; Goldstein et al., 2005). Teens who turn to peers for support due to conflictual relationships at home often engage in risky behaviors. Therefore, a balance between family and peer support is required for optimal development, with moderate levels of parental monitoring and structured peer activities enabling the best contexts for healthy peer interactions.

Providing Multi-Level Support

The majority of interventions designed to enhance social support have taken place on the environmental or network level. Examples include the manipulation of the social environment to increase access to community services, helping people become involved in community activities, making referrals to support groups, teaching others (such as family members) within a person's environment to be more supportive to her/him, and practitioners themselves providing a variety of supports to clients (Ashinger, 1985; Gottlieb, 1981, 1983; Whittaker & Garbarino, 1983).

Clinicians have also turned toward developing models of intervention with a transactional emphasis that take the individual's characteristics and skills into account (Pearson, 1990). The extent to which individual-level interventions can influence network/structural factors, and vice versa, to increase support is unknown, but both micro- and macroconsiderations should be given when making assessments and designing interventions. Whichever level of intervention is employed, some general issues related to adolescent development and the assessment of social support should be taken into account. Adolescence is a critical period for intervention in this area. In this time of dynamic personal and social changes, interventions have the ability to affect long-term trajectories in adolescent and adult relationship quality (Fullerton & Ursano, 1994).

5

Learning the Ropes: Education

Success in school is an indicator of overall well-being and is correlated with future success in the world of work. For children, educational achievement is linked with family characteristics and early childhood experiences. For example, a preschool child whose mother has completed her bachelor's degree is more likely to be read to than a child whose mother has no college degree. This early exposure to literacy is correlated with language acquisition, reading comprehension, and overall school success (Forum on Child and Family Statistics, 2005). And children with educated parents are likely to get strong messages from their parents about the value of formal schooling, and thus perform better in school (Kaplan, Liu, & Kaplan, 2001).

School success depends on experiences outside the home as well. Children who attend high-quality early education programs demonstrate positive gains in IQ, greater achievement in school, and higher rates of graduation. However, kids from low-income families and those with mothers who are not college educated are much less likely to attend early childhood programs (Forum on Child and Family Statistics, 2005).

In the United States, most youth (87%) complete high school. The acquisition of a high school diploma or its equivalent is supposed to mean that students have achieved a basic level of skills needed to function in the social environment. Participation in the education system is seen as preparation for the important adult role of worker. Youth who understand and can carry out basic math and reading tasks are more likely to compete successfully in the job market as adults. High school graduates have more stable and higher status employment opportunities and tend to earn more money over a lifetime than do dropouts. Completing a college degree enhances that potential. In 2004, 28% of young adults had earned a college degree in the United States, but around 10% of youth neither attended school nor worked for some period (Forum on Child and Family Statistics, 2005).

Children spend a lot of time in school and, as the preceding statistics illustrate, school may be one of the most important institutions in their social and economic lives. In their interactions with schools, both parents and children are asked to negotiate an increasingly complex and dynamic social environment. For example, American public schools are becoming more ethnically diverse. African American, Latino, and Native American students have higher rates of poverty than their White counterparts (Marrett, 1990) and may have different resources and levels of support for education in their homes and neighborhoods. Greater diversity in the schools may lead to higher rates of intergroup conflict, as well.

Chase (2002) describes teacher qualifications and overall teacher quality as the most important factors in a child's educational experience. Most parents want their children enrolled in schools with excellent teachers, but overall cuts in education funding means fewer jobs for teachers and a less attractive job market overall. Historically, teacher training programs have not attracted the most qualified students in the university (Heyns, 1990), though, and recent trends toward greater accountability and certification may further influence the labor supply. Concerns about high rates of teacher attrition have been linked to teacher shortages and declines in teacher quality, but Heyns (1990) found that teacher shortages tended to be clustered in chronically underfunded urban schools rather than being a general phenomenon. Teachers were found to be remarkably mobile, however, moving from small suburban schools to larger ones. Thus, some schools may not benefit from the expertise of senior faculty, since many of the best teachers seek employment in the most desirable (suburban, well-resourced) schools.

Another notable trend is the perception of schools as magnets for random, lethal violence among children. Recent highly publicized incidents of gun violence in schools mean that more parents and children may feel unsafe. In fact, overall violence has been on the decline in the United States since the early 1990s, and students are not at any increased risk for gun violence since the rash of multiple-victim shootings began in 1992 (Wooden & Blazak, 2001). Nevertheless, initiatives to increase safety in schools abound, along with so-called zero-tolerance policies for weapons and threats of violence in schools.

SCHOOLS AS SOCIAL INSTITUTIONS

Schools are generally seen as loosely-coupled systems (Weick, 1976). That is, schools are social organizations in which common goals are shared by the participants, but the means to achieve these goals are largely determined through the knowledge and skills of workers acting independently from administrators. Teachers and counselors carry out their professional functions with relatively high degrees of autonomy. Administrators generally do not control every aspect of the production of learning, thus school employees (especially teachers) tend to be characterized by high levels of self-determination. This characteristic of the education institution means that trouble in the system has been hard to pinpoint and needed changes have been difficult to implement (Marrett, 1990).

For the past 25 years, educators and analysts have expressed dissatisfaction with the quality of public education in the United States. This concern was first framed as a problem with falling standards and lack of discipline, then subsequently as a problem with lack of equity for the growing number of students who come from relatively disadvantaged homes and communities (Ekstrom, Goertz, & Rock, 1988). It seems that both concerns are valid. On tests of math and science, American students do not compare favorably with their counterparts in Japan, for example. And changes in the demographics of students are accompanied by significant challenges to the education system. Not all students are achieving a basic education in school; racial-ethnic minority students and those from low-income families often perform much worse than middle class and White students do. On closer examination, though, some schools are recognized as helping at-risk students achieve, even as researchers suggest that such students bring environmental deficits too great to overcome. Clear goals and lofty expectations; strong leadership, structure, and discipline; and systematic assessment mark these "effective schools" (Marrett, 1990).

Since the 1980s, reforms in the U.S. educational system have included a move toward a stronger academic curriculum, especially in high schools, and a general tightening of standards of achievement (Lee, 2001). This movement has culminated in the federal legislation known as the "No Child Left Behind Act of 2001," which includes mandates for testing and measures intended to make schools accountable for each child's learning.

Linked to the move for standards reform, advocates for effective schools call for a change in the ways in which schools are structured, such that improvements in the curriculum are accompanied by improvements in the processes of education. Restructuring involves fundamental change in what schools do (and who does it) to educate children. While such change may be relatively mundane, it challenges assumptions about the goal of education, as well as the basic activities of each of its constituents. For example, restructuring curricula might mean teaching English while studying the environment; learning about reading and writing is integrated into learning about principles of biology and ecology. Students exposed to integrated curricula demonstrate higher academic achievement and more positive attitudes about school (Lewis & Shaha, 2003). Other examples of educational restructuring include using parent volunteers, placing students in multi-grade classrooms, team teaching and service learning (Lee, 2001).

Restructuring in educational systems often highlights the importance of social networks for the success of children in schools. Social networks are vital for passing information, establishing trust among valued members of the network, and conducting knowledge from one member to another (Marrett, 1990). In schools, such networks may experience barriers as the result of widely varying beliefs and values (Haney, Czerniak, & Lumpe, 2003). Social networks that result in teachers communicating with colleagues, parents collaborating with teachers, and community leaders working directly with students exemplify effective schools. Networks exert social control, and they reduce isolation, hopelessness, and apathy—that is, they form the foundation for the culture of the school. This understanding of schools as cultural systems is essential to addressing the important structural changes needed to improve education.

Part of the second wave of the school reform movement is a focus on restructuring school curricula to include attention to the social and emotional skills of vulnerable students. Advocates of social and emotional education suggest that developing skills in self-awareness and responsiveness to others allows children to be more perceptive to social cues and react to problems with flexibility and creativity (Cohen, 2001). Educational research does suggest that cognitive development depends on social and emotional development (Elias & Butler, 1999), and more educators are adopting the stance that real achievement in school requires that students learn more than the standard academic skills.

Although conservative educators and community members may see social and emotional education as wasteful and irrelevant to the mission of public education, studies have shown the methods to be generally successful. Dasho, Lewis, and Watson (2001) described a project to infuse social and emotional learning into an elementary school curriculum. The project goals included helping students to develop interpersonal relationships, teaching values like respect and compromise, and supporting self-motivated behaviors and prosocial actions. Compared to a control group, children in the project showed improvements in a host of positive traits and skills, such as conflict resolution, academic motivation, and respect for teachers.

THE FAMILY–SCHOOL PARTNERSHIP

Participants in our study responded to questions about the family's relationships with the education system, about significant events in members' lives, and about hopes for the future. The responses related to education are presented in this chapter. Themes and topics are presented in Table 5.1.

Families play an important part in encouraging learning. Children learn what the value of education is from their parents, other adult relatives, and siblings. Many of the families in our study expressed strong, unambiguous, positive attitudes toward education. A high school diploma was considered the absolute minimum for their children's survival as adults. This was expressed as a practical

TABLE 5.1
Category: Education in Families With Adolescents

Topics	Themes
Family–school partnerships	Parental expectations
	Parental support for education
	Development of work ethic
	Parental involvement in schools
	Gender differences in parental participation
School as a social environment	Bullying
	Teachers
	Changing teacher-student dynamic
	Negative teacher characteristics
	Clubs and extra-curricular activities
Success in school	Academic achievement and gifted students
	Pathways to careers
	Alternatives to college
	Choosing a college
	Choosing a career
	Marriage and family

matter; people have trouble getting jobs without a high school diploma. For example, one mother told us that she warns her children, "A diploma looks better on an application than if you didn't graduate from high school." Another mother said, "I tell the kids it's easier just to work hard and get good study habits in high school. The more education they have the more options [they've] got." In the atmosphere of economic uncertainty, education was seen as a pathway to a secure financial future. One mother expressed the concern this way, "I've done better than my parents. Will my children be able to do better than me? Will they be able to get to the level that I'm at?" Another father put it this way:

> Any time the boys are involved in a job that's not pleasing to them and they were just moaning and groaning, I stressed upon them that this is the kind of job that somebody who doesn't do well in school does. This is a manual labor job. Somebody that doesn't do well in math and doesn't go to college and doesn't get a good job, this is the kind of work that they do. If you don't want to do this kind of work later in life, do good in school.

Parental Expectations for College

Most parents we interviewed expected that their children would graduate from high school and go on to a traditional four-year college degree program. Many parents and children mentioned graduate school, as well. A few families, especially those with children struggling academically or with children labeled as learning disabled, also mentioned post-high-school programs leading to vocational degrees or technical training, such as those offered by community colleges.

Father: I myself dropped out of school, where I don't see him dropping out of school. I see him going on to college. I told him that if they want to go to college, let us know. It's their decision. My expectations are that they will go to college or a trade school or something to get into a regular career.

While the families' economic resources varied, many parents indicated that they would try to financially support their children's aspirations for college. In fact, money for college tuition was the only practical barrier mentioned to achieving a university degree. Many families indicated that they had concerns about paying for college, and several said that they did not have any savings set aside for their children's education. As one mother put it,

> The only barrier I see is how to pay for it [college]. I try to put some money away now, but it seems like there's no way you can ever put away enough.

While there were some differences in how education goals were envisioned for boys and girls (e.g., fields of study), the fact that one's child is a girl did not seem to preclude her from seeking a college education, even for the most traditional of these families. However, some of these families saw education for their daughters as a "back-up plan," rather than as a desire to see them complete higher education or as a means to pursuing a career goal. The sentiment expressed is best characterized by this mother:

> We've always taken the line that college is not optional. Well, you know, it is. There's no getting around it. I think my expectations for the girls would be to go to college. They would get a marketable degree. If, when they get married, they choose not to use that degree, as long as it's something they can fall back on, that's fine.

Parental Support for Education

Even with the high outcome standards set by these parents, many students felt strong personal support from their parents regarding their performance in school and their plans for the future, whether or not they included post-high-school education. The message they received was exemplified by this statement made by a father:

> Our expectations were just do as good as you can. You know, if you need help, don't be afraid to ask for help, whether it'd be from us or whether it'd be from a tutor or whatever. We just wanted them to do the best they could.

Both boys and girls expressed the idea that their parents' focus on educational achievement was "for my own good," and acknowledged that their parents taught them the value of education through repeated focus on the benefits it would bring them:

> **Female teen:** If I'm having trouble with something, then they find a way of helping me out. If I'm having trouble at school my mom and my dad will find a way to support my decision and support my thoughts and ideas about what that problem is.

Male teen: My parents support me for my schoolwork, even if I feel I've done bad. They're there and they think that whatever I do is the best, and it's fine with them. Although I guess I don't always believe that. I guess they're just kind of there for me. They care about me, I know that. Because they make up rules for me, because if they didn't care they'd let me do whatever I wanted, which they don't. I guess they've supported me and pushed me through school. I mean, kind of pressured me to get into some stuff, but now I'm pretty glad I did. Although at times, I'm not.

Female teen: They don't mind my grades as long as my effort and my conduct are up there. But I always feel proud when they like my report card and stuff like that. It makes me work a little harder in school. I've always had good grades. They usually don't pressure me about that. I mean, if I come home and go, "Oh my God, mom, I just bombed a test," they're like, "What? What for?" They don't check to see if I got my homework done. They don't ask about tests or anything, because they leave that all up to me. They say if I don't get it done, they see it on my report cards. Then they'll start asking, but as long as I'm getting it done, they have no reason to. They said they'd be proud of me as long as I am a good person.

For some, the focus on education was perceived as stressful, although even here most children acknowledged some benefit to the pressure (even while some note that expectations were not always the same for all the children in the family):

Girl: I was always really stressed with education. Until the day that you graduate and even then, education is really a big part of my life and it was always stressed like that. You know, if my step-sister starts slacking off, well my parents let her go. With me, it's not tolerable. They never tolerated it. If I slacked off the slightest bit, it was always you've got to really try harder. It is really important and they explained how important it is. And now I'm beginning to understand how important it is. That education, you know, is really big. It should be really big in my life.

Male teen: My mom and dad put a lot of pressure on me to do well in school. It's positive pressure. It's stress that I need. Dad always wants me to be the best at everything because he looks at me as a lot of things that he couldn't do when he was a kid. It's stressful because they always want me to be the best and I always have to live up to their expectations, even though, a lot of times, they're my expectations too. I've got the hard classes, but I usually can get all my stuff done. I get good grades in school, usually an A– average, probably more if I worked harder. I don't feel I need to because I'm satisfied with my grades as they are. I just feel that an A– is sufficient for me right now.

In at least some cases, the parents' focus on achievement was marked by a great deal of stress and even conflict, as parents worked for children's academic growth. This father commented on the effect this had on his wife's relationship with their son:

It has taken a toll on her relationship with him, as far as pushing him to learn. She has to be divorced from being close to him, because no mother would do to him what she has to do to him to get him to learn and understand and just be as close to normal as we can.

In addition, some students acknowledged that their parents' support was limited by practical concerns, most often related to tentative career choices perceived to be impractical by parents:

> **Female teen:** My parents don't like the fact that I'm uncertain right now because they think I need to have some sort of decision and get a useful degree. It's one of their favorite terms like "You can't get a degree in history or something." God forbid.

> **Male teen:** My parents are very encouraging and say you can do whatever you want. But on the other side of things, sometimes they say that performing arts is an unstable career, you might want to find something to fall back on.

Sometimes the focus on educational success was less supportive, especially when it involved a father-son interaction. For example, one father reported:

> This last year, in science, Joe had a problem with the teacher. It didn't seem so much the science, but he just couldn't stand the teacher. His grades suffered. I told him "tough." "Try to suck up a little bit."

Other times, the focus on education was modified by a child's limitations (or perceived limitations) due to learning problems:

> **Father:** Now he's back in the special ed program and I think it's the best thing for him. We've kind of accepted what he can and can't do and we're going from there. I never had a lot of expectations for him. He's probably done more than I thought he could have done. So he's probably over-achieved my expectations.

Sometimes this difference in expectations resulted in problems for younger siblings who take their cues from parental messages to the older child:

> **Mother:** If Tim had a D and brought it up to a C, it's fine. I wouldn't get mad, you know. It's not like I'd ground him. But I think Kathy thought she could do the same thing. I explained it to her. "Don't fluff off. You can't take a break from school or something because I'm not going to get upset and all uptight. You're only going to hurt yourself. I know you can both do better."

> **Mother:** Knowing that they were both extremely intelligent young men, I really expected my son to perform better academically. He has improved obviously. I've been real pleased by how he's improved, but if I were to say I have a disappointment, that would be one of them. And you know I don't think it's that he is unmotivated. I see in him the problems with focusing that I had, and doing homework.

Development of Work Ethic

An important subtheme running through parents' expectations for their children's education was the idea that school prepares one for the "real world" of work. Parents wanted their children to learn about self-motivation, the value of effort, and the importance of hard work. Thus, many of their stories had to do with times when children were not "applying" themselves. For example, this mother describes her teenaged daughter's comeback from a middle-school slump, which had the whole family concerned for her future:

> **Mother:** Her grades were okay, but I don't think they were as good as she could have done back then. I don't know, in terms of effort, what she was putting into her work. She has exceeded what I thought she was going to accomplish. I never would have thought she'd be in the National Honor Society. She's held some kind of officer positions in several different clubs, so she has exceeded my expectations, and her maturity in making decisions and choosing the right path—I think she has succeeded. She's gone beyond what I thought she would do. I mean, I always expected to know something good, but I didn't think she would be at this particular point being involved in the things she has actually done.

A father compared his son and daughter's potential for success almost exclusively on each child's effort in school:

> We still think Rob has potential, but he doesn't have the drive. He's certainly not an overachiever. He's an underachiever, so I don't think he's gong to end up going to the best schools in the country. Karen works very hard. I don't think she has the innate ability to do as well in school as her brother, but she works a lot harder. Every night she's really working. So she has the work ethic.

In contrast with mothers' narratives of school as a time to uncover potential or make adjustments in expectations, fathers' comments about the importance of the school experience were highly focused on the idea that effort and hard work are character-building experiences and thus constitute a significant part of children's education:

> **Father:** I feel like if they can get the importance of work instilled in them now, when you get on your own and have a job, you'll want to do the best you can, even if you dislike the boss or don't like the work. You want to at least not be ashamed of what you did.

> **Father:** That's all I expected out of them. Try to be the best student you can be. You don't have to be the valedictorian of the school, just be the best student. Apply yourself. I'm probably like my dad. I expect you to work to your full potential.

> **Father:** There were some things involved with school that lead me to believe he's not as dedicated to his school work as what I might have been. I think peer pressure's impressed upon them that it's almost un-cool to do well in school. I think sometimes they don't strive to achieve only because they will achieve and then they'll be made fun of. They're both very concerned with image and self esteem. I don't think they work as hard as they could. If they knew as much about geometry and algebra as they do about skateboards and videogames, they'd be the leader of the pack.

> **Father:** When I was in high school, I always had homework. Every night! These kids never seem to have any homework, but their grades are fairly good grades. I'm trying to instill in him what college will be like. He thinks he knows it all.

Parental Involvement in the Schools

Successful schools depend, at least in part, on strong power-sharing relationships between families and school personnel (Eccles & Harold, 1996; Martin & Hagan-Burke, 2002). Parent expectations for their children's education is a strong predictor of achievement (Kaplan et al., 2001), and recommendations for improvements in schools nearly always include encouragement to strengthen the relationships between parents and their children's education (e.g. Ekstrom et al., 1988). But social class and institutional structures complicate how parents and schools connect with each other. Middle class parents tend to respond to problems in the school with collective action or by mobilizing the authority of professionals known to the family. In contrast, poor families whose social networks were more tied to kinship groups dealt with problems on their own and with less outside social support (Horvat, Weininger, & Lareau, 2003).

Lewis and Forman (2002) found that higher income parents sometimes engaged in condescending or disrespectful interactions with teachers, making effective parent–teacher collaboration difficult and ambiguous. Low-income parents are often unable to offer as many material resources to the school because of logistical issues like distance and day care needs of young children, but a collaborative and responsive school culture can still allow significant interactions regardless of social class. The most inhibiting factor in school–family interactions is a school environment that insists on scripted and proscribed interactions between parents and school personnel (Smrekar & Cohen-Vogel, 2001). Parents can easily become frustrated by expectations that they remain passive recipients of the educators' expertise, who are called only when their children are in trouble.

Efforts to make schools more family-centered involve policies and practices that make schools more welcoming to the input offered by families, as well as more flexible and responsive to family concerns (Dunst, 2002). Models for increasing parental involvement in their children's schools include: opportunities for parents and teachers to interact more frequently (Miretzky, 2004); opportunities for parent volunteers, parent participation in decision-making, and education/support for parenting skills (Jacobi, Wittreich, & Hogue, 2003); use of electronic communication (Hernandez & Leung, 2004); and inviting members of extended family to participate alongside students' parents (Benson & Martin, 2003).

As can be seen from respondents' comments about expectations for children's education, parents were quite supportive overall in terms of giving positive feedback to children's efforts, verbalizing support for college plans and emphasizing the value of education. However, generally parents in our study monitored the schools from home and through structured school events, rather than from the flexible, intensive and nontraditional methods outlined in the literature. In fact, one of the most common types of parental interaction with the schools described by these families was a wholly indirect one: several families mentioned being disenchanted with their local public schools and responded by moving their children into "better" private schools.

Typical descriptions of more direct parental involvement with the schools suggest that parents are likely to attend parent organizations (with little evidence of active participation beyond fundraising) or participate as spectators at sporting events, music or theatre performances, or other activities in which their children participate. Despite their descriptions of parental support and involvement at home, both adults and youth interviewed for this study were quite clear that parents had little direct contact with their schools' teaching or administrative personnel, as these students' comments indicate:

> **Female teen:** My mom goes to PTA meetings and football games and basketball games.

> **Female teen:** My parents were both on the PTA. They helped the craft show and bake sale and party, stuff like that.

> **Male teen**: They [parents] don't really know all my teachers because they just see them in open house.

Gender Differences in Parental Participation.   Parents acknowledged their lack of direct involvement with schools in different ways. For mothers, these comments were likely to be modified by an explanation for the decrease in participation since elementary school. These explanations usually focused on an increase in paid work responsibilities:

> **Mother:** I was a little more involved when Mary was in elementary school, before I had Suzanne. Because I was married, I wasn't working. I was the room mom and stuff then, but not no more. I don't do anything.

> **Mother:** I could go be a PTA member, president or whatever, and do this or that. My time is so limited that if I have the time, I choose to do things that involve my kids directly, whether it's watching them play a game or whatever. I don't have the luxury of being the organizer or arranger behind things. But to me, when your time is precious, you have to prioritize it.

> **Mother:** We went to the open house last night and it was very impressive, with all the teachers. I don't volunteer as much as I used to, of course. I used to volunteer regularly, once a week when I wasn't working. So, it's cut way down now. Last year, I went on a field trip, but this year, I don't know if that's going to work, because I'm working. I was working part-time last year, so this year it's full-time. I think it's important for your kids to see you involved in school. So we try to do evening meetings and the PTA.

> **Mother:** It's hard to interact with teachers. Conferences with school are difficult because of my job. I have written letters. I mean I have communicated with the teachers about certain aspects that I wasn't pleased with. The last one with my son, and they were accessible. I did get a phone call back.

This mother points out that even "showing up" to children's events is a substantial commitment of time for a working parent:

I don't participate on anything as far as committees. I do show up to all the sports activities. We try to show up to track and swim meets. If they're in any activity, we're always there. If they get awards for anything, we go for that. We'll go for the parents'
night, all of those open houses and things like that, and conferences. We'll go to community night, we go for college night. So although we don't join the PTO or anything,
it seems like we're at the high school—at least I am—probably every single week. I
probably don't miss a week.

However, comments from both men and women indicated that most fathers had
never participated regularly in the life of their children's schools, and that this arrangement continued in high school. A sentiment expressed by many men in our
study was, "My wife belongs to the PTA but I don't participate too much myself."
The reason given for much of this gender difference was that fathers' work schedules interfered with their participation, although the same arrangement was observed in families where both parents worked full-time.

Mother: Is he involved with school? No, not usually. That's usually just because of
scheduling. It's not because he wouldn't be. I mean, a point is always made of talking
over what went on at school. He certainly would take off, and he has, if there's any indication that we should both be there.

In spite of this general nonparticipation in the schools, some families pointed
out important roles for fathers in particular incidents regarding their children's
education:

Girl: I had a problem with a teacher here last year and my mom really didn't notice
that he was a problem and really didn't do much about it. My dad went back second semester and had a conference with this same teacher and he really started talking to
him, and really realized that there was a problem. But my mom just said he's a problem and just left it at that. And my dad talked to him and said, "Yeah he really is a problem." But we just had a conference not too long ago, and my dad talked to both of our
sets of teachers, and when he came back he had to give a report to my mom and they
agreed on how to take care of things.

Thus, while these respondents did not indicate that they used collective action to
deal with the schools and they did not seem to be participating in decision making
alongside the faculty and administrators of their children's schools, neither did
they complain that the schools were unacceptable or underperforming in any general way.

SCHOOLS AS SOCIAL ENVIRONMENTS

Students experience schools as social environments in which to meet friends, deal
with conflict, learn social norms and develop identity. As they move through puberty, young adolescents contend with these social tasks simultaneously with bio-
logical/hormonal and cognitive changes—a sort of "normal life crisis" (Elias &

Butler, 1999, p. 75). Central to the processes of adolescence, of course, are changes in ways of interacting with adults as well, so teachers are an important part of the social environment that is school (Solodow, 1999).

Chapter 4 examined the role of social support and peer relationships in the lives of the children interviewed for this study. It is evident that many of the relationships valued by adolescents are established and carried out in the school environment. For the daily challenges that the school environment presents, peers are used for companionship and entertainment and adults are used for instrumental support. The following section discusses some of the particular social opportunities and challenges respondents found in schools.

Bullying

Bullying by classmates is a type of conflict especially common with children and youth. One recent large-scale survey of students in New York State revealed that 98% of youths acknowledge that bullying often occurs, and the majority of respondents said that some sort of intervention was needed to stop the aggression. Many of these students could readily identify places where bullying was likely to occur, and most knew that bullying happens to kids who are labeled as different by virtue of appearance or behavior (Schroeder, 2002). Bullying is usually hidden from adults, but is recurrent and systematic. Most researchers understand bullying to be based on the dynamics of power and control, much like domestic violence. Bullying generally reaches its peak in early adolescence and declines throughout high school, when changes in physical stature and social maturity inhibit victimization (Sullivan, Cleary, & Sullivan, 2004).

Once dismissed as a natural rite of passage in childhood, there is growing understanding of the potential physical and emotional harm that can be inflicted by bullies. Aside from the obvious injury done to children who are physically assaulted, bullying can result in anxiety, social withdrawal, depression, and increased risk for suicide (Sullivan et al., 2004). Sharp (1995) suggests that targets of bullying may respond to the experience with impaired concentration and poor academic achievement, as well.

It is important to note that roles in the bullying dynamic are not fixed: a child may be a victim in one interaction and a bully in another. Where people tend to see bullying as perpetrated by aggressive and irredeemable monsters on passive victims, evidence points to much more complex relationships. The young men who carried out the random shooting at Columbine High School were often the targets of bullying rather than bullies themselves (Bender, Shubert, & McLaughlin, 2001).

Although social researchers frequently focus on bullying as one of the most distressing aspects of childhood, almost none of the respondents mentioned bullying at all. It is possible that some characteristic of these families protected their children from the phenomenon of bullying, but more likely our results are the result of a failure to inquire directly about the issue, and/or students' reticence to report such behavior. A few parents did mention their concern about children's struggles to fit in, and these comments may indicate the presence of some level of interpeer aggression that would merit further study. This mother commented on her daughter's adjustment to a family move and a new school:

> She didn't find the kids acceptable at the beginning. She had a real hard time adjusting. She was in band. There were kids playing tricks on her. You know, taking instruments, hiding them, whatever. I don't know if that's a welcome kind of thing.

Teachers

Teacher attitudes and expectations have a strong impact on student achievement and perceptions of school. Students who believe that teachers and others in the school care about them, and have their best interests at heart, have increased perceptions of worth and are better able to focus on learning (Green, 1999). Teachers' beliefs about students are reflected in their actions and attitudes toward them; analysis demonstrates that teachers actually sustain rather than grow student achievement—thus students who are perceived as low achievers tend to stay that way, while students perceived as successful are reinforced. The result is that students' behaviors are shaped by teacher attitudes, with serious long-term consequences—both positive and negative. Many teachers express negative attitudes toward their students, especially minority and poor children (Warren, 2002). Students who experience their teachers as harsh or insulting are less likely to ask for help in the classroom (Kennedy, 1997). Thompson, Warren, and Carter (2004) found that teachers who blame students for low achievement were also likely to blame students' parents, and to believe that the students themselves did not want to achieve. Contrast that with the caring teacher, who is perceived as attentive, neutral, interested, and hopeful (Wentzel, 1997). Such teachers are correlated with higher achievement in the classroom, as well as increased social responsibility.

Our respondents' comments about teachers reinforced the idea that teacher attitudes and behavior are central to the experience of school. In most of these families, both adults and youth characterized at least some of the children's teachers as helpful, caring or understanding; having specialized knowledge or teaching skill was mentioned much less often.

Changing Relationships Between Teens and Teachers

Both male and female students mentioned the important changes taking place in their relationships with teachers, based on physical and social development. The youth felt affirmed that their teachers treated them more like adults than children, saying, "Now that I'm older, it seems like they are working with you, like you're not just learning off of them. They work with you." Other comments included:

Female teen: I feel more secure talking with teachers about problems I have. And I feel more comfortable around them, because they treat me more like an adult.

Female teen: Because I was getting taller so they happened to notice me a little more, being at eye level, instead of being lower. I got more respect from other people. Teachers couldn't yell down at me. They had to either [look at] eye level or up.

Male teen: Some of the teachers are really good, and you get in a good relationship with them, talk to them about things, fooling around with saying jokes and stuff. It's just kind of fun to have a teacher sort of, not really a friend, but just somebody you can talk to.

Male teen: I would say that now the teachers are your friend outside of the classroom. If you see them in the halls, you can talk to them, and you see them at games and stuff. They are nice to you when you talk to them. But, when I was 10, I never really saw my teachers outside of the classroom.

For these youth, friendly relationships with teachers are seen as a source of support and resources. This young woman described one of her teachers:

The teachers really helped me out. My French teacher helps me out an awful lot. I talk to her about stuff. If I have a bad day, she always … you know. Today was one of my off days. She's real. "Is everything okay? Is there anything I can do? If there is, just tell me." And that's the way it's been all year and last year.

Another aspect of the shift into adolescence was the phenomenon of increasing numbers of male teachers in the middle and high schools. This change was seen as particularly important for boys. One mother commented:

Most of the boys have really changed, because they've all had women teachers. And then in junior high, they get some men teachers and they change every hour. They aren't with the same lady all day. And so it's been a real positive experience in junior high, even though you have to deal with some of this garbage that goes along with it.

This change was not seen as universally positive, though, as some teens reacted to the dilution of the student–teacher relationship in high school. A teen girl commented,

Once you're out of middle school, you've got six teachers rather than just one. So [I'm] not as close to the teachers as I used to be.

Negative Teacher Characteristics

While stories about positive relationships with teachers were common, we also recorded several negative comments about teachers in general. One male teen said, "I don't know my teachers that well, because they just don't like students." Other youth compared high school teachers with professionals at other levels of the educational experience:

> **Teen boy:** When you're in elementary, you always like your teachers, but in middle school I hated all my teachers. And in high school I hated most of them too. But I like them more than I did in middle school. I mean, they just looked down on kids all the time. With elementary teachers, they always try to encourage all the little kids. [In high school], there's only one nice teacher out of all the teachers I had. The other teachers, they think because we are in high school, we're like there to jump off and stuff. Most of them look down on some kids. Some are okay, they just mind their own business.

Others compared "good" teachers with "bad" within the same system:

> **Female teen, discussing her advanced courses:** I felt that it's been like good for me. In my advanced classes especially the teachers have given us a lot more respect than in regular classes. For example, I suppose five of my six classes this year could have been termed more advanced classes. But I had to take Government, which was like the fire for everybody. It had been a long time since I had taken a class that the entire school was required to take. I was glad I was in the advanced classes, because the teacher kind of taught us like we were all a bunch of extremely slow students, and the thing is, I didn't know everybody in the class, but I think some of the people who were having problems in the class, were having problems because of how it was going instead of their abilities. But his entire attitude towards the class was like, "I'm the teacher, I'm the dictator, I'm in power," whereas with my advanced classes, the teachers were more like, "Let's get together and share ideas. I'm not entirely sure how this one's going to work out." They treated us more maturely and I think partly it was the teacher, and partly it was the group of students and the fact that we were advanced and, it was almost humiliating being in that Government class and having the teacher tell me after the first card marking, "Oh you got an A this time. Lucky you." He kind of figured it out after not much longer, but, it was just kind of funny in a sick sort of way that it would be like that.

Girls had quite a lot more to say about teachers than did the boys in our study. Female teen respondents, in particular, had stories to tell about incompetent, inappropriate, or unhelpful teaching staff. These stories were often indirectly focused on feelings of powerlessness and inequity in the student-teacher interaction:

> **Female teen:** The teachers are really bad. We had one fired. One of our teachers was just out of control. He would throw things and he would give us bad grades. I had that teacher for a whole year. I had two C–s and a D– in his class. The last half a month there was a substitute teacher and I brought my grade up to an A. That teacher was just out of control. He was really old and he would hear things. I missed a lot in math. We didn't really learn anything last year. So, I guess you could say I'm a little behind. But the teacher I have now is pretty good, so I can catch up.

> **Female teen:** So, school in general, I'd have to say is positive, but when you get down to individual teachers—well, last year, my science teacher was so ditzy. She's just like an airhead. She's a very intelligent lady, you know, scientific and everything, but she

just kind of swings her hair around. And the gestures she makes used to make me laugh. My homeroom teacher used to make this face, "Seventh grade, settle down!" She used to have the biggest mood swings, very low patience. She was very involved in our lives. I think it got a little too personal, sometimes got a little too involved with us. I don't want to sound like I'm cocky and bragging, but my friends are the popular group, and so she assumes we're mean and stuff like that. She always says how we exclude the other people. And it's not true.

Female teen: I remember in elementary school I'd always have a teacher that I'd like a lot and they'd help you or give you advice or something. But now, you know, it's just like none of the teachers are really there to help you. It's just like go in the classroom, get your homework and go home. And some of the teachers I don't really like at all. I had a problem with a teacher. It was a male teacher. He was a pig, I guess you could say. And I didn't like that at all.

Parents' negative comments about teachers varied from general dissatisfaction to specific descriptions of teacher errors or interpersonal conflicts. For example, this father described why his family chose to send their children to private school:

We just weren't satisfied with the education they were getting in the public schools. It appeared that the teachers primarily just didn't care. There were a lot of substitute teachers. We just didn't see basic fundamentals, like cursive writing. They weren't learning some basic things in the classroom. My wife just wasn't pleased with their attitude. [It] seemed more like a job. I definitely like the Catholic schools much better and the teachers are more involved with the kids. We struggled with the school decisions, but we think we made the right decision.

This man focused on his personal knowledge of teachers' behaviors to support his son's interactions in middle school:

Well, with boys going to the same junior high school that I went to, I know a few of the teachers that are left. I know how they are. The schools will try to say something and I'll say, "Well, wait a minute. I was there, when I was going to school, I had the same teacher and he was the exact same way."

Although the parents that we interviewed seemed to clearly understand the importance of their children's teachers, very few families indicated that they undertook action as the result of problems with teachers. In some cases, however, families indicated that they moved their children to new (usually private) schools. A few other parents described approaching the problem directly with the school. For example, this mother described her intervention when her daughter experienced a troublesome situation at school:

There are a lot more good (teachers) than bad, but if you're unfortunate enough to get one of the bad, I found out you don't have to accept it. You should absolutely go to the top and say, "No. Absolutely not." I mean, why should my child endure a teacher all year who tells them they're small and stupid? I don't need to do that. I'm looking for an understanding teacher. I'm looking for a teacher that my children won't be afraid to go up and say, "You know, I know you explained it 10 times. I don't get it." And there are maybe a quarter of the teachers in the school system that you can't do that to. And when they're looking to cut some people, I don't think they should go by seniority, I think they should go by that.

A few families talked about school personnel other than classroom teachers, most commonly school counselors. In general, these stories were positive and suggested a strong source of support for families struggling with issues ranging from classroom misbehavior and learning disabilities to selecting an appropriate college:

> **Mother:** There's a lot of ding bats that should retire. But I found a counselor, who is not my daughter's counselor, that I go to continuously for support for my daughter. And this lady is everybody's grandma. And she took my daughter under her wing. And I asked her, with my younger daughter coming in next year, will you be my younger daughter's counselor? And she said, "Sure. What's one more?" They have an assistant principal there, same thing. No problem.

> **Father:** We have a very good school counselor. He's been absolutely excellent. He understands everything. He helps us and he understands our boys, and talks to them. We've built a strong relationship with our school counselor.

Clubs And Extracurricular Activities

During adolescence, young people learn new roles and try out interests and skills. Participation in extracurricular activities at school is one way for teens to rehearse various interests. Schools may offer students opportunities for membership in social clubs, sports teams, organizations that perform volunteer work, and theatre, musical, or recreational groups. Participation in these activities is linked with a variety of positive outcomes, such as increased exercise, decreased substance abuse, better mental health, and more positive attitudes about self and others (Harrison, 2003). Involvement in extracurricular activities, particularly volunteer work, is correlated with high levels of social connectedness in the community (Brady, Schlozman, & Verba, 1999) and may predict a lifetime of civic and social involvement. College-bound students often find that these activities enhance their admissions applications, as universities search for students who are well-rounded or who can demonstrate leadership skills.

Many youth in our study indicated that they enjoyed the social and interpersonal aspects of school. For most of the families that we interviewed, school organizations and after-school activities were an important way to engage with peers and develop non-academic skills. Many students' interviews were marked by lists of activities in which they engage enthusiastically:

> **Female teen:** I'm really active in my school. I'm secretary of the French club, president of the school band. I'm on the honor society. I'm in marching band and concert

band. And I help out my teachers. There are other things that I want to get into but I've been moved around so much that it would be awfully hard for me to get into it because you'd have to be there from pretty much the start. Since I moved in Junior year, there's lots of things I couldn't get started in, like sports.

Male teen: I'm in some clubs. I socialize there. Ski club, junior achievement, SADD. I'm planning to join more. My sister's in all sorts of clubs: Spanish, junior achievement, SADD, literary magazine, the student government, everything.

Female teen: My school in general, I love it. But the teachers and the principal, that's a different story. I have lots of school spirit and I love all my friends. I love pep rallies. I love going to school dances. I mean, those are a blast.

Some respondents described sports schedules and other activities that consumed substantial portions of the students' day and evening. For example, this mother talks about her daughter's dedication to swimming:

She's motivated enough that all fall last year, she was in the swimming pool by five in the morning because that's when practice starts. So she was up at 4:30 in the morning. She would sleep in her sweats—that's how they do it—sleep in their sweats, throw their suit on, jump in the pool, wash up afterwards and take a shower there.

And this male teen described his schedule:

I play sports, so I never really have time to do anything like on the weekend or during the week. I talk to my friends a lot. I see them at school, but other than that, we don't really get together.

Parents tended to talk about the benefits of extracurricular activities in terms of their children's improved social contacts and new skills learned, and thus sometimes promoted these activities, even when their children were unenthusiastic. For example, this mother discussed her son's reluctant involvement with a school club:

We wanted Gary to get involved in school with different activities just so that's a way he can meet other people. [Now] I think he knows more people and he had a very positive experience at the end of the school year.

A father described his children's involvement with after-school activities:

Bottom line, they're both really good kids with all the activities they've done. He really enjoys football. As I said, she does dance and gymnastics. They like improving themselves in other sports I've let them do, although he's more laid back. He'll do football and that's it. And I'm real gung-ho on "Join this! Join that! Try this. Try that." He prefers to do things with his friends.

And joining a club or other activity at school was clearly perceived as an appropriate way to deal with being the "new kid" at school:

Mother: She had a really difficult time adjusting to the new school, you know, getting in to meet new people. She was in the band, which did help. But it was just strange trying to move yourself into another group and find acceptance. My son, too, found it a little bit hard. He tried to join in whatever he could in school.

More indirectly, this female teen describes transferring into a new school, where she didn't know anybody in her classes:

I felt kind of left out. I went to high school and then I tried for cheerleading, so I made that. That's given me a lot more self-esteem, because I didn't feel that good about myself when I went to high school. That introduced me to a lot more people. I was scared to go to high school, but I really liked (cheerleading) a lot, so I'm really involved with it.

Some students described their activity schedules as part of an overall self-improvement:

Male teen: This year I got my grades up. I also have a job and I'm in four bands at school. So, it's a real accomplishment for me to be able to do all that stuff and still keep my grades up. It kind of makes me try harder for everything. Before, it was "Oh, I can't do it." Now it's like I can do it and that means I can do other things too. It gives me more of a future to look forward to like in college.

While activities were generally considered beneficial to these youth's future prospects, a couple of students indicated that they were cutting back on activities in order to "get serious" about college. Their comments indicate a perception of some extracurricular activities as somewhat frivolous or impractical unless they lead to scholarship money or career opportunities:

Male teen: I'd like to keep playing soccer but I don't think I'll be able to in college. Maybe I'd like to play soccer on some team that I could organize with people. I don't see myself getting a scholarship for soccer or anything. I don't think I'm good enough. I want to focus more on my education than I do on sports. Even right now it's kind of causing me problems, just like balancing my time and everything. So, I just think I'll want to focus more on just getting a career and everything than playing soccer.

Female teen, who has been skating competitively for several years: I really like skating, but I don't know what I'm going to be doing through high school. I know that I'm not going to be taking that through college because it's going to be important to be focusing on college stuff.

A few students indicated a lack of interest in extracurricular activities, like this boy: "I don't care for the school sports that much. I just go to school so I can just pass high school and get my credentials." But this attitude was very much in the minority. Even students who indicated a lack of current participation often commented on how important the social aspects of school are to them:

Female teen: Well in middle school, I used to play sports. I used to be on track. Now, I just go to school because I have to. I think it's boring unless, maybe like in between class and stuff, you get to talk to your friends. That's cool, but that's about it.

SUCCESS IN SCHOOL

Most of the students in our respondent families demonstrated success in school. Both children and parents reported on students' achievement in terms of grades and honors earned, awards given, and aspirations for future success in the professional world. Families see success in school as a prerequisite to opportunities for college admission and pursuit of these career goals. In the following section, we discuss the interviewees' responses related to school achievement and connections between education and future goals.

Academic Achievement and Honors

A portion of the students in the families interviewed either identified themselves as academically gifted or reported that they enrolled in one or more honors courses in school. Students who have a high level of academic achievement are unique along several variables when compared to average students. "Smart kids" may be socially isolated from their average peers or may underachieve because the social pressures to conform may impede academic progress (Frey, 1998). Nevertheless, gifted students have significantly higher levels of self-actualization than average students (Pufal-Struzik, 1999), and girls in gifted education programs see themselves as more effective with instrumental tasks, have higher levels of motivation, and are less traditional in career aspirations (Mendez, 2000).

Because gifted students often need additional academic challenge in order to learn at full potential, they may require additional encouragement to take advantage of the enrichment opportunities offered in most schools. Educating these students (and their parents) about how to advocate for themselves is seen as one way to enhance the educational experience (Douglas, 2004).

Several families interviewed for this study included children identified as academically talented. In general, these students were presented as doing quite well both academically and socially. This mother's description of her daughter is typical:

In school, she's taking classes that have already surpassed me. I can't even help her with her homework now. She's in these advanced math classes and all advanced classes. She is very hard on herself. She has a lot of homework and seems to be handling it. But then, we just went to her open house last night and sat through all those classes. These seem like a lot is involved. She said, "Mom, I'm doing fine." So she is pleased. I'm pleased that she seems to be getting into high school. She's in the marching band, so a bit more socializing, and she goes to the football games on the weekends.

Students identified as academically gifted in our sample were quite modest about their talents. Many expressed discomfort with being labeled "gifted," as did this young man:

> I'd say that if you're going to talk about being gifted, you should put another term, like "educationally gifted." Because I think most kids are gifted in some area, such as gifted as an artist. I'd say being gifted means someone with a talent. I don't like to take that too literally, but I guess you kind of have to. Because I wasn't gifted with my intelligence, I don't think, because a lot of people have it and don't use it.

Another boy commented,

> I'm in this advanced program for math and science. Right now, to me, it really doesn't mean anything. I really don't see that I'm more special than anyone.

Whether the youth being labeled as "gifted" were modest or not, most acknowledged that they were perceived as different, a condition with which many adolescents are particularly uncomfortable. One male youth put it succinctly: "I was in the gifted program and the people looked down on us because we were smart or something. It was biased. They thought we were smart so we were different." Youth saw themselves as different, too, and expressed varying degrees of ambivalence about their "gifts."

> **Female teen:** My family is proud of me for being smart, but I think they'd be proud if I wasn't all that smart. To me the one thing that's not a real advantage of being an academic student is you tend to think about stuff a lot more in-depth. Whereas some people's biggest concern might be, "Oh, my hair's not okay." That can still be a concern with me, but then you also get into concerns like sometimes I've got into these really deep discussions about stuff like abortion with my friends and we get into these little yelling matches about abortion. It's nice in a way, but in a way, you don't want to have to think about that all the time. But then you don't have a choice, because it just comes naturally. I don't know, if I could be born all over again, if I would make myself smart or not. Now that I'm smart, I like being smart, but then you sometimes wish for that level of ignorance where it didn't really make a difference to you, so you didn't care.

Parents also verbalized an understanding that being perceived as especially smart was not always an advantage, especially for young women. This mother expressed her concerns especially well:

> I get the sense talking to some of the parents that I know from church and school—their sons will say, "Sarah's the smartest girl I know." It's intimidating. One of the boys she went to homecoming and prom with, they applied for the same scholarships, and she got the scholarship. We're aware of those types of things, and I think in that age group, it's intimidating. Sometimes she will say she's not attractive, and I'll say that's not true.

Despite these feelings of difference, the students' experiences of their segregated full- or part-day gifted programs or their advanced placement courses were mostly positive. One benefit discussed by the students is a social one; gifted students got to know one another and could be assured that they would see each other frequently in their classes:

> **Male teen:** Once in a while, I get fed up with being with the same kids over and over again. But I guess it's good for an education, and two of my best friends are in the program with me. Then I always know I'll have some friends in my classes. And I'm friends with almost everyone in my classes, because I've known them.

This female teen reflected on the ways in which this close-knit group allowed her to relax and avoid some of the negative social consequences of achievement:

> They gave us a whole bunch of really advanced classes, and we got to be in a kind of small environment, so nobody was afraid to ask questions or speak up. It gave me a sense that you never felt like an outsider in that type of situation. It was never one of those classes that you walked into on the first day of school and you didn't know anybody at all. I never felt that I had to conform to any sort of social standard in that class. I could be myself or make my own comments or be smart and not worry. I mean, in some of my classes, it would not be all that cool to be smart or to be the kid who always did well on the tests. And in this program, it didn't matter because everyone knew you were smart to begin with, just for being in the program. It was nice being in there, because you were interacting with a lot of high-achieving students. At the end of this year, because it was senior year, everybody was winning all these awards, and you're all happy for one another. And it was unlike a regular class, in that we were all close after that time. There was competition, but it was more competing against yourself than against other students. And just trying to get your personal best because, just to get selected to be in the program, 30 students district-wide, says that you have to be good to begin with, and so nobody felt any pressure.

This young woman identified a unique opportunity offered to her because of her academic achievements as critical to her comfort with attending college in the future. She attended a summer program for gifted high school students:

> And it brought like 50 students together nation-wide. And we were in this National Science Foundation grant program, but it was not a terribly challenging program at all. But, the real experience of being there was that we were there for six weeks. And there were several other [high school] programs there, too, taking regular college classes at the university for credit. Like they had the whole run of the university, and they housed all the students in all the various programs in dorms so we were all living together. They mixed us in together. And like the real experience of that was that I got to meet a lot of people from all over the country who were in all different interests. In areas where I thought I'll never have a friend who's in this [academic] area. And I ended up meeting some of the best friends I've ever made, there, just living with them and stuff. And I still keep in touch with many of them. And it was a good experience for me, because at the time, I was kind of hesitant about going away for college.

Several of the families that we interviewed for this study produced some children labeled as academically gifted, and some children who remained in mainstream classes. Both mothers and fathers discussed the particular difficulty of "having one kid recognized as being in this gifted program, and then not having the other one get in." For some families, having their children labeled as gifted seemed to be treated as a challenge to be met. For example, this mother described her youngest daughter's efforts:

> The older kids were in the academically talented program and she wasn't. I think she felt some of that pressure, because there was an esteem thing there. The older kids would say negative things. She started to pull her grades up with this teacher and started bringing home excellent report cards and found out that she really was academically talented.

Pathways to Careers

Much of parents' and students' discussion about school related to children's future goals and aspirations. Not surprisingly, much of their focus was on school as a pathway to a specific career. Adult respondents' discussions of the world of work are the focus of chapter 6, but here we will provide an overview of the relationships between education and careers mentioned in the interviews.

For the majority of our families, the future looked promising. Parents and youth alike predicted at least adequate academic success and, for most, the near future included a college education or career training. It was clear from the interviews that not all children appreciated education as much as others. Some youth were apathetic about attending school, and a few were in the process of dropping out before graduating. The few families we interviewed where children were not achieving success in school were clearly less optimistic about their children's future. For example, this mother described her son's decision to drop out of school after failing in his classes:

> As a parent it's put a great deal of stress on us the entire year. The disappointment that he didn't even complete school, didn't care about it, and has no interest in it. And [he doesn't have] too much of a desire to work anything regular either. We feel he's just kind of floating, looking for what he's going to do and doesn't seem to be too anxious to get there.

Another mother describes her concern that a romantic relationship is interfering with her daughter's motivation to pursue a college degree:

> We have always discussed college and looked at that. Then about two weeks ago we got, "Well, I'm going to go to trade school." And we're going, "Wait a minute, what's going on here?" I don't believe her boyfriend has any aspirations whatsoever of going to college. We had a real painful end of the last year in school. She ended up flunking out. She ended up skipping classes and this was with him [the boyfriend].

Even where children were expected to successfully complete high school, some parents recognized that immediate enrollment in college was not appropriate for everyone:

Father: He has a couple of various goals. One of them is to go into the military. He knows he has to get out of high school to do that. I think it's great. I think it will help his maturity level tremendously. I think he'll have the opportunity for college after that. That's pretty much the expectations that way.

Students and parents understood that education provided an opportunity for specific preparation for future career goals. A few students mentioned courses they were taking (or not taking) that were needed for college or other job training, and nearly all mentioned "getting good grades" as a prerequisite for future success. Parents' expectations were expressed quite explicitly in this area— work hard in school so you don't need to work hard in a dead-end job later as we saw earlier in the "pep talk" given by the parent whose sons did not like doing "manual labor."

For students not bound for college, the emphasis was on learning job skills for entry into a trade. For example, this mother describes a program her son is enrolled in through his high school:

The intent of the program is that when they get out of high school, they'll be able to take care of themselves and find a trade and be able to go out and at least make a living or feel good about themselves and be productive.

A father with a son who has attention deficit disorder discussed his efforts to use the education system to help prepare his son for a career:

This year, I'm having him take an auto mechanic class, just so he can see. Plus, I think it will be good for him to have a hands-on class because he can only sit so long.

Going to college is a crucial decision and an exciting change for most young people. One mother described this period with her son, "Joe's getting letters from all over the country from different colleges and stuff. He wants to get away from home, you know." Many parents of students who were college-bound described the process of choosing a college and major as a huge task for the whole family:

Mother: As we started to look at colleges and go to lectures and orientations in the area, we talked a lot about picking the school that's not only a good school, but one that's right for you.

Mother: Probably the most trying time that [she] and I have had together was with her choosing a university to attend. She ended up weighing the merits of the two schools for the curriculum that she's interested in and she chose the best academic school. She'll be going to [a top-rated public institution] and I think that, after she spends a week on campus, she'll be happier than hell that that's what she chose.

For some parents, the process of choosing a university to attend is linked as closely with concerns about financing the college education as with grade point averages or test scores. This father describes his daughter's choices:

She wanted to go to an Ivy League school, and Ivy League schools do not give out academic scholarships or any money. It's all based on financial need. The alternative was the state university, [which] also doesn't give out money except for financial-need-type things. Except the longer we delayed, the more money they kept sending us. Honorary scholarships, renewable for four years, alumni people giving us money, and you know, to the point where her first year was free. She's going to the state university, and I think she's still wondering if she should have gone to [the Ivy League school]. She really wanted to go to [another Ivy League school], and they put her on a wait list. Everybody she knows was put on a wait list. I mean people with perfect ACTs. She was one question away from perfect, and she wasn't accepted.

Interviewers specifically asked respondents to consider plans for the students' young adult years. Parents and youth mentioned a wide variety of specific careers in their discussions of future goals, including surgeon, attorney, veterinarian, computer programmer, and others. Interview responses from students clearly showed that the selection of a career goal is an important but dynamic process. Many youth described the winding course by which they chose one or more target careers by observing adults in their everyday lives, talking with peers and parents, and watching movies or television. One young man's description:

I know I want to go to college, and that's a definite. But when I was getting my braces on and stuff, I wanted to be an orthodontist because I saw how much money they made and how much they worked. But it's just that I've talked to people and they've said it's not a good thing for the future because there's going to be so many different changes and stuff, and I just kind of lost interest in that. So right now I really don't know what I'm going to be. I always wanted to be a lawyer when I was little, but I just kind of lost interest in that too, and a doctor for a while, and then an orthodontist. So I'm just throwing around a lot of ideas.

A female teen described her process:

I'm trying to concentrate on my grades more. There's a career day coming up. Someone comes in, like a doctor, and if you want to be a doctor, you can go with them and they'll talk to you about all that. I really like dissecting and science and stuff so I was thinking about being a coroner but, then, that's kind of gross. It's like dead people and stuff, but then I was thinking about being a prosecuting attorney because I like to argue, and I thought that would be a good thing, so if I decide that I could go on the debate team in high school.

A father describes his high-achieving daughter's plan:

She's going into the college of engineering and probably into chemical engineering. She wants a double major with political science. And she wants to go on to medical school after that. But who knows?

This father describes his son's process of determining a career path:

He pretty much knows what he wants to be. Last year he wanted to be a music major. And I really didn't think too much of that, but we didn't say anything. This year he decided that music is hard to have as a job. He wanted to be a music teacher. They cut those jobs first. Music's always the first to go—music and art. So, now he's looking at law enforcement—criminal justice, I think it's called. He's not exactly sure what area he wants to be in, so we talk about that and he's doing some reading. And he says, "Which one pays the most?" And I said, "I don't know. We'll have to go to the library and look that up." But he's looking at colleges—which ones have the best criminal justice programs and things like that.

While our interaction with these families did not allow us to measure the likelihood that students will achieve these goals, some plans seemed more realistic and achievable than others, and some choices seemed quite distinct from one another. For example, one student said she wanted to go to a famous academy of the arts for music, or be a physical therapist. Another teen described more elaborate, but somewhat disjointed, career plans:

> I'd like to become a marine biologist. And me and my friend want to go in business together. And, I would like to get something higher than a master's degree in college. Me and my friend have real strong feelings about doing this. We have a pretty good chance of getting this. We keep up good grades and stuff in school. We planned our whole future out, in a way, because we want to live together in a ranch house and raise horses and breed dogs and stuff. And in my spare time, I either want to be working on a SWAT team or on a bomb squad, or the state police. I like animals a lot, and I'd like to work with dolphins and stuff like that. And I think (I'd like) to do something kind of dangerous, in a way, like work on the SWAT team or the state police.

Contrast that plan with this slightly older student's plan:

> I'd like to get a bachelor's of engineering at the university and I've thought about them [degrees] a lot. Right now, I might go in the Air Force to study basics of aeronautics. I could go right into the Air Force and then later, while I'm in the Air Force, have them pay for my college.

Finally, a few respondents acknowledged that partnering and starting a family may play an important role in the career choices of these students. Interestingly, where this issue was mentioned, it was almost exclusively as a comment that marriage and career can go hand-in-hand:

> **Female teen, on her vision of herself at age 25:** I hope to have a significant other by then. I mean, I hope to be seriously thinking of marriage about that time. I will be definitely a college graduate, if not going on to law school, medical school, whatever training. Career is important to me. If not, a housewife might not be a bad idea, but I still would want to be a college graduate.

> **Father:** I think, even if she were to get married or anything, I think she's determined enough that she would continue her education and graduate. I think it's important enough to her.

SUMMARY AND IMPLICATIONS FOR PRACTICE AND POLICY

The modern system of public education was formed during the Industrial Revolution, a period of mass immigration, urbanization, and social and economic upheaval (Lee, 2001). Contemporary conditions mirror that time, as changes in the social and economic environment are driven by the evolution of technology and the globalization of industry. Schools themselves are transforming, as society attempts to meet the demand for citizens better prepared to participate in an international community. The parallels between the schools of today and the conditions of public education in its infancy are striking for their implications for the future of the quality of life in the United States. The narratives of our respondents indicate that many families do not experience the education system as overtly distressing, but several issues raised in our analysis suggest that social workers and other helping professionals will continue to play an important role in the education system, both locally and on the macro level.

Identifying the System Level for Intervention

The traditional role of school social workers, counselors, and psychologists is to assist school faculty and to insure that all students are provided with the highest possible level of education and ancillary services that will help them succeed in school. As student demographics and school resources have changed dramatically in the past few decades (Ekstrom et al., 1988), this job has grown to include ever more complex and difficult functions, so that the contemporary school social worker, for example, must now address the needs at various levels of systems: needs of various student populations, as well as the needs of faculty and administration, as well as advocating for change in policies on a district, county, or state level.

As this study indicates, the education system is one of the most important in the lives of adolescents. The ancillary service providers are often the heart of the system's support services for students, and they act as a vital protective link between and among the constituents of the school. Thus, although few of our respondents indicated a problem with bullying, an important function of the social worker, counselor, or school psychologist may be to monitor the environment for harassment, educate students and faculty about reporting and responding to bullying, and supporting efforts to teach alternatives to these behaviors.

Helping professionals have a particularly important role to play in mediating between the school as a system and the needs of students and their families. In this role, they may be called upon to assess students' specific needs. Thus, they can assist parents who want to understand their children's educational progress or problems, and they may provide consultation and support to the student's classroom teachers and support personnel, as well. This service to families may also include dissemination of information about the school's resources and programs, helping families to understand which resources are appropriate for their needs, and assisting families to find needed resources within and outside of the school system. Social workers and counselors may be called upon to provide guidance with career selection and choosing a college or an institution for vocational training.

The characteristic of contemporary classrooms as relatively free of the oversight of administrators (Weick, 1976) is both a great strength and a clear weakness. These loosely coupled systems create classroom locations with little or no oversight of the environment, resulting in the possibility of both increased excellence and increased risk to students in the classroom. Indeed, parents and students who participated in these interviews described their experiences with middle- and high-school teachers who were exemplary, as well as those who were poor communicators, unfair to students, or inept educators. Thus, one of the school social worker's most challenging tasks may be in acting as a liaison between families and "bad" teachers whose attitudes or behaviors are causing disruption to the teen's educational progress. They also must be prepared to act as advocates for students when teachers' attitudes and behaviors are abusive or harmful to students in their care, and to work with students and families to use confrontation and mediation skills in their work. In addition, all helping professionals must understand the bureaucracy of the school and the power dynamics of the system in order to negotiate the difficult terrain of the ombudsman role.

Where problems in the schools reach proportions that indicate a larger, system-level problem, such as unequal distribution of resources or the neglect of vulnerable students, the social worker must be able to work with parent groups, the community, and the local school board to address these issues. These advocates should have skills in group process, community empowerment, public speaking, and coalition building to effectively carry out these tasks.

Marrett (1990) emphasized the importance for children's educational success of the development of a culture of communication and collaboration in the schools. To this end, social workers' training and skill base, for example, makes them prime candidates for leading the change from a formal and hierarchical system to one exemplified by networks of communication and trust. Social workers can use their experience in teaching communication skills, team building, and linking to help colleagues develop new ways of interacting with other professionals, students, and parents.

Of course, social workers are also uniquely positioned to provide leadership in the sort of emotional education advocated by contemporary school reformers (e.g., Cohen, 2001; Dasho et al., 2001). Social workers' distinctive focus on person-in-environment and their training in human development and human diversity mean that they should play a major role in the development of curricula to address the emotional development of diverse students.

Outside of the school system, clinicians have an important role to play in supporting families as they negotiate the educational system concurrently with changes in their children's development. Although these families did not report many conflicts with their children's schools, our respondents' indicated that many families struggle with important decisions regarding children's careers, educational plans, and even financial planning for college during this time. While most families in our sample showed a remarkable level of positive relationship skills, parents said that they and their children struggled with career and college decisions. Others said that they had difficulty balancing school or work with social or family activities. Clinicians in a counseling setting can reinforce parents' strong emotional support of their children while assisting in goal setting or teaching skills for time management. For many families, a frank discussion of the financial aspects of their children's education would seem to be very useful, as well.

Concerns With Policies for and Beyond These Participants

As a group, the families interviewed here were remarkably well positioned to take advantage of their communities' educational opportunities. They lived in relatively well resourced, primarily White, middle-class suburban communities. A large percentage of the parents were college educated, most had adequate incomes, and many chose to send their children to private schools. Opportunities for sports, recreation, and other extracurricular activities were available and accessible within their communities. Thus, this study does not contradict Marrett's (1990) conclusion that race and class are predictors of educational success, but neither does it provide much information about the particular factors important to poor and ethnic-minority families' relationships with the education system. Further study of diverse families is needed to draw these conclusions, and funding should be allocated to such in-depth research.

Families with adolescent children would benefit from social policies that mandate appropriate opportunities for students at all levels of academic potential. That is academic programs must address the needs of academically gifted students as well as those with learning disabilities, and must provide for students who will enter vocational training, as well as those bound for Ivy League universities. This is no small order, but these data clearly indicate the importance of such diverse foci in the educational system. With significant resources, most of these families were able to address their children's diverse educational needs. Where families have fewer resources, it is likely that some children would have faltered as they moved into adulthood.

Helping professionals can play an important part in clarifying the role of parents in secondary education. It was clear from these interviews that parents have moved away from active participation in their children's schools, as their youth have moved into middle and highschool. Parents who had been quite active in elementary schools were much less so in their teens' schools. Part of this change was due to changes in mothers' work responsibilities as they returned to work or increased work-for-pay hours (see chap. 6), and part of it seems to be a lack of clarity regarding the purpose of parental involvement at this level. The literature on parental involvement in their children's schools is most focused on conditions in elementary school buildings (e.g., Dunst, 2002; Miretzky, 2004) and indicates that it diminishes as children enter middle and high school (Eccles & Harold, 1996). If parents in the secondary education system are to play a larger role than raising money and coordinating parties, a clear mission and accessible means for their participation must be developed. Such an undertaking must involve system-wide discussions about the particular value of these families, a clear offer to share power, and an explication of the benefits of such participation for the schools, the parents, and the students. Social workers should play a part in leading such a movement.

If parents are to be expected to participate in their children's schools, more opportunities for meaningful engagement must be offered. Parents who work and those who have child-care responsibilities should be deliberately included in the system. Meetings could be scheduled at various times of day and evening, child care must be provided for parents, and outreach to fathers should be encouraged.

Wentzel (1997) characterized the caring teacher as attentive, fair, and positive toward his or her students. Respondents in our study clearly identified teachers as "good" or "bad" based on similar characteristics. Since much of the recent literature on teacher characteristics confirms the commonsense notion that "bad" teachers are detrimental to children's learning, a fundamental goal of school reform should be to increase the number of well trained, caring teachers. (Although our respondents downplayed the importance of teachers' knowledge or technical skill, we took this to be an indication that most of their teachers were well trained, since their school districts fit Heyns' (1990) description of the most desirable districts, where experienced teachers tend to congregate.) Thus, in addition to knowledge about curricula and subject area, teacher training should include an emphasis on the model of the caring educator. Hiring, training, and mentoring practices should include evaluation of these characteristics, as well. The value of teacher excellence as the most important factor in a child's educational experience (Chase, 2002) should be supported by policy decisions that enforce actions linked to real reform in the classroom.

6

Taking on Provisions:
Work in the Lives of Families
With Adolescents

Employment plays an important role in parents' lives and serves as a model for teens' growing sense of identity. Occupational status is linked with social values such as worth, responsibility, maturity, and success, as well as material gain through salary and employment benefits. In the United States, the legacy of the Puritan work ethic and the mythology of the "rags to riches" journey still mold individual and family ideas about who works, how success is achieved, the meaning of one's occupation in the daily social interactions that make up family life, and the roles with which one identifies at home and in the workplace, as referred to in chapter 1.

Gender remains a fundamental element in structuring perceptions of both work and family. Despite enormous changes in society in the past several decades, many contemporary researchers find that their respondents still organize their perceptions of family life around sex and gender (Smith & Beaujot, 1999). That is, people continue to assume, as part of the normal social order, that men should support themselves and their families, while women's first responsibilities lie with their families, especially their children.

Social attitudes about the gendering of work result in real differences in individual experiences of work and family. Men are still better compensated for their work and are more likely to remain focused on their careers throughout their work lives. Women's work, on the other hand, is more likely to be interrupted by family responsibilities, and women themselves express more ambivalence about their work (Fredriksen-Goldsen & Scharlach, 2001; Larson, Richards, & Perry-Jenkins, 1994).

This chapter focuses on the social context of adolescent family transitions as they relate to work by describing views of maternal and paternal employment and how work impacts the family. Much of the literature on work and family relates primarily to the historical movement of women into the paid workforce, and related effects on marital and parent–child relationships. Particularly relevant for our analysis are the correlations, suggested by social science theory and research, between increases in women's work–family demands, perceptions of inequality concerning household work, and increases in marital and family discord. This is pertinent in light of the fact that more mothers reported working during this study than at the time of our first book when their children were in elementary schools.

Additionally, for the first time in their lives, the children interviewed for this study are entering the workforce. Teens must learn new roles and participate in new social relationships to adapt to this context. This chapter describes the teens' experiences with work and parents' feelings about their children entering into this new social milieu.

CHANGING CONTEXTS FOR WORK AND FAMILY

For much of the past century, marriage and mothering were considered the primary jobs and natural roles for women. Social norms enforced the notion that White, middle-class, married women's paid work should be sporadic and secondary to their husbands' employment. When women's income was necessary to their families' subsistence, as with White working-class women and Women of Color, most were relegated to low-paying, low-status jobs. For nearly all families, the ideal was for women to discontinue out-of-home work whenever possible at the birth of a first child (Fredriksen-Goldsen & Scharlach, 2001; Lerner & Noh, 2000).

At the beginning of the 21st century, however, changes in the social environment mean that women's education levels and likelihood of employment have increased significantly. The number of married households where both men and women work now outnumbers "traditional" households by about three to one (Clarkberg & Moen, 1999). Women with infants and preschoolers are still less likely to work outside the home (60%) than women with school-aged children (75%), but the trend seems to be toward greater employment for mothers (U.S. Department of Labor, 1997; U.S. General Accounting Office, 1992). As many as 80% of women who were employed before childbirth return to work within 12 months of their babies' births (Gornick & Meyers, 2001), and 75–80% of preschoolers have mothers who work outside the home (Kajicek & Moore, 1993; Klerman & Leibowitz, 1990). Thus, couples married in the last 25 years are significantly more likely to include a working wife, a wife who works even when there are preschoolers in the household, and less stereotyped gender-role attitudes in both husbands and wives (Rogers & Amato, 2000).

Marriages today are also likely to involve significantly more conflict than marriages made before 1980. Rogers and Amato (1997) studied differences in cohorts of couples married in the periods between 1969–1980 and 1981–1992. After controlling for differences in educational level and age at marriage of respondents, they found that couples married more recently had significantly lower levels of interaction and higher levels of conflict and problems in the marriage than did earlier-married couples (Rogers & Amato, 1997). Work–family demands were found to account for the largest part of the changes in marital quality between the two groups. In particular, marital interaction was found to be particularly low, and marital problems were high, when mothers were employed during children's preschool years.

Many mothers in our research sample left the workforce around the time of their first child's birth, but most returned to work by the time their children became adolescents. Transitions into and out of the workforce are thought to be one reason for women's disadvantage in pay and promotion in the workplace (Baum, 2003). How women manage these interruptions and how they perceive their experiences in the workplace and in the home is much less well understood. It is clear that the women in our study experienced a great deal of ambivalence in deciding whether to work outside the home. It is also clear that they often negotiated solutions to their work–family dilemmas by balancing these roles with creativity and flexibility, organizational skills, humor, and persistence (Mercier & Harold, 2001).

While it is well established that many women respond to motherhood by reducing their emphasis on employment (e.g., Bielby & Bielby, 1989), fatherhood's effect on the work lives of men is less clear. For example, fathers are more likely to be employed than nonfathers, and employed men with traditional (gender-stereotyped) views of fathering and its concomitant responsibilities are likely to increase out-of-home work by more than 10 hours per week. But men with more egalitarian views of parenting are likely to decrease their out-of-home work by the same number of hours, presumably to focus on family work in the home (Kaufman & Uhlenberg, 2000). Interestingly, men with more traditional life views are also more likely to assert that women "prefer" taking care of home and children, or that women do not want to work outside the home (Smith & Beaujot, 1999). In our earlier study of these families' adjustments to parenting, fathers' narratives were remarkable for their perspective that fathering involves long absences from the home and family in order to fill the role of provider. Most women and some men expressed regret or disappointment about time lost during the periods in which fathers' focus on developing a career meant less interaction with other members of the family (Mercier & Harold, 2001).

Women continue to be significantly disadvantaged in the world of paid work; they earn less, achieve less power in the workplace, and have less job stability. Although many explanations for these disparities have been proposed, much of the real difference between men's and women's earnings remains unexplained by differences in qualifications, time spent in family caregiving, years of work experience, or occupation. In 1990, the average weekly pay for women was about 77% of men's earnings (Davidson & Cooper, 1992). Even after controlling for demographic and other differences, significant differences in wages can be found in nearly all occupational categories (Fredriksen-Goldsen & Scharlach, 2001).

Work is identity-making. Choosing an occupation, working toward a career goal, and surviving transitions in the workplace involve changes in self-presentation, social status, and relationship patterns (Barley, 1989). Indeed, the mothers in our earlier study noted that they often forfeited a sense of self and left behind important sources of social support when they left paid employment to concentrate on the work of mothering (Mercier & Harold, 2001). Even when a job is seen as temporary or low-status, individuals often imbue value in their roles as workers when the occupation includes the development of competence (Hall & Mirvis, 1996).

As individual and family development theories have evolved to acknowledge the role of structural and interactional forces in human development, so too has theory about career development expanded to include an understanding of the roles of family and society. Guichard and Lenz (2005) articulate models of career development, in which development of a career choice involves the interaction of social conditions, culturally diverse experiences, varying internal frameworks, and the role of self-consciousness in present and future events. For example, for women, the importance of establishing a career and wage stability is related to the high rate of divorce, as well as the economic risks for women when their partners' become unemployed or disabled (Blumstein & Schwartz, 1983). Thus, decisions about returning to work may well be responses to anxiety about protecting oneself from financial devastation in the event of the loss of a partner.

THE FAMILY–WORK TRAJECTORY

Work is central to family stability and personal identity, but its integration into life plans and a developing sense of self is often challenging. Most young people assume that they will combine career and family as adults, but this goal is complicated by the difficulties inherent in balancing homemaking, child rearing, and career expectations. Young women, in particular, express a great deal of ambivalence about the possibility of having both career success and a conventional family life (Orrange, 2003). As we have discussed previously, such doubts are reasonable, given the high levels of stress and conflict for contemporary working mothers.

Young people leaving the world of education make important choices about the conditions of their work and family lives when they accept their first full-time jobs. As might be expected, young women rate support for family life and pleasant.

working conditions as more important than do their male counterparts (Heckert et al., 2002). This study also showed that young women rated pay and promotion as significantly less important than did young men, although other research has shown the two groups to be more similar.

Family life span development theory is based on the idea that certain experiences are normative for various stages of family life. Thus, in classical family development theory, early stages of family development may be marked by an emphasis on child care and the development of parent–child relationships and roles simultaneously with entry into the workforce and establishment of a career trajectory. Voydanoff (1987) notes, however, that this "normative" progression in family development relies heavily on the maintenance of traditional gender roles and gendered expressions of work (male provider / female homemaker) and that any variance from the normative sequencing of family–career events results in work–family role overloads. Most couples (and researchers) seem to translate this to the notion of women "sacrificing" career for family. For example, White (1999) found that married partners' satisfaction with the balance between work and family was highest when women focused more on home and family when work-family tensions increased.

In addition, contemporary trends in marriage and family formation do not support the linear trajectory assumed by most models of family development. One trend noted in contemporary demographic studies is the emergence of the "trial marriage," characterized by a brief child-free, legal marriage followed by relatively amicable divorce in which both partners appear to be "trying out" the concept of marriage before moving on to a more permanent marital relationship. Whatever the reason for such trends, the institutions of marriage and family are experiencing significant changes in predictability, function, and definition. In fact, two thirds of first marriages result in divorce, and nearly 25% of White children and about 50% of Black children are born to unmarried mothers (Fredriksen-Goldsen & Scharlach, 2001). As more families experience break-up, remarriage, long-term single parenting, and family blending, transitions from one stage of family development to another are less likely to correspond neatly with transitions in career.

ROLE STRAIN VERSUS ROLE EXPANSION

As much of the discussion about the changing context of work and the family makes clear, the relationship between family and the workplace is increasingly complex. The increase in dual-earner families is one explanation for this complexity. A more complete list of reasons might include: the globalization of the American economy resulting in decreased job stability and increased demands on worker mobility; the aging of the Baby Boom generation and increasing concerns with pension funds and work in later life; changes in benefit structures and employer commitment to the worker; and increasing demands for employees trained for high-tech information sector jobs, on one hand, and low-tech service sector jobs, on the other hand.

Most of the literature addressing the job-related stressors experienced by families focuses on the strain experienced by the competing demands of wage work and family caregiving. The vast majority of these studies are built on the premise that such strain is disproportionately experienced by women workers. In fact, women are more likely than their male partners to provide the type of care to both young children and older family members that is most likely to interrupt daily routines, including job performance (Mathew, Mattocks, & Slatt, 1990). Nearly all of the unpaid care (e.g., cooking, bathing, cleaning, supervision) given to family members is provided by women (Fredriksen-Goldsen & Scharlach, 2001). Hochschild (1989) coined the phrase "second shift" to describe the additional full-time burden of homemaking care assumed by women who are employed outside the home. The term "sandwich generation" is also applied to mid-life adults, primarily women, who have caregiving responsibilities for both their children and their parents.

Increases in workplace complexity and changing roles for women are linked to increases in stress related to the work–family relationship. The term "role strain" is used to describe difficulty coordinating the demands of various roles held simultaneously. For example, a working father may try to evaluate and manipulate competing tasks and responsibilities at home and at work, with the goal of achieving a manageable and satisfying pattern of activities and expectations (Warren & Johnson, 1995). Understanding work-family stress as role strain implies that, when faced with such stress, individuals can choose which activity or responsibility will get priority. This model works well to explain demands coming from roles that are discontinuous or sporadic in nature (Gilbert, Holahan, & Manning, 1981).

What happens when role demands occur simultaneously and none can be deferred, as when a child is too ill to go to school or daycare at the same time that an important work deadline occurs? Parents deal with such stressors in a variety of ways, including attempts to redefine roles and responsibilities within and outside of the family. However, Gilbert et al. (1981) found that professional women commonly experienced guilt about not being fully available to their families, and many used the strategy of "role expansion" to deal with conflicts between family and work. That is, they added new tasks and responsibilities to their existing work loads, without deleting existing tasks, in an attempt to do it all (Yogev, 1981).

Real success in achieving career and family goals may be less common than thought. Ferber and Green (2003) analyzed data on college-educated women and found that, depending on one's definition of career and family, only 17% to 44% could be said to have achieved both a career and a family. Faced with the conflicting demands between work and family responsibilities, many women chose to defer or give up their career aspirations. Such a response may represent a "serious step backward" (Ferber & Green, 2003, p. 144) for women's equality, but the reaction may be justifiable. Research clearly indicates that competing demands from work and family, termed *interrole conflict*, are correlated with decreased job and life satisfaction. Thus, when work life interferes with family, decreased family performance is likely to result. When family life interferes with work, role overload and reduced job performance are likely to result (Kossek & Ozeki, 1998).

BUDGETING TIME FOR WORK AND FAMILY

Time is at a premium in family life. Interrole conflict is complicated by the recent trend toward workers of both sexes spending more time "on the job" (Ferber & Green, 2003). For example, in Moen and Dempster-McClain's (1987) study, the majority of dual-earner families worked more than the equivalent of two full-time jobs outside the home. Dual-earner couples are likely to be unhappy with the number of hours they work. In a representative sample of American adults, over half of working mothers and two thirds of working fathers expressed a preference for working less. Not surprisingly, those who reported high levels of role strain were most likely to wish for reduced work schedules.

The implications of time are profound for these families, but work–family stress is experienced differently according to economic status, age, and gender. One significant difference between mothers' and fathers' relationships with time is due to the relegation of housework, child care, elder care, and other homemaking tasks to women in the home. Women spend up to 19 more hours per week on this "family work" than men do, while men spend more time on leisure and other activities (Hochschild, 1989; South & Spitze, 1994). Thus, because men have greater overall reserves of time, increases in family demand are less likely to impact their work lives, while women are more likely to meet increases in family demands with decreased efforts in the workplace (Rothbard & Edwards, 2003).

Work patterns have long-lasting implications for family life. Children's access to parents' time and the financial well-being of the family are linked to employment. Another aspect of work is the part it plays in modeling behaviors emulated by children in later life. Altonji and Dunn (2000) used data from a national longitudinal study to examine work preferences and earnings in families. Their analyses showed strong similarities in patterns of work within families. In particular, they found that the number of hours worked by sons was correlated with the work-hour preferences and work history of fathers. Similarly, daughters work hours were correlated with mothers' histories and experiences.

A major theme in the family literature of the past three decades has been the concern that women's movement into the workforce will have a negative effect on child development. The premise of the argument against such a trend is that women's time in the workplace equates with less time spent bonding with and guiding the development of young children. Assertions that children spend less time with their parents due to maternal employment seem to be unfounded, though. For example, Sandberg and Hofferth (2001) found that American children in 1997 actually spent more time with their mothers than did children in 1981. For two-parent families (like the majority of families we interviewed for this study), time that children spent with their parents increased substantially for this period.

Nevertheless, most working parents use child care when needed. The implications of out-of-family care for workers' children are usually considered along the dimensions of cost, quality, parental preferences, and availability (Folk & Yi, 1994). Casper and Smith (2004) found that cost and family income are the least significant of these predictors, but need for care due to parental work and the quality of care are important factors in choosing care.

Some families prefer to have their children cared for within the family. The most common arrangement to avoid child care expenses and reduce the use of nonparental supervision of children is for mothers to leave the workforce temporarily or permanently when children are too young to be in school during the day. Many of our respondents earlier reported on their decisions to balance work and child care arrangements by leaving work or arranging schedules so one or the other parent would be available to young children (Mercier & Harold, 2001). Hattery (2001) termed this strategy "tag team parenting" (p. 419). Parents who work opposite shifts in order to accommodate child care report positive outcomes, including constant parental presence and opportunities for father involvement in early childhood. Because negative outcomes associated with this strategy included sleep deprivation, reduced time with a spouse, and stress related to solo parenting, many respondents felt that the benefits of this strategy were time-limited.

Clearly, individual- or family-level strategies to address the issues of early childhood family care are limited, at best. Solutions at the level of state and federal policy are more appropriate to the scale and importance of the issues. Gornick and Meyers (2001) suggest that government-supported early childhood parenting leave for both parents, high-quality public preschool and child care programs, and incentives to encourage fathers to provide more caregiving at home are essential to addressing work–family stress. Further, as our data suggest, this work-family stress does not end, but rather changes, as children become adolescents. The need for parental support, presence, and supervision is necessary, even as it is different.

JOB CONTINUITY AND WORKPLACE BENEFITS

The effects of changes in family and work are mediated by employment policies and practices. Social science research is replete with recommendations for specific policies designed to alleviate some of the role strain experienced by contemporary workers. These suggestions may be having some effect. A 1995 survey of over 1000 major U.S. companies found a significant increase in the number of employers offering programs that help employees balance work and family life

(Single ton, 2000). Family-friendly policies might include support for dependent care, flexible work schedules, paid family leave, counseling, and information programs. Fredriksen-Goldsen and Scharlach's (2001) family-care model indicates that workers' preference for and use of these programs varies with the types of family needs being experienced. In particular, employers' efforts to make work schedules more flexible may be missing the point, since many workers really need less to do, rather than a shift in work hours or location.

Employer-sponsored benefits represent as much as 40% of the value of a full-time position, but changes in the American economy and the marketplace mean that many workers are no longer guaranteed health insurance and paid vacations, much less family leave, child care assistance, or flexible work schedules (Caputo, 2000; Fredriksen-Goldsen & Scharlach, 2001). Nonetheless, access to benefits remains critical to most workers.

For most families, the most important workplace benefit is access to medical insurance. Family decisions about working may hinge on the availability of health coverage for a worker's family; and among heterosexual couples, husbands' health insurance significantly reduces the number of hours that wives work for pay (Buchmueller & Valletta, 1999). Society continues to perceive men as the primary breadwinners in families, resulting in fewer "women's jobs" with full family benefits. In a study comparing access to benefits for a modal women's profession (nursing) to a modal men's profession (auto mechanic), Berggren (2003) found that men continue to have an advantage in access to most employer benefits, especially major medical health coverage.

The United States is one of only six countries surveyed by the United Nations without mandatory paid maternity leave (Olsen, 1998). Nevertheless, as noted earlier in this chapter, many mothers leave the paid workforce around the time of childbirth, and most return to the same employer after their children are born. In the absence of paid leave, employees may use accrued sick leave and vacation time to approximate a paid family leave, but many parents' access to paid sick leave is jeopardized by changes in employment conditions in recent years. Heymann, Earle, and Egleston (1996) found that more than one fourth of working mothers have no sick leave; rates for poor and non-White mothers were as high as 31%. Lack of access to sick leave means that options for perinatal and other types of family leave are limited for many families.

Recent state maternity leave legislation and the federal Family and Medical Leave Act of 1993 (FMLA) were intended to protect the jobs of mothers who take perinatal leave or workers who need time off to care for ill relatives. The FMLA requires employers to allow at least 12 weeks of unpaid leave to workers caring for a new child or ill dependent. Because legislation limited the act to employers with 50 workers or more, the FMLA covers only 11% of private employers (Fredriksen-Goldsen & Scharlach, 2001). Even for those workers covered by the policy, the unpaid nature of the leave means that women are no more likely to take maternity leave since the law was enacted, and utilization rates for family leave policies remain in the single digits (Fredriksen-Goldsen & Scharlach, 2001). However, data indicate that these policies increase the probability that mothers will eventually return to jobs held before the births of their babies (Baum, 2003; Klerman & Leibowitz, 1999).

In addition to the financial strains associated with unpaid family leave, workers may be reluctant to use leave to which they are entitled for social or environmental reasons. Men are much less likely to take family leave than are women. Men who choose family over work are still suspect in the contemporary workplace. Further, since much family leave is unpaid, and because men typically make substantially higher salaries than their wives, maternal leave will continue to be seen as a more sensible option for families (Dorman, 2001).

Taking family leave may be seen as a sign of weakness, a lack of loyalty to the employer or a willingness to impose an additional burden on co-workers. In a study of financial professionals, for example, Blair-Loy and Wharton (2002) found that employees were unlikely to use employment policies designed to ease work–family role strain. Employees with access to colleagues and supervisors who are perceived as powerful enough to protect the employee from the negative effects of such policies on their careers were most likely to use the benefit.

ADAPTIVE STRATEGIES

As stress associated with work and family increases, options to move away from traditional full-time jobs are likely to be considered by families. Women, in particular, may consider lengthy leaves of absence, part-time employment, moving into lower level jobs and working in fields perceived to be more family friendly (Arai, 2000). Another strategy for addressing work–family conflict is to become self-employed, an option perceived by many workers as offering flexibility and independence. However, Hundley (2000) found that self-employed women's wages declined as family demands increased. The opposite is true for males who are self-employed. (Recall the finding by Kossek and Ozeki (1998) that reduced job performance is likely to result when family life impinges on work responsibilities. Since women are more likely to be working the "second shift," it follows that their self-employment is more likely to be affected by nonremunerative responsibilities.)

Flexible work arrangements are being offered by more employers, and considered by more workers. Ranging from part-time work schedules to alternative work hours or locations for full-time employees, these alternatives are often mentioned as concessions to the work-family dilemma. However, the growth in part-time employment has been mostly involuntary on the part of the workers—and many permanent part-time positions now offer none of the benefits traditionally offered to permanent employees in the past. And working from home, once common for agricultural families and craftsmen, may result in increased role strain for workers who are no longer able to regulate the boundary between work and family life.

Only flexible scheduling is perceived by most workers to be a truly family-friendly workplace policy. Organizations where flexible work schedules are offered are more attractive to applicants with high role conflict, while jobs with opportunities for telecommuting are attractive to workers with low role conflict (Rau & Hyland, 2002). This may also relate to the type and status of jobs that allow for telecommuting.

Attitude and perception are essential to managing the stress associated with balancing work and family roles. Dual-earner couples and families who are successful in this endeavor have several characteristic strategies: They prioritize family life and marital partnership, engage in purposeful and productive work that is well separated from family time, value simple and enjoyable life choices, maintain a firm sense of control over decisions that affect family members, and hold a positive view of the dual-earner family model (Haddock, Ziemba, Zimmerman, & Current, 2001).

THE STORIES

Using the eco map technique described in chapter 2, interviewers were able to elicit data on participants' work situations, concentrating on changes in work during children's adolescence. Relevant text was coded into the "Work" category by informant status (e.g., mother, father, and child), and then topics within the data were identified. Themes emerged from the data and are explicated in Table 6.1 and in the following pages. Analysis revealed that the majority of the data relevant to work were found in mothers' and fathers' interviews. Thus, the themes described in this chapter are derived from adult interviews.

BENEFITS OF WORK

Many respondents reported experiencing enjoyment, fulfillment, or other forms of gratification from their work lives. More fathers than mothers reported enjoying the challenges of the workplace, and described work as fulfilling or rewarding. Men were much more likely to describe their accomplishments on the job, sometimes in great detail. And men were the only interviewees to mention compensation as a major factor in liking their jobs. Several fathers mentioned that their work provided a "comfortable living" for their families. One father said that he loved his job because he is "loaded." Another father described his job as stressful, but said his "family likes the money."

Only one father admitted that work functioned as a social outlet for him. He describes spending extra time at work, because he could depend on his wife to take care of things at home:

> I enjoyed my job. I just tended to. That was an out for me, too. I mean, that was the only really social interaction I had was if I could spend a few hours—extra hours—at work socializing with people there. And get paid for it at the same time.

TABLE 6.1
Category: Parents' Work in the Lives of Families With Adolescents

Topic	Father's themes	Mother's themes
Benefits of work	• Accomplishments and challenges • Compensation • Flexibility to attend to occasional family needs	• Self-esteem • Financial power • Availability for family obligations
Prioritizing family	• Separation of work and family • Response to family crisis–personal development	• Husband's directives • Valuing family • Focus on family welfare

Managing work–family connection	• Working overtime
	  Impact on family connections
	  Efforts to change work schedules
	• Father as provider
	  Specific financial obligations
	  Supportive wives
	• Threats to employment stability
	• Dealing with stress
		• Husband's attitudes
		  Gendered division of labor
		  Denigration of house-wife role
		  Anxiety about loss of resources
		• Increases in self-esteem
		• Returning to world of work
		  Loss of parenting role
		  Disruption in family patterns
		• Balancing work and family
		  Guilt and anger
		  Interpersonal conflict
		  Staggered work schedules

For women, positive feelings about work were usually linked to increasing self esteem or achieving a good fit with family responsibilities. A few mothers discussed the positive factors of work for the sake of fulfillment or financial benefit to the family:

> **Mother:** It's been real helpful financially, and'I think it's been good for me too. I don't feel tied to the house, and I don't have any worth in whether my house looks nice and whatever. So, it's been good to get to know some new people and find out that I'm capable of doing a job and earning money. It's been a change for me because I really did like being home, I liked the freedom of what I could do. I liked to cook. I liked to be home with the kids. And so a lot of these things have changed, where I don't have time to cook. I'm not always there when the kids get home. I oftentimes have a lot of things on my mind from work. So, I'm not always focused on the family. I think it's been good for the kids to see me working and it's been good for my self-esteem to be working and earning some money.

However, nearly all mothers who spoke unambivalently about their work lives were those whose work was limited to sporadic self-employment or part-time work. One self-employed mother described her work:

> I love it! I work only a few days a month, and my salary is triple from when I worked for another company.

Another mother said:

> I've got the best job in the world. It fits with all (our) schedules and with the kids' needs.

And one more:

> I work in the home, but I do a lot of other stuff. Not really work, per se, but I do drapes for people. I paint. I want a job where I have control of my time because, with the hours that my husband works and he's never here and with the activities the kids are in, I need to be aware of that. From the minute they walk in the door from school, I'm basically the one getting everybody where they need to be. So basically, I take these jobs just to keep me from being bored, I make a little extra money. Nothing substantial, but it still gives me a sense of worth—self worth.

In spite of these women's focus on the relationships between home and family, their comments indicate that work for pay had important meanings for their sense of identity, as well as offering valued alternatives to homemaking:

> **Mother:** Well, I think in terms of my personal growth. This has added another dimension to my professionalism.

> **Mother:** I tell you, even though I am not the major income earner here, losing my job hurt because it was ... I was there for almost five years and evolved in such a way, and I loved my work, you know, I didn't get paid a whole lot, but still. Self-pride and all that. Your self esteem. It hurt. For a while, I had ... emotions that I had to deal with.

> **Mother:** My husband is 13 years away from retirement and what am I going to do? I don't shop! I can't see filling 10 years with that. I'm actually, in the long run, going to be a happier person because I feel that I will be doing something other than sitting around and—not that I would have ever sat around—but I just feel that it'll help me as a person. Sooner or later I'm actually going to look forward to getting up and going [to work]. I also think that my working is going to be a real positive thing because, when I don't have my life wrapped up in my kids, I will have something other than just what he's doing or where he is.

> **Mother:** I like it. I think it's challenging and I just find it positive. A lot of time I get bored around the house, I guess.

> **Mother:** So within this past year there's been a change. There's been an increase in pay, increase in responsibility that goes along with it. But it hasn't been a strain; it's been

positive coming home, because I feel so good about my job. I feel good about the people I work with. So I'm upbeat, I think I tend to feel less strain when I come home so that affects all of us, of course. And even if I have a stressful day, it's not like a bad stress.

Work conditions that offer flexibility for men to attend to family needs was acknowledged as a real reason to like the job. When a father's workplace allows him to take children to appointments or to attend an event at school, this is considered a significant advantage. For example, this mother describes her ex-husband's workplace:

He's been there enough time, long enough at this one place that if he has something to do with the kids, he makes arrangements with his boss to have that time to be with the kids and then when he's not, he makes up those hours elsewhere.

A father described his new job this way:

I believe 90% of the time there's less stress [in the new job] because I control more or less what I do and what I don't do. Sometimes when things don't go right, go my way, I bring that home just as I did on my other job, but because I have more control over what could happen and what doesn't happen, and I have more freedom to vary my schedule and be with the kids more, and help them or be with them—actually socialize with them more—I think it helps a great deal.

In contrast, women's availability for family obligations was seen as a necessary condition of employment, rather than a reason to like or dislike the job. These issues are discussed in detail later in the chapter.

MAKING FAMILY NUMBER ONE

Just as many participants described their jobs in positive terms, most emphasized the importance of their family lives. In fact, when discussing work, many respondents described their careers as secondary to their family lives and interpersonal relationships. Some men described particular efforts they made to "keep work at work" or to "go in early so I can be home with the family at dinnertime." One father put it concisely: "It's nine to five and forget about it."

Some men mentioned a change in focus from work to family as a result of illness or other family circumstances that changed their views of the family. A man whose wife had cancer described how he "tries to balance work and home. There's a shift away from work being number one." Another father told a story of his wife's disability:

I used to be strongly focused. Work was something I had to do, and I had to do it well, and it took up a lot of my strength and focus. But now, I'm detaching myself. I have a job that's nice and, while I'm there, I give it what I have. However, there's more important things—home and people in the home.

A few fathers mentioned that work had helped them grow, either through adversity or age-related maturity, with the result that family emerged as top priority. One father talked about growing older and learning to do more for himself, including taking time to really enjoy his children:

> I'm not as hard-driven. Everyone has tensions at work. But I always wanted to own a company, or be a president of a company, and now I don't care if I ever do. In fact, I don't want to. I just want to get away from it. I want to enjoy things a little more. And, you know, I've gotta go with the philosophy that headstones never say, "I didn't put as many hours into work as I thought I should." The goals have changed. I have no goals other than to keep earning enough money so we can live a certain lifestyle. If I do what I'm doing the rest of my life, fine. And if I don't—if I have to do something else, it's not a big deal. The career has gotten to the point where it's not that important what I do. It's important that I can give these kids and this family what they need. But I don't have aspirations like I used to and that doesn't bother me at all. In fact, I wish it would have come to that sooner.

Nearly all women respondents focused on the prioritization of family over work in their interviews. This focus on family as a first priority had a different tone for women than for men. Women made much greater concessions in their careers in order to spend time at home (e.g., left careers to raise small children, took part-time jobs in order to be home after school). In addition, women were much more likely to be directed to home life by their husbands than vice versa. For example, one man defended his objection to his wife's new job, "My wife doesn't have to work unless she wants to. But I don't want her employment to have negative impact on the family."

In any case, many women clearly expressed the value of family over work in their descriptions of their own choices. For example:

> **Mother:** I really believe that my not working full-time has helped a lot. I think you miss a lot now; as long as you have enough money to meet your bills and be semi-secure, I really think its important to be home when the kids are home. It's cool if you can find a job the same hours while they're away at school, that's terrific. But there aren't many jobs like that, where you can get off at 2:30. And I think being home when they come home and they're disgusted about a test grade or happy about something that happened, I think it's important to be here.

> **Mother:** I try and stress to [the kids] that, some people, their lives are their work. This family is our life. This is what's important to us. So, if we lost our jobs tomorrow, we'd probably find other ones and we'd be okay.

In addition to these general comments, some mothers specified that they chose family over work as a way to focus on the welfare of their children or their roles as parents. The idea is: "If you have kids you should take care of them."

> **Stay-at-home mother:** I figure, you know, you bring the children into the world and you put down the best ground work you can, and then you cannot say, "I wish I had done that [staying with the kids]," because I did the best of my ability.

Mother with part-time home-based employment: I had kids because I wanted them and I want to raise them. I tell you, there's some negative things going on because I think those parents work and leave these kids alone all the time. Especially the teenagers. It just makes me sick. All these people, they want kids, they want everything, but they don't want to take time to raise their kids.

MANAGING THE WORK–FAMILY CONNECTION

Interviewers asked family members to describe major changes in their families in the five years preceding the interviews. Respondents described a variety of life events, but most mentioned a change in work patterns as one of the family's important changes. Both mothers and fathers mentioned these changes as part of the family's transition from the "young children" stage into "life with adolescents."

Parents' comments indicate that these families perceived changes in the work–family interaction as closely related to their everyday experiences of family life. Changes in work life were mentioned as they related to work schedules, power and responsibilities on the job, and work conditions, as well as a variety of negative experiences with work. In addition, fathers' comments about their wives' work suggested that this period was critical to the couples' definition of women's role in the work life of the family.

FATHERS' WORK LIVES

Fathers discussed many changes in their job responsibilities during the years around their children's adolescence, particularly where transitions meant greater commitments of time or increased responsibilities for the families' workers. Some men mentioned increased or decreased time spent commuting to work as important changes in family life. Other notable changes included achieving promotions or seniority, gaining perquisites such as increased flexibility or benefits, and changes in job duties. For example, one father mentioned that his promotion was especially welcome because he no longer had the duty of supervising hourly employees, a responsibility he had found stressful and time-consuming. Another man mentioned that he had switched from a traditional job to working at home in a self-employment situation. While this arrangement was described as positive, he reported working more hours than before the change and described experiencing additional stress related to starting a business.

Fathers Working Overtime

Most fathers describe work as stressful because of the time requirements of their jobs. Both men and women mentioned the fathers' work schedules as a major stressor in family life, although few of the women's jobs were characterized in this way. Many of the stories about fathers' work schedules suggest that family routines are frequently carried out without fathers present. One woman described her husband as "gone 15 days out of the month." A father described traveling for work "three or four days a week." Another father, who works a second job after his shift at the plant, talked about spending very little time with his children, although he gets to see his wife during the day. A woman reported that her husband is "never home in the evening." She was "lonesome" and so was considering a part-time second job herself to deal with the isolation. Another wife describes her husband as "gone before we get up in the morning and home after we go to bed." This woman described how her husband's work schedule, which included a lot of evening overtime, increased her stress level:

> It probably affects me more than it affects the kids, because I have to do everything. Like last night, we had a swim meet and baseball game. So I'm trying to cover all the bases. So that makes it harder on me.

Respondents of both sexes described men's work weeks of 50 to 70 hours as common. One man talked of routinely working 110 hours per week in the past, so 55-hour work weeks feel "normal" to him now. Most of the parents that were interviewed acknowledged that fathers' work schedules interfered with the connections between fathers and children, and indirectly, with overall family relationships. Many respondents made clear that the long hours at work were a negative factor in their lives:

> **Mother:** On a normal basis, the man sees his children probably eight hours a week, maybe ten. In that ten hours, or whatever it might be, we have a pretty stressful house because dad doesn't always agree in the way I run the household.

> **Father with two jobs:** When I'm at my job, I'm gone most of the time before the girls get up, and then I come home for supper and then I go on duty at six o'clock in the evening, and I'm on duty until six a.m. And so there are times that I will be gone. Other times it's quiet and I'm available. So, that's a big change because not only don't I have any free time. It also affects the family in the fact that I'm not available to do a lot of things.

> **Mother:** When we were first married, he was working full-time, going to school full-time, and taking as many as 17 credits and he came within a half point of graduating with honors. So he was gone all the time, and after he graduated, I thought, "This will be great! I'll have a husband." Well, that's a myth. That's when the overtime started.

> **Father:** If there's any stress, it's only due to our schedule. Between our work schedules and the three kids and their schedules, that's the only stress we have, is trying to get three kids to three places with two cars at the same time. My wife is a school teacher, so she works like a 35-hour week, but she probably does another 15 hours at home. I'm probably away from the house for about 70 hours. Depending on the week—some weeks I'm here at 4:30, other weeks, I'm not home until midnight every night. We can be like ships

passing in the night. It's probably shown the kids that working won't kill you. At least not yet. It's taken time away from the kids to some degree. Even though we devoted a lot of time to their activities, we don't have a lot of casual time.

Father: From my aspect, work has not been going well. I'm not enjoying it. And so, I can tell that it's really had an effect on me and my relationship at home here. The thing that has affected me is the hours I'm putting into the office. Because of the current structure of our organization, we don't have any resources, so I'm just literally putting in 12-hour days. We try to do as much as we can, but you can't replace the hours when you're not home for dinner around the table. You know, those times when family gets together and when that bonding takes place. And one-on-one. So I try to do as much one-on-one as I can and also family outings on weekends and stuff, but its still not the same as being together on a daily routine basis.

Father: We're in a better financial position than probably we've ever been in our entire lives. And I think the kids'll benefit from that, whether you want to equate it to vacations or the ability to pay for college down the road. Maybe I'm not there for some sort of family activity. Maybe consciously you might worry that, somewhere down the road, they're going to throw it in your face and say, "Well, you made a choice to work hard, as opposed to spend time with us."

Father: The end of the week, I'm just dead. My family says, "Let's go do something," and I'm like, "Okay." And I'm like falling asleep in the movie or something like that. There have been times when my wife has said, "Why don't you find a new job?"

Some respondents talked about attempts to change their work schedules:

Father: I was in a situation where I was working in our administrative office. And because I was doing well, I kept getting transferred from one problem area to another. And basically got sick from cleaning up everybody else's messes and all the politics that went along with it. And that was putting a strain on the family, and I was working, like 12 or 13 hours a day with no extra pay, and that sort of thing. And so I finally got sick of that affecting my health and the family as a whole and I transferred out of that situation to a job where I knew I'd be more comfortable. It's a lot different. I'm in a job now where basically I set my own hours and my own appointments. So I can just see things have improved both at work and at home because of that. I'm much more easygoing with the kids again.

Mother: We started a business out of the home. So he was home everyday, which was kind of nice, actually. I mean we had less money coming in, but I think he got to know the kids a little better.

There were comments indicating an understanding that some work schedules are not conducive to healthy families. For example, a father admitted that his working out of state for a few months resulted in his young daughter developing depression and school problems "because she missed me." Other interviews suggested that fathers' chronic absence from the home caused rifts in family connections:

Wife: I think six years ago, I probably wasn't as tolerant of his job. You know, the kids were little and when your kids are little, they take more of your time and energy just because they're little and you're taking care of them. And I started to really resent how much time he spent at work. I've just come to accept it. I'm not on his case. … It's kind of like I'm used to it now. It's just like I don't live my life for the minute you walk in the door. You know, he kind of gets upset when he comes home and we're all gone. You know, it's like "I finally got home and no one's here." Well, daddy, if we sat and waited for you to come home all day, we'd be sitting here every day.

Father as Provider

Gendered roles for families and work are alive and well. Comments about men's work were strongly suggestive of family perceptions of men as the primary financial providers for these families. Men's comments on this theme tended to center around specific financial obligations that validate their roles as providers—for example, the tuition bill for a child's private school education. A few men articulated more generally that they want to be a "strong, positive, stable, financial foundation" for their families. Others expressed anxiety about earning enough to support their families' needs and desires. As one father put it, he felt "pressure because I am the one making the money and it's spent so quickly!"

Women's comments strongly reinforced this view of husbands as providers. Most of their descriptions of men's efforts to provide financially were both sympathetic and supportive:

> **Mother:** It's a lot of responsibility to have financial responsibility for your own family. Owning your own business and being the type of person that he is, I think he feels very strongly the responsibility for the people that work for him, for their financial success.

> **Mother:** I think that maybe it's because he is the dad and feels responsible for the working, bringing home the money, and he probably thinks I look at things kind of high in the sky and he's down to earth.

> **Mother:** We couldn't do these [kids' activities] if he didn't work so much. I mean, I don't think the man dies to work on Saturday and Sunday. He would rather not. But (he works) for his kids to have the things that they have, and I haven't worked since I've had [the youngest child]. Basically he does what he thinks he has to do. And he's giving up a lot.

> **Mother:** My husband goes through some periods where he wishes he could do something else. That's like, how awful where you're in a position where other people are depending on you, and you're kind of strapped and stuck in a situation taking on so many hours of your life to be spending at something you don't want.

Threats to Job Stability

Fathers' experience of unemployment and threatened lay-offs were mentioned by several male respondents. Some men mentioned extended sick leave for major illness, surgery, or injury as an important event in their work lives. A father who had been laid off for more than five months due to work slow-downs in his industry described the time as "traumatic." Threats to employment were perceived as important events by other family members, as well. A woman described her unemployed husband's depression with some sympathy and the comment that his reaction was "normal. I mean, a job is what you are." Another father of four described his family's reaction to his period of unemployment:

> It was just stressful and there were lots of times when there was a big change in the kids, where there was a recognition an awful lot of times, when dad was going berserk. They were mature beyond their years in recognizing that, "Well, he's nuts because he's out of work."

A few descriptions of job instability were surprisingly positive. One father described being laid off his job three times. His wife also lost her job because her employer moved the company out of state during this time. Despite these events, he described the outcome as positive, since circumstances led him to seek work with a different employer, where he got a "better job with better benefits, retirement, travel… ."

Demotions were particularly difficult transitions for several men. A father described his career changes as moving from being a "marketing authority to just a salesman" as a major "ego change as well as financial strain." Another man demoted from a supervisory position in his department said he was "disappointed" by his new role.

Another theme that was related to job stability was concern about the economy, a reasonable apprehension given that many of these families are working in a declining auto industry. One respondent, who described how hard he had worked to finish his college education, commented that he now worries about the stability of his employment and viability of his employer's company. He noted that he "spends money more carefully" now, with an eye for a time when he may have "less money and less vacation time." Another father who was worried about his employer going out of business was thinking about returning to school to prepare for a career change. And still another father talked about giving up his business to take a job in a local company, a move that he once saw as a loss. He has since come to see that the career change (and a period of unemployment) allowed him to spend more time with his daughter:

> It probably brought us closer. Yeah. And I say that because, when I was at my own business, I would be gone a lot more. I would drink a lot more. I'd be on business trips. I'd be marketing and hiring people and wheeling and dealing. It kind of put my family secondary.

Dealing With Fathers' Work Stress

Fathers articulated a great deal of stress in their interviews. Long hours, time away from the locus of family life, changes in the work environment, economic insecurity, and other factors made their work lives a source of much of this stress. A few men also mentioned specifically that coming home from work to a household where they may be expected to help with cooking, cleaning, or child care was an additional source of strain in their lives. Interestingly, much of the in-depth descriptive narrative about dealing with the work-related stress came from wives talking about how their husbands' reactions are played out in interpersonal relationships in the family:

> **Wife:** He would take it out on us, you know, just stress that he had at work. He'd bring it home with him, or else he would just keep it all inside and not say anything, but you know something was wrong.

> **Wife:** My husband's job is very stressful for him and consequently I think it becomes stressful for me because I'm dealing with the stress when it comes home.

> **Wife:** You know, I've done everything I can. There just aren't enough hours. But when my husband had a lot of stresses at work, everybody's kind of picked up and we've all kind of (been) quiet at certain hours. I certainly get dumped on a lot. I mean, it happens—rearranging carpools, canceling lessons, so I can pick up where he can't be.

MOTHER'S WORK LIVES

Women talked about their work lives by focusing on the relationships between the two spheres of work and family. Nearly all these comments included overt connections to the stress of balancing these aspects of their lives—and often the mothers' narratives were clearly anguished.

Changes in the family circumstances of these women were the most frequent precipitators of changes in their work lives. Many women mentioned that children who moved into adolescence didn't need them as much. Other women described separation or divorce as precipitators. For example, one mother talked about returning to work for the first time in 15 years following her divorce.

Many mothers mentioned husbands' job changes or lay-offs as factors in their returning to work. Women who returned to work because of financial need in the family were most likely to express ambivalence about the move. Ambivalence seemed to be related to feelings of guilt about not working, on one hand, with feelings of guilt about leaving home and family on the other. In addition, some women expressed shame about choosing or preferring family over career. For example, a mother whose husband's job situation had become unstable described her reluctance about returning to school to prepare for re-entry into the job market: "I love to stay home—as horrible as that might sound to some people. I'm very happy with my life." Another woman told of working two jobs because her husband was laid off: "The house isn't getting cleaned. I got to get my act together on that!"

Fathers' Attitudes Toward Mothers' Work

Men had a lot to say about their wives' work lives. A common theme expressed by male respondents in this study was that women's unique role in the family was in running the home, including providing a comfortable and attractive environment, organizing family activities, and making sure that children's lives were enriched by activities and relationships that helped in development. Some explained their preference for wives to remain in the home as a "natural" division of labor. For example, this husband explains why he dislikes his wife's return to work:

> She has primary responsibility for the children. I think she's vastly superior at that than I am. I think she's smarter than I am, but, on the other hand, I'm much better equipped to deal with the world from both a business standpoint and a social standpoint even, than she is.

Other male participants indicated more negative attitudes toward their wives' work, in general. One husband described his wife's transition into the nursing profession as making her "kind of cocky." Another woman described her husband's reaction to her promotion at work, which meant more responsibility as well as increased pay:

> The kids seemed a little bit proud about it. But then my husband says, "You'll just want to be at work everyday." But that's not so. I'm going on vacation for two weeks soon.

Many husbands expressed strong feelings about their wives' roles as homemakers and mothers, while minimizing the complexity or importance of the tasks performed by stay-at-home parents. Another woman's story demonstrates the paradoxical attitudes toward home-based work:

> My husband was laid off. I told him once it was the best thing that ever happened to him. Because he used to come home from work and say, "What did you do all day?" And this was when I was still working part-time or whatever. And the kids were little in diapers. "How come you didn't wash the walls while you were cleaning today?" He just didn't have a concept of what it was like staying home with kids all day. I remember one day I came home and the kids were still in pajamas. Nothing had gotten done and I said, "Oh, my God, what happened here today?" And he goes, "You don't know what it's like watching kids all day."

Some husbands' comments were overtly unsupportive or angry about wives' work. For example, one man explained that his wife sometimes has to work late, so he tells her to quit her job:

> When the boss is supposed to be there and she's supposed to be off early, he calls in sick or doesn't show up. So she has to stay later. I get angry at them, and I just tell her, "I work two jobs, so quit. Tell them that this happens so often that you're not going to put up with it anymore." But she won't quit!

A few men commented that their wives' work contributed to divorce. One recently divorced man explained that his wife "started working, making pretty good money. So that was a contributing factor in our divorce. She was more independent."

Even when they reported little conflict in the relationship, men's reactions to their wives' work lives were often framed by comments about the impact of the woman's job schedule on her ability to complete domestic chores. For example, one man reported that his wife's work providing private music lessons in the home resulted in "less time for the family." Specifically, he complained that, with her students in the house, "I can't even sit down and have dinner." Another man, whose wife has a new, demanding employer, reports being relieved that his wife's pay "removes some of the financial stress," but complains that she uses the job as an excuse to cut back on her household responsibilities:

> Well, she thinks now that just because she's got a job, I have to start doing everything. Well, baloney, I've had a job all my life and I had to work. Welcome to society. You've still got to go shopping. You've still got to do the laundry. I mean, you've still got to do things. So, hey, let's just get with the program. Kick it up a step, instead of just passing the buck to everyone.

Another father commented on his children's reactions to their mother's job. His perspective seems to support the view of mother's return to work as challenging family expectations about "women's work" in the home:

> They're very proud of her. But I think they would like to have her at home when they need her help. They need her home when they are ill and those kinds of things. It has caused a change in relationships because, now that she is a full-time employee, she can't do as much or can't be depended upon to do as much in terms of clean-up. "Well, mom, are you going to be home? Could you do this for me today?" or "Could you pick that up for me today?" "Could you run this errand for me?" And I haven't been able to depend on her to do that either.

This man described the family's reaction to his wife's career change:

> She spends more time away from the house. So, consequently, I've been doing more of the domestic stuff than I was doing before. And for a while there, our relationship was strained. And it's been coming back around, so it isn't quite so strained. A lot of the time, our son feels he's been neglected. I think he feels that his mother deserted us or was neglectful of us.

Some women attributed the husband's ambivalence about the wife's return to work as a perceived loss of the wife as a resource at home. This seems to fit with the narratives in which some men admitted that they pushed their wives to work only when the family was experiencing periods of financial need or insecurity. For these husbands, the trade-off for increased income was the perceived negative impact on the smooth functioning of the household. This man, whose wife recently started back to work as a classroom aide, described his conflict:

> One of the things I always said was that she didn't have to work unless she wanted to work. Um, that changed right now with a son at [a private college]. It's nice having a little extra income coming in. I never particularly wanted her employment to have a major, negative impact on the household. Just because she worked, we had to look for ways the house still needs to get clean. She basically does that. She does the laundry and stuff and I don't care if she does it or somebody else does it, now. I'm changing the way I look at this, too. It's best that we jointly get this done, but I prefer actually that she buy the services so that it just happens.

This father, whose wife is a teacher, described how her job provides "extra income" that takes pressure off of him financially, but:

> Sometimes I wish that she could stay home so she could do more for the kids. You know, like be the room mother or something like that. She will still do things—special activities for them—but she won't be that room mother that hangs around the school.

A final theme expressed by several male respondents was the idea that paid employment was beneficial to a woman, as it increased her sense of worth. This husband commented that, while he would prefer that his wife not work, he could see a benefit to her personally:

> I see a rise in her self-esteem. She feels that she's a contributor and that she's intelligent. And that she's respected in her office. I think she feels more important. There was a time when she was not working, she'd get in a group of women, and they'd kind of look at her and say, "You're not working?" And it would make her feel small, whereas it used to be that she felt good because she was raising the kids. It got to the point where she had to find some kind of in-between. Now, you almost have to (work), or you can't keep up with the Joneses. I'd like it if she didn't have to work at all. Not being a male chauvinist or anything. I'd like to see her relax, but if it's a trade-off for her self-esteem, she should work and be involved.

Another husband commented on his wife's recent promotion:

> I have mixed emotions about it. I had the traditional role of being sole supporter. I wanted to create enough income to do it all on my own so that she'd have the freedom to be able to just stay home and those kinds of things. As the children become older, less dependent, now outside the home, she would need something much more fulfilling for herself. Overall, I would say that I feel very positive about her working outside the home. It's a positive impact in terms of salary. It's enabled me to make up some of the difference in terms of salary because of the change in my position. It is something that she loves to do. I've seen her develop and grow as an individual as a result of it. Her sense of confidence has grown immeasurably over the last year because of it. She went out, she developed her resume, and applied, interviewed, got the job. But at the same time, there's that wounded pride because dad couldn't do it all.

Fathers also recognized that their wives' work had an impact on the perceptions of the children. For example, one father commented that he felt his wife's work meant that their children would see their mother as more than "just a dumb housewife."

Mothers Returning to the World of Work

A major issue for women we interviewed was the re-emergence of paid employment as a focus of activity when children grew into adolescence. Mothers who had chosen to leave the workforce at the birth of a child began to consider returning to work. Some of these transitions were relatively smooth, but many were marked by resistance inside the family, as well as in other relationships. Many mothers verbalized the process of thinking through the transition from mother to worker and described some of the factors in making choices for work. A mother who is building a business in her home:

> I always think, "What will I do?" In a few years, my kids will be pretty grown up and maybe I can go back to work. I've gotten to the point where I'm kind of spoiled. If I have a job, it's going to be on my terms. If I don't want to do it, I can say no. And I like it, sure, because I have control.

Another mother said:

> I think I'm going through a battle with myself over what I'll do next, you know. It feels like I should work part-time or I should go back to school. So, if I'm having any changes, it's actually within myself.

In addition, returning to work meant increased financial and material resources for these families. For example, one mother excitedly described her new job by mentioning that she is a member of the union for the first time, a condition that means "a decent salary, even benefits."

A major consideration for women moving into the world of work was concern about balancing work and family responsibilities. Many women respondents expressed their understanding that a focus on homemaking in the past had created a sense of dependency in the family. This mother described her concern about doing less for her children when she returns to work: "Because it's so nice to have mommy do all the laundry. And it's so nice to have mommy do all the cooking and just run to the store." Another mother who described starting a part-time job was quick to point out that the work was restricted to school-day mornings "so it doesn't interfere with school."

Mothers who had worked part-time when their children were small discussed increasing work hours or responsibilities as their children's needs for supervision and physical care decreased. For these women, the move from part-time to full-time work seemed less riddled with ambivalence, yet many offered acknowledgement that the change might create disruption in their family lives. One mother currently working part-time discussed taking a full-time job:

> I still haven't decided whether I want to work full-time or not. You know, [my part-time job] hasn't made much of an impression that I can tell. If I was working full-time, it would be completely different.

Another mother: I've started working full-time for the first time in 18 years. We're in turmoil. We're just in a real big state of flux right now. I haven't gotten used to working full-time to the point of getting schedules down pat. Until this year, I never wanted to work full-time. Actually, before my mom died, I started considering it because my oldest son is gone. My youngest gets his license in December and, you know, he needs me even less.

And another mother: It's a matter of trying to fit paid work in and take care of the household and do what I need to do, so it does get very stressful in trying to balance, trying to juggle all of these things to do, trying to find the time and being tired from what has to be done here in the house and making sure the kids are taken care of.

Balancing Work and Family

As can be seen by the preceding comments, the dilemma for many of the mothers in our study was in finding a way to maintain balance between the demands of the family and the demands of a job. Many women respondents indicated that their primary concern about returning to work was the impact of their jobs on the family's routine, comfort, and convenience.

Many women had strong emotional reactions to questions about their work lives. Often, these narratives were accompanied by expressions of guilt, anger, shame, or anxiety. Guilt was the most common theme. For example, one mother who works cleaning houses while her children are in school expressed guilt when her older daughter has to watch her younger child on the rare occasion when her job keeps her past 2:00 in the afternoon.

Mother: I had to have babysitters and that kind of thing. I wish I didn't have to work so I could be home with the kids. I didn't like leaving them with babysitters, but I had good babysitters throughout the years.

The concern that women's careers implied child neglect was an important theme in the stories of both men and women respondents. Some mothers acknowledged that these negative feelings prevented them from working outside the home before their children's adolescence. For example, one mother "took a job for 2 days, but knew it wouldn't work out. I couldn't be home for the kids." She quit because she felt so guilty.

A few parents reported children who had significant difficulty adjusting, such as this mother:

The first year that I was working was real difficult for our youngest, It seemed like she just couldn't adjust real well, and we had a lot of school problems, behavior problems, social problems, all kinds of things. The next year seemed to iron things out.

But most of the families' responses to mothers' working were more low-key adjustments to having mother around less, such as learning to get themselves ready for school in the mornings, making themselves snacks in the afternoons, or taking on additional chores.

Many women stated that, as their children grew older, the anxiety and guilt for leaving the children with other adults decreased, but did not disappear. For example, this mother who chose to work nights when her children were small so that she would not have to use babysitters, commented on her current work arrangement:

> I don't like it when my job takes me away a whole day, like say, 10 to 4 or whatever. I'm afraid something might happen where they may need an adult there and there isn't one at the time. That's what worries me the most. It's more positive, though, because I'm home at night, which I wasn't for a long time.

Another mother, whose husband is on-call for work in the evenings, noted that she wants to attend church functions in the evenings. She acknowledged that she felt "bad" about leaving her teens home alone sometimes, but chooses to attend the activities anyway.

Anger was another common theme, particularly as it related to a lack of assistance with household chores. This mother describes her workday routine:

> When I come home, I'm exhausted. You still have to keep the house running and make sure whatever activities are going on, to fulfill all the other obligations.

This woman works four days a week:

> Gee, if I came home and the laundry was done. Wouldn't that be wonderful? So I said, "If I ever get a full-time job, you better believe things are going to change around here." We haven't really discussed that. I just started subbing and am hoping to get full-time. But whatever discussion is going to have to take place, is going to have to be this way. You see, he grew up in a family with one brother and four sisters. So the girls had the women's work, and the boys had the painting and yard work and the driveway, the snow clearing. That was it. My daughter will sometimes say, "Dad, why don't you ever clear the table?" And it frustrates me sometimes when I have to go to a meeting, and I don't have time to wash the pans and stuff. And I come home and they're dirty. ... Now he can manage to put things in the dishwasher, but it's going to take some training for him, as well as for the girls, on how to do things.

Many women interviewees were quick to justify their work with an explanation that it doesn't keep them from their parenting responsibilities. For example, this woman defended her part-time job:

> The work I do is only a couple hours a day at school, so it's not really affected the family. To the point where they don't even know I'm gone because they're usually gone.

Defensiveness and other forms of anxiety about interrole competition are compounded by the reality that, for these women, work outside the home is disruptive to getting chores accomplished. And it causes friction with spouses and children:

Mother: Everyone's used to me being here. Everybody comes to me for everything. So, it's going to be a real adjustment this fall.

Mother: I used to do child care in the home and that kept me quite busy during the school year. And by the time I got rid of the kids (at the end of the day), I was too tired to do a whole lot of anything.

Mother: I had a major change in my job and I had more hours that I'm away from home now and that's put a lot more stress on the family. They had to figure out that there were certain things they had to do on a daily basis. I suddenly was not doing the majority of the cooking. I was not the person handling the laundry any more. I'm not the person that really takes care of getting most of the stuff done in the house. And, you know, I notice stresses in the relationships I was having with my husband and the children because of that. It was harder. My husband absolutely resented having to do all of that.

Mother: My work has had some real good points in that it's helped them become more independent, and I've learned to take some of the guilt off of myself for not always living up to everybody else's expectations.

A few families reported that they attempted to minimize the impact of both parent's working by staggering their schedules so that one parent could be available for the children at all times. Although most of these stories reflected the couples' efforts to cover parenting responsibilities earlier in their marriages, a few couples were still working opposite shifts. These stories were marked by comments about feelings of isolation and separation between spouses. For example, this mother worked the night shift and spent afternoons with her children. Her husband arrived home from work about the time that she was going to bed. The schedule made her peripheral in the family: "It's kind of made me like a nonparent. Kind of like a ghost parent. I'm kind of like a part-time parent for now."

As a result of women returning to work, family members reported having to adjust their own routines and workloads to compensate for mothers' decreased focus on housework and family maintenance. Mothers who started working full-time during this period admitted that they were not as involved with their children's schools, and that the family meals were less elaborate. Fathers complained that they had to come home from work and make dinner or do laundry. Generally, respondents' comments seemed to indicate that these families continued to conceptualize housework as "women's work." There were some instances, however, when members of the family engaged in the tasks to assist the woman when her schedule prevented her attention to the chores. For example, this father reported that his wife's part-time job at a day care center was acceptable for the family:

She comes home in time for supper, and it doesn't really create any kind of hardship. I think she feels it's important for her to get extra income of her own. And she's able to enjoy a relationship with children whom she loves, and obviously it's part of her life.

We've got it worked out so smoothly. The kids are all big enough now. This would be a much worse condition if the children were younger, but it's not a problem with them.

THE NEXT GENERATION OF WORKERS

Many of the interviews revealed parent concerns about the emerging work lives of their adolescent children. Parents expressed concern that children would not make good choices about careers, would not take career preparation seriously enough, or would have too few opportunities for financial success. Other parents worried that their children were already overwhelmed by the competing demands of work, school, and relationships.

One theme that emerged from the interviews was the focus on parents as models for work behavior. Parents described themselves and their spouses as both positive and negative models for their teen children. For example, one mother who described herself as "happy and successful" expressed her concern that she never really had to think about her career, and worried about her children learning to be planful: "Things just fell into place for me. It's kind of scary when I think about my kids." A father hoped his son would not follow in his "workaholic footsteps."

Some of the narrative about modeling related to the career interests of children. Several families mentioned that children were interested in college study of fields in which their parents worked, including engineering, health services, law enforcement, and business. A few parents mentioned that opportunities for children to see their parents working was valuable in that it offered children the chance to determine if they would like to "do that job." One mother commented that her son's interest in the military was understandable, since her son "kind of picks up what his father likes and wants to emulate him."

Parental Influence on Children's Work

A number of the children in the respondent families were working at part-time jobs. Most jobs mentioned were typical for suburban teens, including bagging groceries, babysitting, and working in fast-food restaurants. Most parents provided support for their children's work with encouragement, advice, and transportation. For most of the children, the motivation for working seemed to be the desire for spending money, although parents also expressed the sentiment that "working is good for you" or that working "keeps kids from floating around." One mother stated:

> I think with Tim working it's made a difference, because his dad shows a little more respect for him, or something, where before he was always saying "Get a job!"

Some parents discouraged their teens from working because of the belief that school was their first priority, and others advised youth to cut back on hours in an effort to help balance work with other responsibilities. One youth who wanted to get a job at a local retail store was actively discouraged by his mother; she felt "he will be working soon enough." Another mother described her son "going from school to golf to work to hockey. And finally I just said that I really think you should give up the job. And he did. He says, 'I can't do it all.'"

Expectations for the Future

While parents often expressed ambivalence about their own work lives, their dreams for their children's careers were touchingly optimistic and clear. They wanted their children to be happy in their work and financially secure. As one mother put it:

> I really didn't care what they achieved in life as far as their career. It wasn't important to me that they become doctors, lawyers, that kind of thing. As long as they were happy, content people and could take care of themselves. And any family, if they choose to have their own family—that they're able to take care of them in a financial sense.

A father with some regrets about his own career choices said:

> I don't want them to do what I do. They may not make as much money, but I want them to do something they enjoy. I don't care if they are violinists the rest of their lives and they don't make any money. I'll support them. I just want them to get up in the morning and go where they're going and enjoy it and get some satisfaction out of it, which I don't.

An interesting side note is that fathers were especially likely to note that their visions of the future for their daughters included both the recognition that a daughter might have career plans delayed by child bearing as well as an acknowledgment that "The world's changed, especially having three girls. They have to recognize that a woman's place is not just in the kitchen, but it has to be in the workforce."

SUMMARY AND IMPLICATIONS FOR PRACTICE AND POLICY

Despite decades of change in individual and social patterns of behavior related to work, the intersections of family, gender, and work continue to be influenced by traditional (i.e., gendered) expectations of men and women. In addition, as these interviews illustrate, the work–family dynamic is increasingly complex. Personal variables, such as education, job opportunities, number and timing of children, and family support influence how families manage members' employment, as do structural variables such as employment practices and family-friendly workplace policies (Mercier & Harold, 2001). In addition, as our respondents' narratives indicate, family development and changing interpersonal relationships contribute to the unique construction of the work–family relationship for each family.

The Work–Family Dimension at the Micro Systems Level

Social workers and other helping professionals have an important role to play in addressing the divergence between work and family. Clinicians may provide assessment in a counseling setting or health care facility, provide short-term intervention or referral from an employee assistance program, or present educational or preventative materials to families. In each of these settings, the practitioner has an opportunity to intervene to minimize the potential impact of the many stressors described by our informants in this study.

Some of the most striking narratives from our interviews were descriptions of guilt, anger, and other emotions experienced by family members as they dealt with changing roles and expectations related to work. As Gilbert et al. (1981) suggested, the women in our study who were confronted with competing demands from work and family experienced profound guilt. They also used the strategy of role expansion to deal with these two important aspects of their lives, effectively increasing their work loads at a time when they were already feeling overwhelmed. Work–family demands contribute to a significant amount of most couples' marital conflict (Rogers & Amato, 1997). Our participants' reports of anger, resentment, and anxiety regarding work changes support this observation.

Thus, an important task for clinicians in working with families is the assessment of current and past roles and expectations related to work. When changes in the work–family connection occur, it may be especially important to assess members' feelings about the transition, with an eye to offering opportunities to clarify emotions, provide support, and bolster problem-solving strategies. In families where the expression of emotion is difficult, or when family roles block effective communication of feelings, the clinician may be needed to mediate the communication. When historical and current factors related to work and the family are well understood, the clinician may want to engage in goal-setting with the family as well.

Since interrole conflict is correlated with decreases in satisfaction and role performance (Kossek & Ozeki, 1998), attention must be paid to the level and types of demands being experienced by family members. Such work–family issues are often embedded in cultural norms and internalized as ideals for gender or class. Because of the covert nature of these processes, many families may experience interrole conflict as a vague discomfort or generalized uneasiness. Thus, many couples could benefit from increased awareness of the source of the problem, as well as education about the range of reactions to the conflict itself. The clinician's role is to collect sufficient data to place interrole conflict in the context of the family development cycle, the couple's values, children's needs, and individual desires so that the family may make informed choices about their response.

Most of the women in our study were actively moving from a focus on parenting to an increased focus on the world of work. This movement represents a significant change in identity, with resultant transformations in status and interpersonal relationships (Barley, 1989). Social workers and other practitioners should address these developmental changes on the individual and interpersonal levels in order to facilitate a smoother transition for each member of the family. Individual and family counseling, psychoeducation, and even prevention strategies may be used to accomplish this goal. Working from an eco systemic perspective and being cognizant of social role and family life span development theories, as discussed in chapter 1, will help both the clinician and the family understand the issues with which they are dealing and place them in context.

The amount of time that men in our study spent at work, coupled with their expressed self-perceptions as "providers" supports Kaufman and Uhlenberg's (2000) finding that men with traditional attitudes toward family and gender increase their work time when they have families. In this sample, the stories of absent provider-fathers were compelling in their implications for the relational consequences for these families. Besides creating long absences for these men, work roles were clearly linked to the very high levels of stress expressed by fathers in our study. Since families may be angry or resentful about the father's time away from home, the clinician may be invaluable in providing a neutral space for communication about the problem. In the short run, couples and their children may need assistance in developing coping skills for managing the separation imposed by work schedules. In the long run, clinicians can provide wellness strategies, opportunities for clarification of values and goals, and communication skills training. Some families would also benefit from support groups or facilitated group intervention, especially if the groups offered modeling of strategies for more effectively balancing work and family.

The Work–Family Dimension at the Macro Systems Level

In our earlier writing about these families, we called for the ungendering of parenting and work roles as a way to address the gender stratification of the family and the workplace (Mercier & Harold, 2001). Both increased equity in job classification and pay and increased opportunity for female workers are needed to accomplish this objective. But structural changes are not sufficient to address this issue. Attitudes about the relative value of work-for-pay versus family caregiving must change in order for women and men to be freed from the constraints of sexism in the work–family dynamic. Public and family education, media representation, and the availability of role models may prove invaluable in creating change, especially for youth just developing their identities as workers. Essential to this process will be a cultural dialogue about the role of fathers in the day-to-day life of the family, as well as an examination of stereotypes regarding women workers.

Almost none of our respondents mentioned the availability of workplace benefits when discussing their jobs. This may be an artifact of our sample, which was solidly middle class and in a region well known for union activity. Nevertheless, we know that many communities need jobs with benefits, most importantly access to health insurance. Given the severity of the health care crisis in the early 21st century, the government has an obligation to address the issue of health care for one- and two-worker families who struggle to provide coverage for themselves and their children. Practitioners should engage in the political advocacy process to support change in the current health care and insurance systems.

The issue of the "family friendly" workplace is a complex one (Fredriksen-Goldsen & Scharlach, 2001), but it is essential to addressing the concerns expressed by these families. Both mothers and fathers in our sample valued flexibility in work scheduling, though they were likely to use the flexibility in different ways. Fathers wanted jobs where they were not penalized for occasional family-related absences. Mothers wanted workplaces that offered schedules that worked with children's school schedules. Women were also more likely to want part-time jobs that were interesting, challenging, and well paid. Workplaces that can offer options for hours of work, flexibility in number of hours scheduled, or location of work would be seen as desirable by these families. Availability of part-time jobs with benefits would be especially useful for some of the mothers interviewed. In light of the stories conveyed by many of our respondents, workplace policies concerning paid overtime and compensation for unpaid overtime may be beneficial to these families as well.

It is clear from our analysis that change is needed in the work-related aspects of family life. Social workers and others engaged in policy analysis and development have an important role to play in creating these changes in the family and in the community in order to improve the quality of life for families today.

7

Sailing Toward the Horizon:
Moving Into Adulthood

The preceding chapters have described our process of talking with adolescents and their parents to gather their narratives and understand this important period of development as the children and their families make the transition to adolescence. Family members were very generous as they shared with us their individual perceptions of relationships within and outside of the family system, and we were able to get a glimpse of the bidirectional effect of microsystems to meso- and macro- systems, and back. Within that context, we also found that although the "changing dynamics of family relationships over the life course ha[ve] concentrated on how parents affect their children …, processes of influence in families flow in both directions—parents affect their children, to be sure, but children also affect their parents" (Steinberg & Steinberg, 1994, p. 261).

Our data also support Steinberg's (1985) contention that many theorists "view identity development during adolescence as the result of the interplay between the young person's growing self-awareness and society's changing view of that individual" (p. 113). Further, he talks about the social redefinition that takes place during adolescence, and the need for increasing contact between adolescents and adults, including parental figures, to make sure that observational learning continues to take place on the developmental path begun in childhood and sustained during the transitional life periods. These assertions also support the theoretical foundations of our work: family life span development, role theory and, primarily, an ecological systems perspective.

In addition, our family and teen narratives also illustrate these interactions and perspectives:

1. Thomas (2001) states that both individual family members and the family as a whole have a life course. He proposes that there are developmental tasks across the life span, and that by understanding that both the individual and the family have these tasks, we can better understand changes in family relationships during periods of transition, such as we have examined in this book.

2. Leaper (2000) tells us that in taking an "interactionist position that assumes that both person attributes and situational factors have a dynamic relationship in a person's development," which our theoretical models dictate, we must "look at the impact of both proximal factors in the immediate setting ... as well as the cumulative impact of historical factors" (p. 136), that is, social construction and socialization.

3. Bronfenbrenner, Moen, and Garbarino (1984) emphasize the role of the outside systems in adolescent and family development as we have described in our chapters. They suggest that the community impacts development by providing opportunities and challenges for growth.

4. Family relationships impact adolescent relationships in all other areas of their lives (Collins & Laursen, 2004). However, family members' individual differences, for example, characteristics and processes, elicit differential responses from their environment, and in turn they interpret these experiences differently (Scholnick & Miller, 2000).

5. Further, as Luster and Okagaki (1993) point out, characteristics of both the immediate context (e.g., psychological well-being) and the larger contexts (e.g., economic circumstances) can influence individual family members' behavior toward one another and with their external environment.

CHAPTER SUMMARIES

What have we learned? Chapter 3 tells us that adolescence is a period of self-development that includes learning about and adjusting to social, physical, cognitive, emotional, and behavioral changes, for both the teen and her/his family. It involves a process of being aware of new opportunities, choosing which ones to follow, and evaluating those choices (Nurmi, 2004). Parents and teens discussed individual changes that adolescents faced and the importance of person–environment fit to help each unique teen navigate new territory. These included changes related to puberty, new ways of thinking and reasoning, levels of autonomy, emotions, and testing out new, sometimes risk-taking behaviors and limits. The concept of "fitting" each individual teen's needs is particularly important in the areas of warmth and support from adults, parental monitoring without being too restrictive, opportunities for input into decision making, and opportunities for structured activities within and outside school.

Chapter 4 illustrates the interconnection between adolescent and family relationships, and the impact of these relationships on interactions in other contexts. As Collins and Laursen (2004) point out: "Adolescent development, like many other putatively individual changes, can be understood more fully in the context of relationships with significant others" (p. 354). The goal of that chapter was to focus primarily on social support in teens' lives as one, broad way of understanding relationship processes. It reviews how relationships change in quality and quantity from late childhood to late adolescence, with older teens reporting having fewer close friends, but with greater intimacy, trust, mutuality, and support in these relationships. It also provides information about teens' receipt of emotional, instrumental, and companionship support from parents, peers, and other adults. The importance of these relationships for emotional, academic, and social outcomes cannot be underestimated, and the chapter provides practice and policy considerations for ensuring that adolescents have consistent, diverse, supportive networks of both peers and adults to keep them afloat during stormy times.

Many authors (e.g., Eccles, 2004) consider schools, as described in chapter 5, as the place where adolescents spend the most time outside of their homes, and look at the issue of "stage-environment fit." Middle, junior high, and high schools are organized in such a way that they are meant to be congruent with the developmental tasks and challenges of adolescence. The influence of teachers, both "good" and "bad," the academic and social opportunities and climates provided in the schools, and the structure of the schools and particular programs are all important to teens and their parents. Parent involvement in the schools, as in most studies of this age group (e.g., Eccles & Harold, 1996), was much less in the present study than when the children were younger. Parents had less time to devote to this and saw it as less essential, but were also less certain of how to be involved in a meaningful way. Both parents and teens commented on the role of school to prepare them for the future, for example, higher education and/or a vocation, and most felt that their high school education/diploma would provide entrée to the road to the future.

Societies socialize their children to fill adult roles (Hoffman, 1984, 2000), and the role of worker is one of the key roles, as we saw in chapter 6. Parents' work status, that is, employed or unemployed, and type of job impact the family and the individual members financially, socially, and psychologically. This is also an area where gender stereotypes are still prevalent among our adult participants, in particular. Most mothers reported working either part- or full-time. However, most continue to struggle with the complicated relationship between work and family, and balancing the expectations, obligations, and responsibilities of both (Crouter, 1994). In addition to their own ideas about this, they also report being aware of and influenced by societal notions. Fathers reported understanding the need to provide for their families, and although some mentioned wishing they had more time to spend with the family, most expressed that it was necessary to maintain their work schedule as is. In this developmental period, adolescents are beginning to explore their own productivity in the work arena, and both parents were cognizant of the need to role model a work ethic and help adolescents make choices and prepare for the kinds of employment/careers they might seek.

The work contained in this volume speaks to some of the contexts in which the adolescent and the family develop. To be sure, there are others upon which we could have focused—many of which are represented by other circles on the eco map shown in chapter 2. We selected those that appeared to be most critical for this life stage (Silbereisen & Todt, 1994). However, religion, health care, and the legal system, among others, all may be important connecting systems for families. Within each context, we note the bidirectionality of influence and the multiple linkages between the individual, the family, and the outside systems, as well as the possibility that some systems will have independent effects on adolescent development (McCarthy, Newcomb, & Bentler, 1994; Parke, 1994; Parke, Burks, Carson, Neville, & Boyum, 1994). These effects, the types and degrees of influence, will probably change as adolescents and families move toward and through other life stages.

EMERGING ADULTHOOD

In our first book, *Becoming a Family: Parents' Stories and Their Implications for Policy, Practice, and Research*, we described the initial formation of new families after individuals transitioned from their childhood families of origin into independent adults and created new family systems through partnership and raising young children. In this book we have discussed our interviews with these same families years later and their experiences of children's transitions into adolescence. The next major developmental transition for these families will be their adolescents' transitions into adult social status and moving out of the family home. These normative developmental transitions shift the nature of relationships between individuals within a family and require further adaptation on emotional, social, and behavioral levels. Noteworthy, though, is that over the last century the timing of adolescence and the shift to adulthood has lengthened, calling for a redefinition of this transition as a developmental period of its own (that is, ages 18 to 25), known as *emerging adulthood* (Arnett, 2000).

Life span development unfolds from birth to death, and involves both continuity and change. However, life *stages* (that is, childhood, adolescence, adulthood, elderly) are culturally constructed and defined. Emerging adulthood, as a stage, is a cultural construction that is characteristic of industrialized societies where, for example, over the last 100 years, puberty has occurred at younger ages, marriages have taken place at older ages as have childbirths, and there is a higher percentage of adolescents in post-secondary education, which has delayed commitment to long-term work roles and identity development.

Many experiences and developmental tasks that characterize adolescence now extend into early adulthood (that is, through the mid 20s), and some tasks characterizing adulthood are now begun during adolescence. In particular, the processes of role and identity formation from adolescence to adulthood substantially overlap. However, this emerging adulthood period is theorized to have some unique features (Arnett, 2000). These include:

- Greater demographic variance or diversity among individuals than any other age, including variations in *living arrangements* such as married, living alone or with peers, and living with parents; in amount and type of *education* from high school dropouts with and without GEDs, to vocational training, community college attendance, and university-based programs; *work status*; and *childbearing*. There is little variability during adolescence and little after age 30 across these demographic characteristics, and it should be noted that this variability is strongly influenced by social inequities and economic status.

- Greater experimentation with new, often risky, behaviors such as sex and drugs, as many emerging adults are less constrained by parental monitoring or the demands of marriage or parenting.

- Greater variability in social roles and self-definition such that 18 to 25 year olds do not typically define themselves as adolescents or as adults. Erikson (1968) defined this stage as a time of psychosocial moratorium "during which the young adult through free role experimentation may find a niche in some section of society" (p. 156). Although social roles are not yet integrated into identity formation, Regan et al. (2004) note that adjustment to new roles looms large. This includes learning role-based behaviors and expectations related to independent living, adult partnerships and sexual intimacy, adult friendships, work roles (e.g., boss, worker, colleague, etc.), and parenthood (although not a necessary criteria, parenthood is often viewed as a key marker of adult social status). During this time, some individuals experience extended adolescent roles as a result of post-secondary education and continued parental support; while for others full adult roles are necessary much earlier, such as for those who drop out of high school, have teenage pregnancies and/or marriage, runaway from, or are thrown out of, their family homes, and those youth who are sentenced to adult jails for criminal behavior. Again, this variability is strongly influenced by social inequities and economic status.

- Greater emotional and sexual intimacy with peers; for example, our data show the changing nature of relationships between adolescents and their peers, as well as with adults. Nevertheless, the development of romantic partnerships and the dating process were only minimally discussed. Other research supports this finding such that romantic relationships, intimacy, and identity develop more fully in emerging adulthood than during adolescence (Montgomery, 2005; Regan et al., 2004).

* More in-depth identity development such that identity processes are barely begun during adolescence (ages 10–18), but are substantially undertaken during emerging adulthood. Nonetheless, characteristics of identity are still fluid, and individuals begin to define themselves more in terms of individual characteristics than in terms of social roles. For example, these characteristics include responsibility for one's actions, decision making, financial independence, and trying on new world views. Marcia (1980) described this period of identity development as a time of extensive exploration and little commitment in the areas of career, interpersonal relationships, and political and cultural ideas. Development of the self is posited as a critical component affecting the interrelationship between the individual and her/his environment, which includes finding a balance between individual autonomy and social connectedness/interdependency. Thus, the interrelationship between intimacy and identity is significant during this period, and this experience is influenced by gendered social processes.

IMPORTANT PREDICTORS OF ADULT OUTCOMES: RISK AND PROTECTIVE FACTORS

Risk and protective factors can be individual characteristics or social context variables. They are factors that have proximal and/or distal effects on teens' physical and mental health, social success, and/or overall quality of life. Statistically, the most frequent risks during adolescence are depression, low self-esteem, suicide, violent victimization, accidents, and substance abuse (National Research Council, 1995). Table 7.1 lists other common risks that are common in adolescence.

Our data reflect parents' and teens' concerns about a number of these risks, especially depression, substance abuse, and victimization. Also, the home environment and the nature of parent–teen relationships are evident in the data. It is important to note that while emotional variability and transient, mild depression are normal, severe psychological turmoil is experienced by about 20% of teens and should not be considered benign (Offer et al., 1981; Powers et al., 1989). For example, as discussed in chapter 3, serious depression that begins in adolescence is more likely to recur in the future and is associated with other mental health problems such as substance abuse, anxiety, eating disorders, obsessive-compulsive disorders, conduct and oppositional disorders, and hyperactivity and attention deficit (Kovacs, 1996; Petersen et al., 1993). Furthermore, when these problems co-occur, there is a much higher risk for suicide (Kovacs & Devlin, 1998).

TABLE 7.1
Common Risk Factors for Youth

Risk factors
Substance abuse
Familial conflict with high criticism, negativity, and hostility
Lack of adult supervision
Limits set too high without opportunity for input or too permissive without sufficient guidance
Depression
Eating disorders
Vicitimization
Teen pregnancy
Poverty
Academic difficulties and/or dropout
Early sexual behaviors
Early puberty for girls and late puberty for boys
Negative peer group
Low self-esteem

A combination of pubertal timing, discrimination, victimization, and poverty are all associated with depression (Buchanan et al., 1992; Nolen-Hoeksema, 1994; Roberts et al., 1997). And, while depression is a frequent problem for both male and female teens, females and minority youth have higher rates of depression during adolescence and adulthood (Angold et al., 1998; Lewinsohn et al., 1993). Most depressed and/or suicidal teens who receive support and mental health treatment can have positive outcomes in the future. Therefore, intervention, attention to warning signs, and dispelling myths can be critical for helping teens (McGuire, 1984). Substance abuse is also linked with other problem behaviors such as delinquency, running away from home, academic failure, and teen pregnancy, as well as poor mental and physical health, and higher rates of injury and death (Newcomb & Bentler, 1989; Palmer & Liddle, 1996).

The family environment is a place of both potential protection and risk. In this context, the importance of person–environment fit becomes crucial. Teens need stability and a balance between autonomy and decision-making as well as guidance and safety. Parents must find a balance between providing guidance, monitoring, and behavioral control, while not being intrusive, negative, and controlling. Tolerance for disagreement and discord is better than avoidance or control of conflict. This involves engaging in problem solving and mutual empathy and understanding between parents and teens, which promotes teen identity and ego strength. Alternately, arguments that are devaluing, judgmental or constraining, hostile, impulsive, or inconsistent are associated with poor outcomes for all family members (Hauser et al., 1991). The degree of teen autonomy and decision making shifts continuously throughout the adolescent period as individual teens are capable of more and more independence. For parents, the tasks and challenges of raising an adolescent are centered around adjusting to new roles of their teens and for themselves as parents, coping with change and loss as teens separate and individuate from parents, and ultimately with changes in the household composition as emerging adults move out of the family home.

Despite the number of risks that adolescents and their families encounter, these risks can be moderated by protective factors, which enhance an individual's resiliency in the face of hardship and her/his ability to function socially and academically, and to improve health. Table 7.2 lists a number of protective factors that have been found across the research (Benson, 1997). Policy and practice should focus more on increasing the quality and number of protective factors and decreasing risks through primary prevention, rather than on punitive responses after problems occur (such as zero-tolerance policies, trying juveniles in adult courts, removing pregnant teens from public schools, etc.).

PRACTICE AND POLICY OVERVIEW

Chapters 3 through 6 review practice and policy issues that are specific to the chapter topics. We will not repeat all the specifics here, but highlight some critical areas of focus for overall positive development. "Positive development is defined as the engagement in prosocial behaviors and avoidance of health-compromising and future-jeopardizing behaviors" (Roth, Brooks-Gunn, Murray, & Foster, 1998, p. 426). Goals for positive development include:

- Intellectual skills including reflection, problem solving, and critical thinking.
- Productivity or engagement in meaningful work.
- Good citizenship (e.g., ethical behavior and civil participation).

TABLE 7.2
Common Protective Factors for Youth

Protective Factors

Sports and other structured, supervised peer activities
Open communication, empathy, and warmth
Tolerance for disagreement and adolescent autonomy, but with expectations of
    adult-like behaviors and monitoring of limits and rules that are age-appropriate
    and fit the individual needs of the adolescent
Joint decision-making
Adult mentors
Academic involvement and success
Parental involvement in schools
Peer support, positive peer groups
Strong sense of self, self-esteem, ethnic pride

- Interpersonal caring and social relationships (e.g., social integration into communities and organizations, ability to empathize, etc.).
- Overall quality of mental and physical health.

Social policies and practices should be enacted to promote these positive goals. Several policy and research institutes and organizations, such as the National Association of Social Workers, the American Psychological Association, the Search Institute, and the National Research Council, to name just a few, have outlined recommendations. Benson (1997), from the Search Institute, delineates 40 assets that such policies and practices should enhance, which involve:

- Enhancing social support.
- Empowering sociopolitical improvement for self and community.
- Maintaining boundaries and expectations.
- Constructive use of time that includes structured and monitored activities with peers and adults.
- Commitment to education.
- Instilling social values.
- Strengthening social skills.
- Enhancing positive self image, optimism, and hopefulness.
- Access to health care education and services.

These assets can be promoted by professionals including social workers, psychologists, teachers, counselors, and health care providers, as well as by parents and other adults (e.g., mentors, extended family members, community leaders, and others). These interactions can occur through individual relationships or through community programs and services. Promotion of assets serves to protect youth from developing problems such as substance abuse, violence, early sexual activity, depression, and school problems. Additionally, these assets influence positive outcomes such as leadership, good health, academic success, and the development of values and ethics (Benson, 1997; Roth et al., 1998).

Adolescence, as our participants have told us, is a time when social contexts shift with school and family transitions and other life events, and the need to adapt to new relationships becomes central to their ability to gain social support, academic, and perhaps work success. Interventions that increase adolescents' abilities to develop and maintain supportive relationships may be needed to help teenagers adapt to normative, developmental changes in social contexts such as school transitions and moving away from home.

In addition to developmental concerns, intervention plans must consider the effects of gender, culture, and socioeconomic status. For example, adolescents are rarely socially isolated, but lower socioeconomic status (SES) teens may be isolated from some kinds of support or opportunities as compared to upper SES teens by virtue of social structural boundaries that separate lower SES people from having access to the kinds of resources that upper SES supporters can offer (such as professional knowledge or advice, financial resources, and access to opportunities).

Cultural practices and/or language barriers may also restrict access to a variety of different kinds of support and opportunities. As Pearson (1990) notes, "There may be enormous variation among cultural groups with regard to which attitudes and actions are considered to be supportive and from whom such action may appropriately come. [Clinicians] should be careful to enter their work free of too many assumptions about what clients do, or do not, view as supportive. Individual, family, or cultural factors may lead clients to overlook or discount support that they may already have access to in their network" (p. 47). Finally, gender-role restrictions may also serve to keep people isolated from some support networks or opportunities. This may be based on more informal structures that maintain gender segregation, like the discouragement of girls from participation in sports, math, and sciences, or of boys from engaging in support groups or other group activities designated as feminine. Maguire (1991) notes that "a young man who acts differently than his social group permits will have to conform or develop an alternative support system or to withdraw" (p. 132).

Preventive Interventions: Practice and Policy

Prevention can be through informal or formal interactions with teens, and includes primary, secondary, and tertiary interventions. Primary prevention involves strategies that prevent problems from beginning altogether. Secondary prevention intervenes at the early stages of problems or at the initiation of risk behaviors. Tertiary prevention are those interventions that seek to treat established problems in order to prevent the continuation, escalation, or worsening of a problem. We recommend primary prevention for youth throughout the years of primary and secondary education to build strengths and resilience, and to obstruct negative pathways to problems for all youth. Additionally, universal screening for the most prevalent problems during childhood and adolescence, such as depression, victimization, and substance abuse, can identify those youth who are at risk and offer secondary and tertiary preventions. Finally, increasing access to services while empowering adolescents to recognize their own needs and self-refer for a variety of health and mental health services with a greater degree of autonomy and confidentiality protections (especially in the areas of reproductive health, victimization, and substance abuse) is advised in order to reduce barriers to prevention.

Formalized interventions take a variety of forms or treatment modalities, including mentorship programs, group work, youth development programs focusing on skill development, knowledge and attitude changes, and individual health and mental health treatments. Roth et al. (1998) notes that, in particular, "Youth development programs go beyond traditional prevention or intervention models by stressing skill and competency development rather than focusing on specific problems. These programs strive to influence an adolescents' developmental path toward positive outcomes by countering risk factors and enhancing protective factors. The ages of 10 to 16 are often the focus for competency building" (p. 425). Although schools are the major institutions serving youth, development programs are typically initiated by community-based organizations.

One policy approach to adolescent development is to promote a shift in research funding from the investigation of separate disorders to the promotion of general healthy living skills within a competence-based perspective as a means of preventing many disorders with a single intervention. Another policy approach would be to promote and fund prevention and treatment programs that focus on positive adolescent development and support. Primary goals of programs that seek to reach multiple populations of adolescents should be both school- and community-based and focus on increasing competencies and building social support.

Programs could take a universal approach to building competencies and general well-being or a targeted approach to identify at-risk adolescents in schools and communities that could benefit from support interventions. Both universal and targeted approaches have benefits and drawbacks. The most common argument against universal approaches is the cost of implementing large-scale programs to provide services to people who are not reporting problems. However, overall costs may be reduced over time as a result of creating relationship skills that teens can use to deal with a variety of problems, across situations and over time.

Policy initiatives should develop services for adolescents that are easily accessible, which often means within a school or community setting where they are easily utilized by adolescents. For instance, universal prevention programs focused on social support could be integrated into the school curriculum as part of a life skills or social science class. Also, peer activities such as support groups, skills training, and interactive activities could be facilitated by schools, community centers, or religion-based groups. Likewise, professional mental and physical health services should be geographically accessible and affordable for adolescents and should provide confidential services to create an environment of trust and safety.

Policies that seek to enhance programs should make sure that interventions are adapted to developmental roles and tasks of the population being served (that is, services must be tailored to meet age-appropriate needs rather than forcing clients to fit categorical, adult-based services). Services should take a multimodal approach to treatment and define problems and solutions with sensitivity to family systems, culture, ethnicity, and heritage. To this end, research suggests that building external assets in families, schools, and communities will increase positive outcomes for adolescents (Benson & Martin, 2003). Policies should help decrease obstacles to access, adequately fund programs, require that service providers be trained in the proper assessment and treatment modalities, involve teens and families in the development and evaluation of programs, and require that services address not only symptoms but also the conditions that cause them (Maguire, 1991).

Finally, programs, policies, and practices vary widely and are not always based on the best available evidence of effectiveness. Evidence-based practice is based on knowledge developed through the rigorous testing of assumptions and through the systematic collection and analysis of data and replication of findings (see Gambrill, 1999). It involves knowing when and how to use knowledge specifically and efficiently to achieve the desired outcomes, and thus inform the use of best practices with youth. Programs may be developed through the use of evidence-based knowledge about assets and developmental outcomes, but it must be further tested for effectiveness through program evaluation. Although some programs have been evaluated, most have not. Moreover, there are a number of challenges when evaluating programs, which may affect the quality of the research. The most common problems include:

- Tracking youth outcomes over time.
- The lack of integration between theory and practice, and clear protocols for intervention.
- Ability to determine which parts of an intervention are effective for what issues through the systematic comparison of program differences in length, type, and intensity.
- The lack of control group studies.
- The lack of consistent criteria and measures across evaluation studies.
- Quality control mechanisms for validated programs.
- Insufficient documentation and dissemination of information to providers.

An increase in the degree to which funding sources not only support evaluation research but require that treatment providers utilize evidence-based practice will improve overall quality of services to youth. This does not always mean that the best interventions will be the least expensive. Implementing high-quality, effective primary, secondary, and tertiary preventive services on a large scale (i.e., available to all youth regardless of socioeconomic status) will require an up-front social and economic investment, with the payoffs coming later in the form of reductions in crime, mental illness, teen pregnancy, substance abuse, and other social problems.

CONCLUSION

The nature of a qualitative study is to provide information about the sample at hand; it is not intended for generalization to the population at large. Additionally, the homogeneity of this study's sample in terms of race, ethnicity, and socioeconomic status further restricts its descriptiveness to a specific population. However, the findings in this study are consistent with data that are statistically generalizable to large portions of the population and can be used to provide personal accounts of statistical findings.

The nature of qualitative data is also such that no assumptions can be made about what was not discussed by students because there is no way of knowing what might have been talked about if the interview protocol included different questions or different probes. Even the age and gender of the interviewers could have made a difference in the amounts or kinds of disclosure made by adolescents. Qualitative research is naturalistic by design, creating a situation where human interaction may influence the nature of the emerging data. The qualitative researcher is the primary instrument for data collection and analysis and therefore information is mediated through the human interaction rather than through standardized survey measures.

So, is adolescence a period of *smooth sailing or stormy waters?* It seems that it is both. It is a dynamic period of development for the teen and the family and is experienced in all of its positiveness and negativeness by both the youth and adults in our study. What our data show are that individual adolescent and family characteristics and environmental systems interact to make the adolescent transition easier or more difficult. For some, the waters are gentler, for others, more wavy, and the pattern of today is often changed tomorrow. There are many truths, as told by our participants, and each enriches our understanding of adolescent and family development in the context of their larger environments, and helps us see these experiences from a risk and resilience perspective (Allen-Meares & Fraser, 2004).

The bottom line, perhaps, is that this period of life is one of "unusual normality" often leaving parents, friends, schools, work, and the adolescents themselves attributing experiences, both good and bad, to the fact of being "teens." It is clearly, also, a time of life that everyone wants to understand better. But we do not need to "fix" adolescence. It is not broken. And the majority of adolescents make the transition successfully into the adult world!

> It is all a problem of *how to be adolescent during adolescence.* This is an extremely brave thing for anybody to be, and some of these people are trying to achieve it. It does not mean that we grown-ups have to be saying: "Look at these dear little adolescents having their adolescence; we must put up with everything and let our windows get broken." That is not the point. The point is that we are challenged, and we meet the challenge as part of the function of adult living. But we meet the challenge rather than set out to cure what is essentially healthy. (Winnicott, 1965, p. 87)

Steinberg and Levine (1990, p. 2) echo this sentiment. They begin their work, and we end ours, with the following "myths of adolescence" :

• Adolescence is not an inherently difficult period.

- The evils of peer pressure have been overrated.
- The decline of the family has also been overstated.

And, finally, with the importance of considering:

- Youth self-advocacy and empowerment,
- Adult advocacy on behalf of youth,
- Access to social, psychological, legal and economic resources for all youth with a greater degree of confidentiality protections, and
- Treating youth as resources to be developed, rather than problems to be managed.

References

Allen-Meares, P., Colarossi, L. G., Oyserman, D., & DeRoos, Y. (2003). Assessing depression in childhood and adolescence: A guide for social work practice. *Child and Adolescent Social Work Journal, 20*(1), 5–20.

Allen-Meares, P., & Fraser, M. W. (Eds.). (2004). *Intervention with children and adolescent: An interdisciplinary perspective.* Boston: Pearson Education.

Allessandri, S. M., & Wozniak, R. H. (1987). The child's awareness of parental beliefs concerning the child: A developmental study. *Child Development, 58,* 316–323.

Altonji, J. G., & Dunn, T. A. (2000). An intergenerational model of wages, hours and earnings. *The Journal of Human Resources, 35*(2), 221–258.

American Psychological Association. (2002). *Diagnostic and statistical manual of mental disorders* (4th ed., Rev.). Washington, DC: Author.

Angold, A., Costello, E., & Worthman, C. (1998). Puberty and depression: The role of age, pubertal status and pubertal timing. *Psychological Medicine, 28,* 51–61.

Antonucci, T. C. (1983). Social support: Theoretical advances, recent findings, and pressing issues. In I. G. Sarason & B. R. Sarason (Eds.), *Social support: Theory, research, and applications* (pp. 21–38). Boston: Martinus Nijhoff.

Antonucci, T. C. (1994). A life-span view of women's social relations. In B. F. Turner & L. E. Troll (Eds.), *Handbook of aging and social sciences* (pp. 205–226). New York: Academic Press.

Antonucci, T. C., & Akiyama, H. (1987). Social networks in adult life and a preliminary examination of the convoy model. *Journal of Gerontology, 42*(5), 519–527.

Antonucci, T. C., Akiyama, H., & Lansford, J. E. (1998). Negative effects of close social relations. *Family relations: Interdisciplinary Journal of Applied Family Studies: Special Issue: The Family as a Context for Health and Well-Being, 47*(4), 379–384.

Arai, A. B. (2000). Self-employment as a response to the double day for women and men in Canada. *The Canadian Review of Sociology and Anthropology, 37*(2), 125–142.

Arnett, J. J. (2000). Emerging adulthood: A theory of development from the late teens through the twenties. *American Psychologist, 55*(5), 469–480.

Ashinger, P. (1985). Using social networks in counseling. *Journal of Counseling and Development, 63*, 519–521.

Baer, M. F., Connors, B. W., & Paradiso, M. A. (1996). *Neuroscience: Exploring the brain.* Balitmore: Williams & Wilkens.

Barley, S. R. (1989). Careers, identities, and institutions: The legacy of the Chicago School of Sociology. In M. B. Arthur, D. T. Hall, & B. S. Lawrence (Eds.), *Handbook of career theory* (pp. 41–65). New York: Cambridge University Press.

Barrera, M. (1986). Distinctions between social support concepts, measures, and models. *American Journal of Community Psychology, 14*, 413–445.

Barrera, M., & Garrison-Jones, C. (1992). Family and peer social support as specific correlates of adolescent depressive symptoms. *Journal of Abnormal Child Psychology, 20*, 1–16.

Barrera, M., Sandler, I. N., & Ramsay, T. B. (1981). Preliminary development of a scale of social support: Studies on college students. *American Journal of Community Psychology, 9*(4), 435–447.

Baum, C. L. (2003). The effects of maternity leave legislation on mothers' labor supply after childbirth. *Southern Economic Journal, 69*(4), 772–799.

Bell, R. R. (1981). *Worlds of friendship.* Beverly Hills: Sage.

Belle, D. (1982). The stress of caring: Women as providers of social support. In L. Goldberger & S. Breznitz (Eds.), *Handbook of stress: Theoretical and clinical approaches* (pp. 496–505). New York: The Free Press.

Bender, W. N., Shubert, T. H., & McLaughlin, P. J. (2001). Invisible kids: Preventing school violence by identifying kids in trouble. *Intervention in School and Clinic, 37*(2), 105–111.

Benson, P. L. (1997). *All kids are our kids: What communities must do to raise caring and responsible children and adolescents.* Minneapolis, MN: Search Institute.

Benson, F., & Martin, S. (2003). Organizing successful parent involvement in urban schools. *Child Study Journal, 33*(3), 187–193.

Berggren, H. M. (2003). Women's and men's access to employer-provided benefits: An assessment of women's acceptance as breadwinners. *The Review of Policy Research, 20*(1), 153–173.

Berndt, T. J. (1982). The features and effects of friendship in early adolescence. *Child Development, 53*(6), 1447–1460.

Berndt, T. J., & Perry, T. B. (1986). Children's perceptions of friendships as supportive relationships. *Developmental Psychology, 22*(5), 640–648.

Bielby, W. T., & Bielby, D. D. (1989). Family ties: Balancing commitments to work and family in dual earner households. *American Sociological Review, 54*, 776–789.

Bigelow, B. J. (1977). Children's friendship expectations: A cognitive-developmental study. *Child Development, 48*, 246–253.

Blair-Loy, M., & Wharton, A. S. (2002). Employees' use of work–family policies and the workplace social context. *Social Forces, 80*(3), 813–845.

Blau, G. M. (1996). Adolescent suicide and depression. In G. M. Blau & T. P. Gullotta (Eds.), *Adolescent dysfunctional behavior: Causes, interventions, and prevention*, (pp. 187–205). Thousand Oaks, CA: Sage.

Blumstein, P., & Schwartz, P. (1983). *American couples: Money, work, sex*. New York: William Morrow.

Borden, W. (1992). Narrative perspectives in psychosocial intervention following adverse life events. *Social Work, 37*(2), 135–141.

Bowen, M. (1974). Toward the differentiation of self in one's family of origin. In F. Andres & J. Lorio (Eds.), *Georgetown family symposium* (Vol. 1). Washington, DC: Georgetown University Medical Center.

Brady, H. E., Schlozman, K. L., & Verba, S. (1999). Prospecting for participants: Rational expectations and the recruitment of political activists. *American Political Science Review, 93*, 153–169.

Bronfenbrenner, U. (1979). *The ecology of human development: Experiments by nature and design*. Cambridge, MA: Harvard University Press.

Bronfenbrenner, U. (1986). Ecology of the family as a context for human development: Research perspectives. *Developmental Psychology, 22*, 723–742.

Bronfenbrenner, U., Moen, P., & Garbarino, J. (1984). Child, family, and community. In R. D. Parke (Ed.), *The family* (pp. 283–328). Chicago, University of Chicago Press.

Brooks-Gunn, J. (1988). Antecedents and consequences of variations in girls' maturational timing. *Journal of Adolescent Health Care, 9*(5), 1–9.

Brooks-Gunn, J., & Reiter, E. O. (1990). The role of pubertal processes. In S. S. Feldman & G. R. Elliot (Eds.), *At the threshold: The developing adolescent*, (pp. 16–53). Cambridge, MA: Harvard University Press.

Buchanan, C. M., Eccles, J. S., & Becker, J. B. (1992). Are adolescents the victims of raging hormones: Evidence for activational effects of hormones on moods and behavior at adolescence. *Psychological Bulletin, 111*, 62–107.

Buchmueller, T. C., & Valletta, R. G. (1999). The effect of health insurance on married female labor supply. *The Journal of Human Resources, 34* (1), 42–70.

Buhrmester, D., & Furman, W. (1990). Perceptions of sibling relationships during middle childhood and adolescence. *Child Development, 61*, 1387–1398.

Bureau of Justice Statistics. (2003). *Teens experience the highest rates of violent crime*. Washington, DC: U.S. Department of Justice, Office of Justice Programs.

Bush, D. M., & Simmons, R. G. (1981). Socialization process over the life course. In M. Rosenberg & R. H. Turner (Eds.), *Social psychology: Sociological perspectives* (pp. 133–143). Basic Books.

Byrnes, J. P. (1988). Formal operations: A systematic reformulation. *Developmental Review, 8*, 1–22.

Byrnes, J. P., & Overton, W. F. (1986). Reasoning about certainty and uncertainty in concrete and causal and prepositional contexts. *Developmental Psychology, 22*, 793–799.

Caldwell, M. A., & Peplau, L. A. (1982). Sex differences in same-sex friendships. *Sex Roles, 8*, 721–731.

Caputo, R. K. (2000). The availability of traditional and family friendly benefits among a cohort of young women, 1968–95. *Families in Society, 81*(4), 422–436.

Carter, B., & McGoldrick, M. (1988). Overview: The changing family life cycle: A framework for family therapy. In E. A. Carter & M. McGoldrick (Eds.), *The changing family life cycle* (2nd ed., pp. 3–28). New York: Gardner.

Casper, L., & Smith, K. (2004). Self-care: Why do parents leave their children unsupervised? *Demography, 41*(2), 285–301.

Cauce, A. M., Reid, M., Landesman, S., & Gonzales, N. (1990). Social support in young children: Measurement, structure, and behavioral impact. In B. R. Sarason, I. G. Sarason, & G. R. Pierce (Eds.), *Social support: An interactional view* (pp. 64–94). New York: Wiley.

Center on Juvenile Justice. (2004). *Myths and facts about youth crime.* Retrieved 10/1/04 from http://www.cjcj.org/jjic/myths_facts./php

Centers for Disease Control. (2003). *Youth Risk Behaviors Social Survey: Online comprehensive results.* Retrieved 9/16/2004 from http://apps.nccd.cdc.gov/yrbss/

Chandler, M. (1987). The Othello effect: Essay on the emergence and eclipse of skeptical doubt. *Human Development, 30*, 137–159.

Chase, B. (2002). *The new public school parent: How to get the best education for your child.* New York: Penguin Books.

Cicirelli, V. G. (1995). *Sibling relationships across the life span.* New York: Plenum.

Clarkberg, M., & Moen, P. (1999). The time-squeeze: The mismatch between work-hours patterns and preferences among married couples. *American Behavioral Scientist, 44*, 1115–1136.

Coates, D. (1985). Relationships between self-concept measures and social network characteristics for Black adolescents. *Journal of Early Adolescence, 5*, 319–338.

Cohen, J. (2001). Social and emotional education: Core concepts and practices. In J. Cohen (Ed.), *Caring classrooms/Intelligent schools: The social emotional education of young children* (pp. 3–29). New York: Teachers College Press.

Cohen, S. (1992). Stress, social support, and disorder. In H. O. F. Veiel & A. Baumann (Eds.), *The meaning and measurement of social support* (pp. 109–124). New York: Hemisphere.

Cohen, S., & Syme, S. L. (1985). Issues in the study and application of social support. In S. Cohen & S. L. Syme (Eds.), *Social support and health* (pp. 3–22). New York: Academic Press.

Cohen, S., & Wills, T. A. (1985). Stress, social support, and the buffering hypothesis. *Psychological Bulletin, 98*(2), 310–357.

Colarossi, L. G. (2001). Adolescent gender differences in social support: Structure, function, and provider type. *Social Work Research, 25*(4), 233–241.

Colarossi, L. G., & Eccles, J. S. (2000). A prospective study of adolescent peer support: Gender differences and the influence of parental relationships. *Journal of Youth and Adolescence, 29*(6), 661–678.

Colarossi, L. G., & Eccles, J. S. (2003). Differential effects of support providers on adolescents' mental health. *Social Work Research, 27*(1), 19–30.

Colarossi, L. G., & Lynch, S. (2001). Changes in support networks throughout family development. In R. D. Harold (Ed.), *Becoming a family: Parents' stories and their implications for practice, policy, and research* (pp. 115–153). Mahwah, NJ: Lawrence Erlbaum Associates.

Cole, A., & Kerns, K. A. (2001). Perceptions of sibling qualities and activities of early adolescents. *Journal of Early Adolescence, 21*(2), 204–226.

Collins, W. A. (1989). Parent–child relationships in the transition to adolescence: Continuity and change in interaction, affect, and cognition. In R. Montemayor, G. Adams, & T. Gullotta (Eds.), *Advances in adolescent development* (Vol. 2). Beverly Hills: Sage Publications.

Collins, W. A., & Laursen, B. (2004). Parent–adolescent relationships and influences. In R. M. Lerner & L. Steinberg (Eds.), *Handbook of adolescent psychology* (2nd ed., pp. 331–361). Hoboken, NJ: Wiley.

Collins, W. A., & Russell, G. (1991). Mother–child and father–child relationships in middle childhood and adolescence: A developmental analysis. *Developmental Review, 11,* 99–136.

Compas, B. E. (1987). Coping with stress during childhood and adolescence. *Psychological Bulletin, 101,* 393–403.

Cooper, C. R. (1994). Cultural perspectives on continuity and change in adolescents' relationships. In R. Montemayor, G. R. Adams, & T. P. Gullotta (Eds.), *Personal relationships during adolescence* (pp. 78–100). Thousand Oaks, CA: Sage.

Cooper, C. R., & Ayers-Lopez, S. (1985). Family and peer systems in early adolescence. *Journal of Early Adolescence, 4,* 155–181.

Crouter, A. C. (1994). Processes linking families and work: Implications for behavior and development in both settings. In R. D. Parke & S. G. Kellam (Eds.), *Exploring family relationships with other social contexts* (pp. 9–28). Hillsdale, NJ: Lawrence Erlbaum Associates.

Csikszentmihalyi, M., & Nakamura, J. (1989). In R. E. Ames & C. Ames (Eds.), *Research on motivation in education: Goals and cognition* (pp. 45–72). New York: Academic Press.

Cumsille, P. E., & Epstein, N. (1994). Family cohesion, family adaptability, social support, and adolescent depressive symptoms in outpatient clinic families. *Journal of Family Psychology, 8*(2), 202–214.

Dasho, S., Lewis, C., & Watson, M. (2001). Fostering emotional intelligence in the classroom and school: Strategies from the child development project. In J. Cohen (Ed.), *Caring classrooms/Intelligent schools: The social emotional education of young children* (pp. 87–107). New York: Teachers College Press.

Davidson, M. J., & Cooper, C. L. (1992). *Shattering the glass ceiling: The woman manager.* London: Paul Chapman.

Deater-Deckard, K., Dunn, J., & Lussier, G. (2002). Sibling relationships and social-emotional adjustment in different family contexts. *Social Development, 11,* 571–590.

Degirmencioglu, S. M., Urber, K. A., Tolson, J. M., & Richard, P. (1998). Adolescent friendship networks: Continuity and change over the school year. *Merrill-Palmer Quarterly, 44*(3), 313–337.

Denton, K., & Zarbatany, L. (1996). Age differences in support processes in conversations between friends. *Child Development, 67*(4), 1360–1373.

Dorman, P. (2001). Maternity and family leave policies: A comparative analysis. *The Social Science Journal, 38*(2), 189–201.

Douglas, D. (2004). Self-advocacy: Encouraging students to become partners in differentiation. *Roeper Review, 26*(4), 223–228.

Dubow, E. F., Tisak, J., Causey, D., Hryshko, A., & Reid, G. (1991). A two-year longitudinal study of stressful life events, social support, and social problem solving skills: Contributions to children's behavioral and academic adjustment. *Child Development, 62,* 583–599.

Duncan, P. D., Ritter, P. L., Dornbusch, S. M., & Siegel-Gorelick, B. (1982). Educational correlates of early and late sexual maturation in adolescence. *Journal of Pediatrics, 100*(4), 633–637.

Dunkel-Schetter, C., & Bennett, T. L. (1990). Differentiating the cognitive and behavioral aspects of social support. In B. R. Sarason, I. G. Sarason, & G. R. Pierce (Eds.), *Social support: An interactional view* (pp. 267–296). New York: Wiley.

Dunst, C. J. (2002). Family-centered practices: Birth through high school. *Journal of Special Education, 36*(3), 139–147.

Eccles (Parsons), J. (1983). Expectancies, values, and academic behaviors. In J. T. Spence (Ed.), *Achievement and achievement motives* (pp. 75–146). San Francisco: W. H. Freeman and Co.

Eccles, J. S. (2004). Schools, academic motivation, and stage-environment fit. In R. M. Lerner & L. Steinberg (Eds.), *Handbook of adolescent psychology* (2nd ed., pp. 125–153). Hoboken, NJ: Wiley.

Eccles, J. S., Barber, B. L., Stone, M., & Hunt, J. (2003). Extracurricular activities and adolescent development. *Journal of Social Issues, 59*(4), 865.

Eccles, J. S., & Blumenfeld, P. C. (1984). *Psychological predictors of competence development.* (Grant No. 2 R01 HD17553–01). Bethesda, MD: National Institute of Child Health and Human Development.

Eccles, J. S., Blumenfeld, P. C., Harold, R. D., & Wigfield, A. L. (1990). *Ontogeny of self and task concepts and activity choice.* (Grant No. 2 R01 HD17553–06). Bethesda, MD: National Institute of Child Health and Human Development.

Eccles, J. S., & Harold, R. D. (1996). Family involvement in children's and adolescent's schooling. In A. Booth & J. Dunn (Eds.), *Family–school links: How do they affect educational outcomes?* (pp. 3–34). Hillsdale, NJ: Lawrence Erlbaum Associates.

Eccles, J. S., Wigfield, A., Midgley, C., Reuman, D., MacIver, D., & Feldlaufer, H. (1993). Negative effects of traditional middle schools on students' motivation. *The Elementary School Journal, 93*(5), 553–569.

Ekstrom, R. B., Goertz, M. E., & Rock, D. A. (1988). *Education and American youth: The impact of the high school experience.* New York: Falmer Press.

Elias, M., & Butler, L. B. (1999). Social decision making and problem solving: Essential skills for interpersonal and academic success. In J. Cohen (Ed.), *Educating minds and hearts: Social emotional learning and the passage into adolescence* (pp. 74–94). New York: Teachers College Press.

Elkind, D. (1967). Egocentrism in adolescence. *Child Development, 38,* 1025–1034.

Elkind, D. (1994). *Ties that stress: The new family imbalance.* Cambridge, MA: Harvard University Press.

Epstein, H. T. (1974). Phrenoblysis: Special brain and mind growth periods. *Developmental Psychology, 7,* 207–216.

Erikson, E. H. (1968). *Identity: Youth and crisis.* New York: Norton.

Erikson, E. H. (1982). *The life cycle completed.* London: Rikan Enterprises Ltd.

Feinberg, M., McHale, S., Crouter, A., & Cumsille, P. (2003). Sibling differentiation: Sibling and parent relationship trajectories in adolescence. *Child Development, 74*(5), 1261–1274.

Feiring, C., & Lewis, M. (1991). The development of social networks from early to middle childhood: Gender differences and the relation to school competence. *Sex Roles, 25*(3/4), 237–253.

Feld, S., & Radin, N. (1982). *Social psychology for social work and the mental health professions.* New York: Columbia University Press.

Ferber, M. A., & Green, C. A. (2003). Career or family: What choices do college women have? *Journal of Labor Research, 24*(1), 143–151.

Fiese, B. H., & Marjinsky, K. A. T. (1999). Dinnertime stories: Connecting family practices with relationship beliefs and child adjustments. In B. H. Fiese, A. J. Sameroff, H. D. Grotevant, F. S. Wamboldt, S. Dickstein, & D. L. Fravel, (Eds.), The stories that families tell: Narrative coherence, narrative interaction, and relationship beliefs. *Monographs of the Society for Research in Child Development, 64*(2, Serial No. 257), 52–68.

Fiese, B. H., & Sameroff, A. J. (1999). The family narrative consortium: A multidimensional approach to narratives. In B. H. Fiese, A. J. Sameroff, H. D. Grotevant, F. S. Wamboldt, S. Dickstein, & D. L. Fravel, (Eds.), The stories that families tell: Narrative coherence, narrative interaction, and relationship beliefs. *Monographs of the Society for Research in Child Development, 64*(2, Serial No. 257), 1–36.

Flannery, D. J., Williams, L. L., & Vazsonyi, A. T. (1999). Who are they with and what are they doing? Delinquent behavior, substance use, and early adolescents' after-school time. *American Journal of Orthopsychiatry, 69*(2), 247–253.

Folk, K., & Yi, Y. (1994). Piecing together child care with multiple arrangements: Crazy quilt or preferred pattern for employed parent of preschool children. *Journal of Marriage and the Family, 56*, 669–680.

Forum on Child and Family Statistics. (2005). *America's children: Key national indicators of well-being, 2005.* (Federal Interagency Forum on Child and Family Statistics.) Washington, DC: U.S. Government Printing Office.

Franco, N., & Levitt, M. J. (1998). The social ecology of middle childhood: Family support, friendship quality, and self-esteem. *Family Relations, 47*, 315–321.

Fredriksen-Goldsen, K. I., & Scharlach, A. E. (2001). *Families and work: New directions in the twenty-first century.* New York: Oxford University Press.

Frey, C. P. (1998). Struggling with identity: Working with seventh- and eighth-grade gifted girls to air issues of concern. *Journal for the Education of the Gifted, 21*(4), 437–451.

Frey, C. U., & Rothlisberger, C. (1996). Social support in healthy adolescents. *Journal of Youth and Adolescence, 25*(1), 17–31.

Fullerton, C. S., & Ursano, R. J. (1994). Preadolescent peer friendships: A critical contribution to adult social relatedness? *Journal of Youth & Adolescence, 23*(1), 43–63.

Furman, W. (1982). Children's friendships. In T. Field, G. Finley, A. Huston, H. Quay, & L. Troll (Eds.), *Review of human development* (pp. 327–342). New York: Wiley.

Furman, W., & Bierman, K. (1984). Children's conceptions of friendship: A multidimensional study. *Developmental Psychology, 20*, 925–931.

Furman, W., & Buhrmester, D. (1992). Age and sex differences in perceptions of networks of personal relationships. *Child Development, 63*, 103–115.

Furstenberg, F. (1990). Coming of age in a changing family system. In S. S. Feldman & G. R. Elliot (Eds.), *At the threshold: The developing adolescent* (pp. 147–170). Cambridge, MA: Harvard University Press.

Gambrill, E. (1999). Evidence-based practice: An alternative to authority-based practice. *Families in Society, 80*(4), 341–350.

Garguilo, J., Attie, I., Brooks-Gunn, J., & Warren, M. P. (1987). Dating in middle school girls: Effects of social context, maturation, and grade. *Developmental Psychology, 23*(5), 730–737.

Garnefski, N., & Diekstra, R. (1996). Perceived social support from family, school, and peers: Relationship with emotional and behavioral problems among adolescents. *Journal of the American Academy of Child and Adolescent Psychiatry, 35*(12), 1657–1664.

Garner, D. M., Rosen, L. W., & Barry, D. (1998). Eating disorders amongh athletes: Reearch and recommendations. *Child and Adolescent Psychiatric Clinical of North American, 7*, 839–857.

Garnier, H. E., & Stein, J. A. (2002). An 18–year model of family and peer effects on adolescent drug use and delinquency. *Journal of Youth and Adolescence, 31*(1), 45–56.

Germain, C. B. (1979). *Social work practice: People and environments.* New York: Columbia University Press.

Germain, C. B., & Gitterman, A. (1980). *The life model of social work practice.* New York: Columbia University Press.

Gilbert, L. A., Holahan, C. K., & Manning, L. (1981). Coping with conflict between professional and maternal roles. *Family Relations, 30*(3), 419–426.

Glaser, B. (1978). *Theoretical sensitivity.* Mill Valley, CA: Sociology Press.

Goldberg, W. A. (1988). Introduction: Perspectives on the transition to parenthood. In G. Y. Michaels & W. A. Goldberg (Eds.), *The transition to parenthood: Current theory and research.* Cambridge, England: Cambridge University Press.

Goldstein, S. E., Davis-Kean, P. E., & Eccles, J. S. (2005). Parents, peers, and problem Behavior: A longitudinal investigation of the impact of relationship perceptions and characteristics on the development of adolescent problem behavior. *Developmental Psychology, 41*(2), 401–413.

Gornick, J. C., & Meyers, M. K. (2001). Support for working families: What the United States can learn from Europe. *American Prospect, 12*(1), 3–7.

Gottlieb, B. H. (1981). *Social networks and social support.* Beverly Hills, CA: Sage.

Gottlieb, B. H. (1983). *Social support strategies: Guidelines for mental health practice.* Beverly Hills, CA: Sage.

Graber, J. A., Brooks-Gunn, J., Paikoff, R. L., & Warren, M. P. (1994). Prediction of eating problems: An 8-year study of adolescent girls. *Developmental Psychology, 30*, 823–834.

Gray, W., Duhl, F. J., & Rizzo, N. D. (1969). *General systems theory and psychiatry.* Boston: Little, Brown.

Green, J., & Ennett, S. T. (1999). Prevalence and correlates of survival sex among runaway and homeless youth. *American Journal of Public Health, 89*(9), 1406–1410.

Green, R. L. (1999). Nurturing the self that students bring to school. *Guidance and Counseling, 14*(3), 21–23.

Guichard, J., & Lenz, J. (2005). Career theory from an international perspective. *The Career Development Quarterly, 54*(1), 17–28.

Haddock, S. A., Ziemba, S. J., Zimmerman, T. S., & Current, L. R. (2001). Ten adaptive strategies for family and work balance: Advice from successful families. *Journal of Marital and Family Therapy, 27*(4), 445–458.

Hall, D. T., & Mirvis, P. H. (1996). The new protean career: Psychological success and the path with a heart. In D. T. Hall & Associates (Eds.), *The career is dead—long live the career* (pp. 15–45). San Francisco: Jossey-Bass.

Hamilton, G. (1951). *Theory and practice of social casework*. New York: Columbia University Press.

Hammer, H., Finkelhor, D., & Sedlak, A. J. (2002). Runaway/throwaway children: National estimates and characteristics. *National Incidence Studies of Missing, Abducted, Runaway, and Throwaway Children*. Washingon, DC: U.S. Department of Justice.

Haney, J. J., Czerniak, C. M., & Lumpe, A. T. (2003). Constructivist beliefs about the science classroom learning environment: Perspectives from teachers, administrators, parents, community members, and students. *School Science and Mathematics, 103*(8), 366–377.

Harold, R. D. (2000). *Becoming a family: Parents' stories and their implications for practice, research, and policy*. Mahwah, NJ: Lawrence Erlbaum Associates.

Harold, R. D., Colarossi, L. G., & Mercier, L. R. (1996, March). *A picture of the parent–teen relationship within the family context*. Paper presented at the biennial meeting of the Society for Research on Adolescence, Boston, MA.

Harold, R. D., & Eccles, J. S. (1989). *A study of intra-family similarities and differences*. (Grant). Director's Discretionary Fund, Institute for Social Research, The University of Michigan. Ann Arbor, MI.

Harold, R. D., Mercier, L. R., & Colarossi, L. G. (1997). Using the eco-map to bridge the practice–research gap. *Journal of Sociology and Social Welfare, 24*, 29–44.

Harold, R. D., Palmiter, M. L., Lynch, S. A., & Freedman-Doan, C. R. (1995). Life stories: A practice-based research technique. *Journal of Sociology and Social Welfare, 22*, 23–44.

Harrison, P. A. (2003). Differences in behavior, psychological factors, and environmental factors associated with participation in school sports and other activities in adolescence. *Journal of School Health, 73*(3), 113–120.

Hartman, A. (1978). Diagrammatic assessment of family relationships. *Social Casework, 59*, 465–476.

Hartup, W. W. (1993). Adolescents and their friends. In B. Laursen (Ed.), *Close friendships during adolescence: New directions for child development* (pp. 3–22). San Francisco: Jossey-Bass.

Hattery, A. J. (2001). Tag-team parenting: Costs and benefits of utilizing nonoverlapping shift work in families with young children. *Families in Society, 82*(4), 419–427.

Hauser, S., Powers, S., & Noam, G. (1991). *Adolescents and their families: Paths of ego development*. New York: The Free Press.

Hawkins, J. D., Catalano, R. F., & Miller, J. Y. (1992). Risk and protective factors for alcohol and other drug problems in adolescence and early adulthood: Implications for substance abuse preventions. *Psychological Bulletin, 112*, 64–105.

Heckert, T. M., Droste, H. E., Farmer, G. W., Adams, P. J., Bradley, J. C., & Bonness, B. M. (2002). Effect of gender and work experience on importance of job characteristics when considering job offers. *College Student Journal, 36*(3), 344–355.

Heller, K. (1979). The effects of social support: Prevention and treatment implications. In A. P. Goldstein & F. H. Kanfer (Eds.), *Maximizing enhancement in psychology* (pp. 353–387). New York: Academic Press.

Heller, K., & Swindle, R. W. (1983). Social networks perceived, social support, and coping with stress. In R. D. Felnes, L. A. Jason, J. N. Noritsugu, & S. S. Farber (Eds.), *Handbook of counseling psychology* (pp. 87–103). New York: Wiley.

Heller, K., Swindle, R. W., & Dusenbury, L. (1986). Component social support processes: Comments and integration. *Journal of Consulting and Clinical Psychology, 54*, 466–470.

Henderson, S. (1981). Social relationships, adversity and neurosis: An analysis of prospective observations. *British Journal of Psychiatry, 138*, 391–398.

Henshaw, S. K. (2003). *U.S. teenage pregnancy statistics with comparative statistics for women aged 20–24.* New York: Allen Guttmacher Institute.

Hernandez, S., & Leung, B. P. (2004). Using the internet to boost parent-teacher relationships. *Kappa Delta Pi Record, 40*(3), 136–138.

Heymann, S. J., Earle, A., & Egleston, B. (1996). Parental availability for the care of sick children. *Pediatrics, 98*(2), 226–230.

Heyns, B. (1990). The changing contours of the teaching profession. In M. T. Hallinan, D. M. Klein & J. Glass (Eds.), *Change in societal institutions* (pp. 123–142). New York: Plenum.

Hobfoll, S. E. (1986). *Stress, social support, and women.* New York: Hemisphere.

Hochschild, A. R. (1989). *The second shift: Working parents and the revolution at home.* New York: Viking.

Hoffman, L. W. (1984). Work, family, and the socialization of the child. In R. D. Parke (Ed.), *The family* (pp. 223–282). Chicago: University of Chicago Press.

Hoffman, L. W. (2000). Maternal employment: Effects of social context. In R. D. Taylor & M. C. Wang (Eds.), *Resilience across contexts: Family, work, culture, and community* (pp. 147–176). Mahwah, NJ: Lawrence Erlbaum Associates.

Holahan, C. J., & Moos, R. H. (1987). Risk, resilience, and psychological distress: A longitudinal analysis with adults and children. *Journal of Abnormal Psychology, 96*, 3–13.

Hollis, F. (1972). *Casework: A psychosocial therapy.* New York: Random House.

Horvat, E. M., Weininger, E. B., & Lareau, A. (2003). From social ties to social capital: Class differences in the relations between schools and parent networks. *American Educational Research Journal, 40*(2), 319–351.

Hundley, G. (2000). Male/female earnings differences in self-employment: The effects of marriage, children and the household division of labor. *Industrial and Labor Relations Review, 54*(1), 95–114.

Imber-Black, E. (1988). *Families and larger systems.* New York: Guilford.

Inazu, J. K., & Fox, G. L. (1980). Maternal influences on the sexual behavior of teenage daughters. *Journal of Family Issues, 1*, 81–102.

Ingersoll-Dayton, B., & Antonucci, T. C. (1988). Non-reciprocal social support: Contrasting sides of intimate relationships. *Journal of Gerontology, 43*(3), 65–73.

Jacklin, C. N., & Reynolds, C. (1993). Gender and childhood socialization. In A. E. Beall & R. J. Sternberg (Eds.), *The psychology of gender* (pp. 197–214). New York: Guilford.

Jacobi, E. F., Wittreich, Y., & Hogue, I. (2003). Parental involvement for a new century. *New England Reading Association Journal, 39*(3), 11–16.

Jessor, S. L., & Jessor, R. (1975). Transition from virginity to nonvirginity among youth: A social-psychological study over time. *Developmental Psychology, 11*(4), 473–484.

Johnston, L. D., O'Malley, P. M., Bachman, J. G., & Schulenberg, J. E. (2004). *Monitoring the future national survey results on drug use, 1975–2003. Volume 1: Secondary school students* (NIH Publication No. 04–5507). Bethesda, MD: National Institute on Drug Abuse.

Jones, D. C., & Costin, S. E. (1995). Friendship quality during preadolescence and adolescence: The contributions of relationship orientations, instrumentality, and expressivity. *Merrill-Palmer Quarterly, 41*(4), 517–535.

Jones, G. P., & Dembo, M. H. (1989). Age and sex role differences in intimate friendships during childhood and adolescence. *Merrill-Palmer Quarterly, 35*(4), 445–462.

Kahn, R. L., & Antonucci, T. C. (1980). Convoys over the life course: Attachment, roles, and social support. In P. B. Baltes & O. G. Brim, Jr. (Eds.), *Life-span development and behavior* (Vol. 3, pp. 253–286). New York: Academic Press.

Kajicek, M., & Moore, C. (1993). Child care for infants and toddlers with disabilities and chronic illnesses. *Focus on Exceptional Children, 25*(8), 1–16.

Kaplan, D. S., Liu, X., & Kaplan, H. B. (2001). Influence of parents' self-feelings and expectations on children's academic performance. *Journal of Educational Research, 94*(6), 360–370.

Katchadourian, H. (1990). Sexuality. In S. S. Feldman & G. R. Elliot (Eds.), *At the threshold: The developing adolescent* (pp. 330–351). Cambridge, MA: Harvard University Press.

Kaufman, G., & Uhlenberg, P. (2000). The influence of parenthood on the work effort of married men and women. *Social Forces, 78*(3), 931–947.

Keating, D. P. (1990). Adolescent thinking. In S. S. Feldman & G. R. Elliott (Eds.), *At the threshold: The developing adolescent* (pp. 54–90). Cambridge: Harvard University Press.

Kennedy, E. (1997). A study of students' fears of seeking academic help from teachers. *Journal of Classroom Interaction, 32*, 11–17.

Kessler, R. C., & McCloud, J. D. (1984). Sex differences in vulnerability to undesirable life events. *American Sociological Review, 49*, 620–631.

Kessler, R. C., McCloud, J. D., & Wethington, E. (1983). The costs of caring: A perspective on the relationship between sex and psychological distress. In I. G. Sarason & B. R. Sarason (Eds.), *Social support: Theory, research, and applications* (pp. 491–506). Dordrecht, The Netherlands: Martinus Nijhoff.

Kessler, R. C., Price, R. H., & Wortman, C. B. (1985). Social factors in psychopathology: Stress, social support, and coping processes. *Annual Review of Psychology, 36*, 531–572.

Klerman, J. A., & Leibowitz, A. (1990). Child care and women's return to work after childbirth. *American Economic Review, 80*, 284–288.

Klerman, J. A., & Leibowitz, A. (1999). Job continuity among new mothers. *Demography, 36*(2), 145–155.

Kobak, R. R., & Sceery, A. (1988). Attachment in late adolescence: Working models, affect regulation, and representations of self and others. *Child Development, 59*, 135–146.

Kossek, E. E., & Ozeki, C. (1998). Work–family conflict, policies, and the job-life satisfaction relationship: A review and directions for organizational behavior-human resources research. *Journal of Applied Psychology, 83*, 139–149.

Kovacs, M. (1996). Presentation and course of major depressive disorder during childhood and later years of the life span. *Journal of the American Academy of Child and Adolescent Psychiatry, 35*, 705–715.

Kovacs, M., & Devlin, B. (1998). Internalizing disorders in childhood. *Journal of Child Psychology and Psychiatry, 39*(1), 47–63.

Kunkel, A. W., & Burleson, B. R. (1999). Assessing explanations for sex differences in emotional support: A test of the different cultures and skill specialization accounts. *Human Communication Research, 25*(3), 307–340.

La Greca, A. M., & Harrison, H. M. (2005). Adolescent peer relations, friendships, and romantic relationships: Do they predict social anxiety and depression? *Journal of Clinical Child & Adolescent Psychology, 34*(1), 49–61.

Laird, J. (1989). Women and stories: Restorying women's self-constructions. In M. McGoldrick, C. Anderson, & F. Walsh (Eds.), *Women in families.* New York: Norton.

Lakey, B., & Cassady, P. B. (1990). Cognitive processes in perceived social support. *Journal of Personality and Social Psychology, 17*(4), 503–519.

Lakey, B., & Heller, K. (1988). Social support from a friend, perceived support, and social problem solving. *American Journal of Community Psychology, 16*(6), 811–824.

Landry, D. J., & Forrest, J. D. (1995). How old are U.S. fathers? *Family Planning Perspectives, 27*, 159–161, 165.

Larson, R., Richards, M., & Perry-Jenkins, M. (1994). Divergent worlds: The daily emotional experience of mothers and fathers in the domestic and public spheres. *Journal of Personality and Social Psychology, 67*(7), 1034–1046.

Leaper, C. (2000). The social construction and socialization of gender during development. In P. H. Miller & E. K. Scholnick (Eds.), *Toward a feminist developmental psychology* (pp. 127–152). New York: Routledge.

Lee, V. E. (2001). *Restructuring high schools for equity and excellence: What works.* New York: Teachers College Press.

Lerner, J. V., & Noh, R. R. (2000). Maternal employment influences on early adolescent development: A contextual view. In R. D. Taylor & M. C. Wang (Eds.), *Resilience across contexts: Family, work, culture, and community* (pp. 121–145). Mahwah, NJ: Lawrence Erlbaum Associates.

Levitt, M. J., Guacci-Franco, N., & Levitt, J. L. (1993). Convoys of social support in childhood and early adolescence: Structure and function. *Developmental Psychology, 29*(5), 811–818.

Levitt, M. J., Weber, R. A., & Guacci, N. (1993). Convoys of social support: An intergenerational analysis. *Psychology and Aging, 8*(3), 323–326.

Levy, B. (Ed.). (1998). *Dating violence: Young women in danger* (2nd ed.). Seattle, WA: Seal Press.

Lewinsohn, R. M., Hops, H., Roberts, R. E., Seeley, J. R., & Andrews, J. A. (1993). Adolescent psychopathology: Part 1. Prevalence and incidence of depression and other DSM–III–R disorders in high school students. *Journal of Abnormal Psychology, 102*(1), 133–144.

Lewis, A. E., & Forman, T. A. (2002). Contestation or collaboration? A comparative study of home-school relations. *Anthropology and Education Quarterly, 33*(1), 60–89.

Lewis, V. K., & Shaha, S. H. (2003). Maximizing learning and attitudinal gains through integrated curricula. *Education, 123*(3), 537–547.

Lockwood, R. L., Kitzmann, K. M., & Cohen, R. (2001). The impact of sibling warmth and conflict on children's social competence with peers. *Child Study Journal, 31*(1), 47–69.

Luster, T., & Okagaki, L. (1993). *Parenting: An ecological perspective.* Hillsdale, NJ: Lawrence Erlbaum Associates.

Maccoby, E. E. (1990). Gender and relationships. *American Psychologist, 45,* 513–520.

Maguire, L. (1991). *Social support systems in practice: A generalist approach.* Silver Springs, MD: NASW Press.

Marcia, J. E. (1980). Identity in adolescence. In J. Adelson (Ed.), *Handbook of adolescent psychology* (pp. 159–177). New York: Wiley.

Marrett, C. B. (1990). The changing composition of schools: Implications for school organization. In M. T. Hallinan, D. M. Klein, & J. Glass (Eds.), *Change in societal institutions* (pp. 71–90). New York: Plenum.

Martin, E. J., & Hagan-Burke, S. (2002). Establishing a home–school connection: Strengthening the partnership between families and schools. *Preventing School Failure, 46*(2), 62–65.

Mathew, L. J., Mattocks, H., & Slatt, L. M. (1990). Exploring the roles of men caring for demented relatives. *Journal of Gerontological Nursing, 16,* 20–25.

Mauzey, E., & Erdman, P. (1995). Let the genogram speak. *Journal of Family Psychotherapy, 6,* 1–11.

McCarthy, W. J., Newcomb, M. D., & Bentler, P. M. (1994). The contribution of personal and family characteristics in adolescence to the subsequent development of young adult competence. In R. D. Parke & S. G. Kellam (Eds.), *Exploring family relationships with other social contexts* (pp. 169–197). Hillsdale, NJ: Lawrence Erlbaum Associates.

McGoldrick, M., Pearce, J., & Giordano, J. (1982). *Ethnicity and family therapy.* New York: Guilford.

McGuire, D. (1984). Childhood suicide. *Child Welfare, 63*(1), 17–26.

McMahon, M. O. (1990). *The general method of social work practice: A problem-solving approach* (2nd ed.). Englewood Cliffs, NJ: Prentice-Hall.

Mendez, L. M. R. (2000). Gender roles and achievement-related choices: A comparison of early adolescent girls in gifted and general education programs. *Journal for the Education of the Gifted, 24*(2), 149–169.

Mercier, L. R., & Harold, R. D. (2001). Job talk: The role of work in family life. In R. D. Harold (Ed.), *Becoming a family: Parents stories and their implications for practice, policy and research* (pp. 155–193). Mahwah, NJ: Lawrence Erlbaum Associates.

Minuchin, P. (1988). Relationships within the family: A systems perspective on development. In R. A. Hinde & J. Stevenson-Hinde (Eds.), *Relationships within families* (pp. 7–26). Oxford: Clarendon Press.

Miretzky, D. (2004). The communication requirements of democratic schools: Parent–teacher perspectives on their relationships. *Teachers College Record, 106*(4), 814–851.

Moen, P., & Dempster-McClain, D. I. (1987). Employed parents: Role strain, work time and preferences for working less. *Journal of Marriage and the Family, 49*(3), 579–590.

Montgomery, M. J. (2005). Psychosocial intimacy and identity: From early adolescence to emerging adulthood. *Journal of Adolescent Research, 20*(3), 346–374.

Morrow, D. F. (2004). *Families in Society, 85*(1), 91–100.

Murstein, B. I., & Azar, J. A. (1986). The relationship of exchange-orientation to friendship intensity, roommate compatibility, anxiety, and friendship. *Small Group Behavior, 17*(1), 3–17.

Mussen, P. H., & Jones, M. C. (1957). Self-conceptions, motivations, and interpersonal attitudes of late- and early-maturing boys. *Child Development, 28*, 243–256.

National Research Council, Panel on High Risk Youth. (1995). *Losing generations.* Washington, DC: National Academy Press.

Nelson, L. J., & Barry, C. M. (2005). Distinguishing features of emerging adulthood. *Journal of Adolescent Research, 20*(2), 242–262.

Newcomb, M. D., & Bentler, P. M. (1989). Substance abuse and abuse among children and teenagers. *American Psychologist, 44*, 242–248.

Nichols, M. P., & Schwartz, R. C. (2001). *Family therapy: Concepts and methods.* New York: Allyn & Bacon.

Nolen-Hoeksema, S. (1994). An integrative model for the emergence of gender differences in depression in adolescence. *Journal of Research on Adolescence, 4*, 519–534.

Noller, P. (1994). Relationships with parents in adolescence: Process and outcome. In R. Montemayor, G. R. Adams, & T. P. Gullotta (Eds.), *Personal relationships during adolescence* (pp. 37–77). Thousand Oaks, CA: Sage.

Nurmi, J-E. (2004). Socialization and self-development. In R. M. Lerner & L. Steinberg (Eds.), *Handbook of adolescent psychology* (2nd ed., pp. 85–124). Hoboken, NJ: Wiley.

Offer, D., Ostrov, E., & Howard, K. (1981). *The adolescent: A psychological self-portrait.* New York: Basic Books.

Olsen, E. (1998, February 16). U.N. surveys paid leave for mothers. *New York Times*, (pp. 1, 3).

Orrange, R. M. (2003). The emerging mutable self: Gender dynamics and creative adaptations in defining work, family and the future. *Social Forces, 82*(1), 1–34.

Ozer, E. M., Park, M. J., Paul, T., Brindis, C. D., & Irwin, C. E. (2003). *America's adolescents: Are they healthy?* San Francisco: University of California Press.

Padgett, D. K. (1998). *Qualitative methods in social work research.* Thousand Oaks, CA: Sage.

Palmer, R. B., & Liddle, H. A. (1996). Adolescent drug abuse: Contemporary perspectives on etiology and treatment. In G. M. Blau & T. P. Gullotta (Eds.), *Adolescent dysfunctional behavior: Causes, interventions, and prevention* (pp. 114–138). Thousand Oaks, CA: Sage.

Parke, R. D. (1994). Epilogue: Unresolved issues and future trends in family relationships with other contexts. In R. D. Parke & S. G. Kellam (Eds.), *Exploring family relationships with other social contexts* (pp. 215–229). Hillsdale, NJ: Lawrence Erlbaum Associates.

Parke, R. D., Burks, V. M., Carson, J. L., Neville, B., & Boyum, L. A. (1994). Family-peer relationships: A tripartite model. In R. D. Parke & S. G. Kellam, (Eds.), *Exploring family relationships with other social contexts* (pp. 115–145). Hillsdale, NJ: Lawrence Erlbaum Associates.

Parke, R. D., & Kellam, S. G. (1994). Introduction and overview. In R. D. Parke & S. G. Kellam (Eds.), *Exploring family relationships with other social contexts* (pp 1–8). Hillsdale, NJ: Lawrence Erlbaum Associates, Publishers.

Parker, J. G., & Gottman, J. M. (1989). Social and emotional development in a relational context: Friendship interaction from early childhood to adolescence. In T. J. Berndt & G. W. Ladd (Eds.), *Peer relationships in child development* (pp. 95–132). New York: Wiley.

Pearson, R. E. (1990). *Counseling and social support: Perspectives and practice.* Newbury Park, CA: Sage.

Perlman, H. (1957). *Social casework: A problem solving process*. Chicago: University of Chicago Press.

Peskin, H. (1967). Pubertal onset and ego development. *Journal of Adnormal Psychology, 72*, 1–15.

Petersen, A. C., Compas, B. E., Brooks-Gunn, J., Stemmler, M., Ey, S., & Grant, K. E. (1993). Depression in adolescence. *American Psychologist, 48*, 155–168.

Petersen, A. C., & Crockett, L. (1985). Pubertal timing and grade effects on adjustment. *Journal of Youth and Adolescence, 14*(3), 191–206.

Petersen, A. C., & Spiga, R. (1982). Adolescence and stress. In L. Goldberger & S. Breznitz (Eds.), *Handbook of stress: Theoretical and clinical aspects* (pp. 515–528). New York: The Free Press.

Piaget, J. (1972). Intellectual evolution from adolescence to adulthood. *Human Development, 15*, 1–12.

Pierce, G. R., Sarason, B. R., & Sarason, I. G. (1992). General and specific support expectations and stress as predictors of perceived supportiveness: An experimental study. *Journal of Personality & Social Psychology, 63*(2), 297–307.

Pipher, M. (1994). *Reviving Ophelia: Saving the selves of adolescent girls*. New York: G. P. Putnam's Sons.

Potvin, L., Champagne, F., & Laberge-Nadeau, C. (1988). Mandatory driver training and road safety: The Quebec experience. *American Journal of Public Health, 78*, 1206–1212.

Powers, S., Hauser, S., & Kilner, L. A. (1989). Adolescent mental health. *American Psychologist, 44*, 200–208.

Procidano, M. E., & Heller, K. (1983). Measures of perceived social support from friends and from family: Three validation studies. *American Journal of Community Psychology, 11*(1), 1–24.

Pufal-Struzik, I. (1999). Self-actualization and other personality dimensions as predictors of mental health of intellectually gifted students. *Roeper Review, 22*(1), 44–47.

Qualitative Solutions & Research Pty Ltd. (1997). *NUDIST*. [Computer software for qualitative data analysis]. Melbourne, Australia: Author.

Quadrel, M., Fishhoff, B., & Davis, W. (1993). Adolescent (in)vulnerability. *American Psychologist, 48*, 102–116.

Radke-Yarrow, M., Richters, J., & Wilson, W. E. (1988). Child development in a network of relationships. In R. A. Hinde & J. Stevenson-Hinde (Eds.), *Relationships within families* (pp. 48–67). Oxford: Clarendon.

Rau, B. L., & Hyland, M. M. (2002). Role conflict and flexible work arrangements: The effects on applicant attraction. *Personnel Psychology, 55*(11), 111–136.

Regan, P. C., Durvasula, R., Howell, L., Ureño, O., & Rea, M. (2004). Gender, ethnicity, and the developmental timing of first sexual and romantic experiences. *Social Behavior & Personality: An International Journal, 32*(7), 667–676.

Richman, M. (1917). *Social diagnosis*. New York: Russell Sage.

Roberts, R. E., Roberts, C. R., & Chen, Y. R. (1997). Ethnocultural differences in prevalence of adolescent depression. *American Journal of Community Psychology, 25*(1), 95–110.

Rodwell, M. K. (1998). *Social work constructivist research*. New York: Garland Rubin.

Roeser, R. W., & Eccles, J. S. (2000). School as a context of early adolescents' academic and social-emotional development: A summary. *Elementary School Journal, 100*(5), 443.

Rogers, S. J., & Amato, P. R. (1997). Is marital quality declining? The evidence from two generations. *Social Forces, 75*(3), 1089–1100.

Rogers, S. J., & Amato, P. R. (2000). Have changes in gender relations affected marital quality? *Social Forces, 79*(2), 731–753.

Rook, K. S. (1992). Detrimental aspects of social relationships: Taking stock of an emerging literature. In H. O. F. Veiel & A. Baumann (Eds.), *The meaning and measurement of social support* (pp. 157–169). New York: Hemisphere Publishing Corportation.

Roth, J., Brooks-Gunn, J., Murray, L., & Foster, W. (1998). Promoting healthy adolescents: synthesis of youth development program evaluations. *Journal of Research on Adolescence, 8*(4), 423–459.

Rothbard, N. P., & Edwards, J. R. (2003). Investment in work and family roles: A test of identity and utilitarian motives. *Personnel Psychology, 56*(3), 699–729.

Rutter, M., Graham, P., Chadwick, F., & Yule, W. (1976). Adolescent turmoil: Fact or fiction? *Journal of Child Psychology and Psychiatry, 17*, 35–56.

Ryan, R. M., & Lynch, J. H. (1989). Emotional autonomy versus detachment: Revisiting the vicissitudes of adolescence and young adulthood. *Child Development, 60*, 340–356.

Sameroff, A. J., & Fiese, B. H. (1999). Narrative connections in the family context: Summary and conclusions. In B. H. Fiese, A. J. Sameroff, H. D. Grotevant, F. S. Wamboldt, S. Dickstein, & D. L. Fravel (Eds.), The stories that families tell: Narrative coherence, narrative interaction, and relationship beliefs. *Monographs of the Society for Research in Child Development, 64*(2, Serial No. 257), 105–123.

Sandberg, J. F., & Hofferth, S. L. (2001). Changes in children's time with parents: Uniterd States, 1981–1997. *Demography, 38*(3), 423–436.

Sandler, I. N., & Barrera, M. (1984). Toward a multimethod approach to assessing the effects of social support. *American Journal of Community Psychology, 12*(1), 37–52.

Sandler, I. N., Miller, P., Short, J., & Wolchik, S. A. (1989). Social support as a protective factor for children in stress. In D. Belle (Ed.), *Children's social networks and social supports* (pp. 277–307). New York: Wiley.

Sarason, B. R., Pierce, G. R., Shearin, E. N., Sarason, I. G., Waltz, J. A., & Poppe, L. (1991). Perceived social support and working models of self and actual others. *Journal of Personality and Social Psychology, 60*(2), 273–287.

Sarason, B. R., Sarason, I. G., Hacker, T. A., & Basham, R. B. (1985). Concomitants of social support: Social skills, physical attractiveness, and gender. *Journal of Personality and Social Psychology, 49*(2), 469–480.

Sarason, I. G., Levine, H. M., Basham, R. B., & Sarason, B. R. (1983). Assessing social support: The social support questionnaire. *Journal of Personality and Social Psychology, 44*, 127–139.

Sarason, I. G., Pierce, G. R., & Sarason, B. R. (1990). Social support and interactional processes: A triadic hypothesis. [Special Issue: Predicting, activating, and facilitating social support.] *Journal of Social and Personal Relationships, 7*(4), 495–506.

Sarason, I. G., Sarason, B. R., & Pierce, G. R. (1990). Social support: The search for theory. [Special Issue: Social support in social and clinical psychology.] *Journal of Social & Clinical Psychology, 9*(1), 133–147.

Scales, P. C. (1997). The role of family support programs in building developmental assets among young adolescents: A national survey of services and staff training needs. *Child Welfare, 76*(5), 611–321.

Scharf, M., Shulman, S., & Avigad-Spitz, L. (2005). Sibling relationships in emerging adulthood and in adolescence. *Journal of Adolescent Research, 20*(1), 64–90.

Scheirer, L. M., & Botvin, G. J. (1997). Psychosocial correlates of affective distress: Models of male and female adolescents in a community. *Journal of Youth and Adolescence, 26*(1), 89–115.

Schinke, S., Botvin, G. J., & Orlandi, M. A. (1991). *Substance abuse in children and adolescents: Evaluation and intervention.* Newbury Park, CA: Sage.

Scholnick, E. K., & Miller, P. H. (2000). Engendering development—Developing feminism. Defining the partnership. In P. H. Miller & E. K. Scholnick (Eds.), *Toward a feminist developmental psychology* (pp. 241–254). New York: Routledge.

Schroeder, K. (2002). Examining an aspect of student behavior. *Journal of Jewish Education, 68*(2), 23.

Selman, R. L. (1980). *The growth of interpersonal understanding.* New York: Academic Press.

Shaffer, H. R. (1999). Understanding socialization: From unidirectional to bi-directional conceptions. In M. Bennett (Ed.), *Developmental psychology: Achievements and prospects.* Philadelphia: Psychology Press.

Shafii, M., Carrigan, S., Whittinghill, J. R., & Derrick, A. (1985). Psychological autopsy of completed suicide in children and adolescents. *American Journal of Psychiatry, 142,* 1061–1064.

Shantz, C. U. (1983). Social cognition. In J. H. Flavell & E. M. Markman (Eds.), *Handbook of child psychology* (Vol. 3, pp. 495–555). New York: Wiley.

Sharp, S. (1995). How much does bullying hurt? The effects of bullying on the personal well-being and educational progress of secondary aged students. *Educational and Child Psychology, 12,* 81–88.

Silbereisen, R. K., & Todt, E. (1994). Adolescence—A matter of context. In R. K. Silbereisen & E. Todt (Eds.), *Adolescence in context: The interplay of family, schools, peers, and work in adjustment* (pp. 3–21). New York: Springer-Verlag.

Silverberg, S. B., & Gondoli, D. M. (1996). Autonomy in adolescence: A contextualized Perspective. In G. R. Adams, R. Montemayor, & T. P. Gullotta (Eds.), *Psychosocial development during adolescence* (pp. 12–61). Thousand Oaks, CA: Sage.

Simmons, R. G., & Blyth, D. A. (1987). *Moving into adolescence: The impact of pubertal changes and school context.* New York: Aldine de Gruyter.

Simmons, R. G., Burgeson, R., Carlton-Ford, S., & Blyth, D. A. (1987). The impact of cumulative change in early adolescence. *Child Development, 58,* 1220–1234.

Singleton, J. (2000). Women caring for elderly family members: Shaping non-traditional work and family initiatives. *Journal of Comparative Family Studies, 31*(3), 367.

Slavin-Williams, R. C., & Berndt, T. J. (1990). Friendship and peer relations. In S. S. Feldman & G. R. Elliott (Eds.), *At the threshold: The developing adolescent* (pp. 277–308). Cambridge: Harvard University Press.

Smetana, J., Crean, H., & Camione-Barr, N. (2005). Adolescents' and parents' changing conceptions of parental authority. *New Directions in Child Development, 108,* 31–46.

Smith, P. J., & Beaujot, R. (1999). Men's orientation toward marriage and family roles. *Journal of Comparative Family Studies, 30*(3), 471–488.

Smrekar, C., & Cohen-Vogel, L. (2001). The voices of parents: Rethinking the intersection of family and school. *Peabody Journal of Education, 76*(2), 75–100.

Solodow, W. (1999). The meaning of development in middle school. In J. Cohen (Ed.), *Educating minds and hearts: Social emotional learning and the passage into adolescence* (pp. 24–39). New York: Teachers College Press.

South, S. J., & Spitze, G. (1994). Housework in marital and nonmarital households. *American Sociological Review, 59*, 327–347.

Stanton-Salazar, R. D., & Spina, S. U. (2005). Adolescent peer networks as a context for social and emotional support. *Youth & Society, 36*(4), 379–417.

Steinberg, L. (1985). *Adolescence.* New York: Knopf.

Steinberg, L. (1990). Autonomy, conflict, and harmony in the family relationship. In S. S. Feldman & G. R. Elliot (Eds.), *At the threshold: The developing adolescent* (pp. 255–276). Cambridge, MA: Harvard University Press.

Steinberg, L., & Levine, A. (1990). *You and your adolescent.* New York: Harper & Row.

Steinberg, L., & Steinberg, W. (1994). *Crossing paths: How your child's adolescence triggers your own crisis.* New York: Simon & Schuster.

Stewart, R. B., Verbrugge, K. M., & Beilfuss, M. C. (1998). Sibling relationships in early adulthood: A typology. *Personal Relationships, 5*, 59–74.

Stocker, C., Lanthier, R., & Furman, W. (1997). Sibling relationships in early adulthood. *Journal of Family Psychology, 11*, 210–221.

Strauss, A., & Corbin, J. (1990). *Basics of qualitative research: Grounded theory procedures and techniques.* Thousand Oaks, CA: Sage.

Streeter, C. L., & Franklin, C. (1992). Defining and measuring social support: Guidelines for social work practitioners. *Research on Social Work Practice, 2*(1), 81–98.

Sullivan, K., Cleary, M., & Sullivan, G. (2004). *Bullying in secondary schools: What it looks like and how to manage it.* Thousand Oaks, CA: Corwin.

Tannen, D. (1990). Gender differences in topical coherence: Creating involvement in best friend's talk. *Discourse processes, 13*, 73–90.

Tanner, J. M. (1962). *Growth at adolescence.* Oxford: Blackwell Scientific.

Thatcher, R. W., Walker, R. A., & Giudice, S. (1987). Human cerebral hemispheres develop at different rates and ages. *Science, 236*, 1110–1113.

Thomas, R. M. (2001). *Recent theories of human development.* Thousand Oaks, CA: Sage.

Thompson, G. L., Warren, S., & Carter, L. (2004). It's not my fault: Predicting high school teachers who blame parents and students for low achievement. *High School Journal, 87*(3), 5–14.

Tjaden, P., & Thoennes, N. (2000). *Final report on prevalence, incidence, and consequences of violence against women: Findings from the National Violence Against Women Survey.* Washington DC: U.S. Department of Justice.

U.S. Department of Labor, Women's Bureau. (1997). *Report on the American workforce.* Washington, DC: U.S. Government Printing Office.

U.S. General Accounting Office. (1992). *The changing workforce: Demographic issues facing the federal government* (GAO/FFD-92–38). Washington, DC: Author.

van Beest, M., & Baerveldt, C. (1999). The relationship between adolescents' social support from parents and from peers. *Adolescence, 34*(133), 193–201.

Vaux, A. (1985). Variations in social support associated with gender, ethnicity, and age. *Journal of Social Issues, 41*, 89–110.

Vaux, A. (1988). *Social support: Theory, research, and intervention.* New York: Praeger.

Voydanoff, P. (1987). *Work and family life.* Newbury Park, CA: Sage.

Vygotski, L. S. (1978). *Mind in society.* Cambridge, MA: Harvard University Press.

Wapner, S., & Craig-Bray, L. (1992). Person-in-environment transitions. *Environment and Behavior, 24,* 161–188.

Warren, J. A., & Johnson, P. J. (1995). The impact of workplace support on work–family role strain. *Family Relations, 44*(2), 163–169.

Warren, S. (2002). Stories from the classroom: How expectations and efficacy of diverse teachers affect the academic performance of children in poor urban schools. *Educational Horizons, 80*(3), 109–116.

Watzlawick, P. (1996). The construction of clinical "realities." In H. Rosen (Ed.). *Constructing realities: Meaning-making perspectives for psychotherapists* (pp. 55–71). San Francisco: Jossey-Bass.

Weick, K. (1976). Educational organizations as loosely coupled systems. *Administrative Science Quarterly, 21,* 1–19.

Weiss, R. S. (1974). The provisions of social relationships. In Z. Rubin (Ed.), *Doing unto others* (pp. 17–26). Englewood Cliffs, NJ: Prentice-Hall.

Wentzel, K. (1998). Social relationships and motivation in middle school: The role of parents, teachers, and peers. *Journal of educational Psychology, 90*(2), 202–209.

Wentzel, K. R. (1997). Student motivation in middle school: The role of perceived pedagogical caring. *Journal of Educational Psychology, 89,* 411–419.

Westat, Inc. (1997). *National evaluation of runaway and homeless youth.* Washington, DC: U.S. Department of Health and Human Services.

Wethington, E., & Kessler, R. C. (1986). Perceived support, received support, and adjustment to stressful life events. *Journal of Health and Social Behavior, 27,* 78–89.

White, J. M. (1999). Work–family stage and satisfaction with work–family balance. *Journal of Comparative Family Studies, 30*(2), 163–175.

White, J. M., & Klein, D. M. (2002). *Family theories* (2nd ed.). Thousand Oaks, CA: Sage.

White, M., & Epston, D. (1990). *Narrative means to therapeutic ends.* New York: W. W. Norton.

Whittaker, J. K., & Garbarino, J. (Eds.). (1983). *Social support networks: Informal helping in the human services.* New York: Aldine Publishing Company.

Winnicott, D. W. (1965). *The family and individual development.* London: Routledge.

Winstead, B. A. (1986). Sex differences in same-sex friendships. In V. J. Derlega & B. A. Winstead (Eds.), *Friendship and social interaction* (pp. 81–100). New York: Springer-Verlag.

Wood, J. T. (1994). *Who cares? Women, care, and culture.* Carbondale, IL: Southern Illinois University Press.

Wooden, W. S., & Blazak, R. (2001). *Renegade kids and suburban outlaws: From youth culture to delinquency.* Belmont, CA: Wadsworth Publishing.

Wright, P. H. (1982). Men's friendships, women's friendships, and the alleged inferiority of the latter. *Sex Roles, 8,* 1–20.

Yeh, H., & Lempers, J. D. (2004). Perceived sibling relationships and adolescent development. *Journal of Youth and Adolescence, 33*(2), 133–147.

Yogev, S. (1981). Do professional women have egalitarian marital relationships? *Journal of Marriage and the Family, 43*(4), 865–871.

Youniss, J., & Smollar, J. (1985). *Adolescents' relations with mothers, fathers, and friends.* Chicago: University of Chicago Press.

Young, A. M., & D'Arcy, H. (2005). Older boyfriends of adolescent girls: The cause or a sign of the problem? *Journal of Adolescent Health, 36*(5), 410–419.

Author Index

Subject Index